Advance Praise for
Will Write for Food

"*Will Write for Food* is a concise, illustrative and eminently useful guide to the nuts and bolts of professional food writing. Dianne Jacob gets right to the heart of what it takes not just to write—but to write well—about food. And she's managed to wrangle a remarkable group of veterans to share their experiences and examples."

—Anthony Bourdain, author of the *New York Times* bestseller
Kitchen Confidential

"You'll find everything you need to know about becoming a food writer in this indispensable information-packed book. And if you're already a food writer, this book will help you become a better one. Dianne Jacob takes you by the hand through every step of the process from hatching an idea to getting published. Useful writing exercises concluding each chapter help sharpen your skills. Dozens of quotes from successful food writers tell how they got started and what their working lives are really like. If food writing is your passion, then grab a copy of *Will Write for Food* and get busy!"

—Greg Patent, winner of the James Beard Award for *Baking in America*

"*Will Write for Food* is a great gift, not just for those who are new to food writing, but for those already ensconced in the business. Dianne's clarity, kind suggestions, and nudges and admonitions to work well are truly inspiring."

—Deborah Madison, author of *Vegetarian Cooking for Everyone*

"Dianne Jacob has done a masterful job in this book of amassing everything a fledgling food writer needs to know. Whether one yearns to review restaurants for a local newspaper or turn a passion for food into magazine articles, or even a cookbook, *Will Write for Food* offers invaluable practical advice along every step of the way."

—Fran Gage, author of *Bread and Chocolate*

"This book does a great job of covering the nuts and bolts of food writing, for sure, but Jacob delivers much more than the usual advice: She shoots straight about the realities of the business, provides loads of insider insights and practical exercises, and radiates enough genuine enthusiasm to get both beginning writers and seasoned pros up and at 'em."

—Martha Holmberg, former publisher, *Fine Cooking* magazine

"Dianne Jacob has presented budding food writers with a clear blueprint on how to get started in the business."

—Michael Bauer, Executive Food and Wine Editor, *San Francisco Chronicle*

"My only complaint about *Will Write for Food*—and it's a big one—is that it wasn't around when I started my career. If you're serious about becoming a food writer, save yourself years of banging your head against the wall in frustration and run to the checkout with this book now."

—David Leite, food writer, and publisher and editor of *Leite's Culinaria*

"In *Will Write for Food,* Dianne Jacob combines all the right ingredients for a delectable read."

— Joanne Fluke, author of *Sugar Cookie Murder* and other Hannah Swensen Mysteries

Will Write for

The Complete Guide to
Writing Cookbooks, Restaurant Reviews,
Articles, Memoir, Fiction
and More...

By Dianne Jacob

Da Capo

LIFE
LONG

A MEMBER OF THE PERSEUS BOOKS GROUP

Copyright © 2005 by Dianne Jacob

Designed by Maria Elias
Set in 10.5 point Sabon by the Perseus Books Group

Cataloging-in-Publication data for this book is available from the Library of Congress.

ISBN: 978-1-56924-377-0

Published by Da Capo Press
A Member of the Perseus Books Group
www.dacapopress.com
Note: The information in this book is true and complete to the best of our knowledge. This book is intended only as an informative guide for those wishing to know more about health issues. In no way is this book intended to replace, countermand, or conflict with the advice given to you by your own physician. The ultimate decision concerning care should be made between you and your doctor. We strongly recommend you follow his or her advice. Information in this book is general and is offered with no guarantees on the part of the authors or Da Capo Press. The authors and publisher disclaim all liability in connection with the use of this book. The names and identifying details of people associated with events described in this book have been changed. Any similarity to actual persons is coincidental.

Da Capo Press books are available at special discounts for bulk purchases in the U.S. by corporations, institutions, and other organizations. For more information, please contact the Special Markets Department at the Perseus Books Group, 2300 Chestnut Street, Suite 200, Philadelphia, PA, 19103, or call (800) 255-1514, or e-mail special.markets@perseusbooks.com.

10 9 8

To Rachel and Moses,
who showed me how to love food and writing

Contents

Acknowledgments

his book would not have been possible without the generous responses of the knowledgeable food writers, editors, and agents I interviewed. Almost everyone, no matter how well known, gave me their time and came up with thoughtful responses. They read e-mails and took calls at the office, at home, on the road, on vacation, and after retirement. I am grateful for the time they spent educating me, sharing their sagacity, and giving advice so beneficial to my readers.

Several friends and colleagues gave me useful feedback and advice. Former student Faith Kramer marked up each chapter with intelligent and constructive criticisms. About twenty-five of my closest friends, colleagues, and clients responded to an e-mail plea for a good title. Josh Greenbaum came up with the witty name. Writers Eva Heninwolff, Greg Patent, and Laura Taxel reviewed chapters and made thoughtful comments. Writer Greta Wu provided insights on fiction writing. Writers Mary Margaret Pack and Gary Allen brainstormed ideas and resources. Editor Meredith Arthur improved my book proposal and sense of humor. I give a big thank-you to writer Hannah Miller, who researched and constructed my appendices quickly and professionally. Publisher David Cole helped me sprout the idea.

My friend Kris Montgomery provided a sympathetic ear, encouragement, brainstorming, and resources. Unwavering encouragement also came from Judy Lightstone and Deborah Madison.

My husband, Owen Rubin, provided material, emotional, and technical support. He also gave terrific neck and shoulder massages, laughed with me over the funny parts, and arranged for takeout when necessary.

Agent Carole Bidnick encouraged me from the first mention of this idea. She was a major source of insider information and reality checks. Her vast experience, tenacity, and friendship have been invaluable.

I thank my publisher Matthew Lore for giving me this opportunity, and my editor Kylie Foxx for her editorial expertise. Her gentle edits and recommendations improved the book greatly. Heather and Randa Dubnick painstakingly copy-edited the book and fact-checked so many names and titles. Marc Cohen designed a gorgeous cover. Wendie Carr and Karen Auerbach surpassed my expectations on publicity.

My gratitude goes to all other authors of books and Web sites on good writing, freelancing, proposal writing, self-publishing, and finding agents.

Thanks to all the writers and editors who've kept my skills sharp by hiring me to edit articles, proposals, manuscripts, recipes and Web site content, and to all the magazine and newspaper editors who've taught me what it's like to be on the other side as a writer.

It seems fitting that some of the proceeds of this book should serve the hungry. As an eight-year board member of the Alameda County Community Food Bank (ACCFB), I recognize those who do not have the means or opportunity to obtain, eat, and cook high-quality food of their choice, whenever they want. Ten percent of the proceeds will benefit the ACCFB.

Introduction

I teach classes on food writing in the San Francisco Bay Area, and I coach people all over the United States and Canada on how to get published. Students and clients always ask for a book that shows them how to write about food. I couldn't find one. I decided to write the book I'd recommend, packing it chock-full of sound guidance and wisdom on all kinds of food writing, from fiction to memoir to restaurant reviews and recipes.

Within these pages I'd like to be your friendly guide, encouraging you with enthusiastic yet practical advice no matter what stage of development you're at:

- If you hope to support yourself full-time, you're in for a challenge, but many people do it, and you'll learn how.
- If you are already a food writer, this book builds on your skills and shows you how to branch out to other types of food writing.
- If you'd like to write part-time or as a hobby, you're in good shape. "A day job and a rich husband helps," one agent advised me. You'll find plenty of useful advice about honing your writing skills and how to approach editors.
- If you want to self-publish a family cookbook, you'll find detailed information about how to write recipes and advice on self-publishing.

➤ Even if you come to this book without any desire to
   be published, but with curiosity about how to
   express your passion for food, this book will answer
   questions you've always wanted to ask. At the very
   least, it will help you appreciate the effort that goes
   into writing, selling, and publishing food writing.

Will Write for Food takes you inside the heads of some of
America's most powerful food writers, editors, and agents. Their
wisdom, recommendations, and experiences appear in every
chapter, along with stories of how successful food writers broke
into the business. I've also packed the book with nitty-gritty
tools and resources designed to move you forward. Understanding the process behind food writing, the characteristics of
those who succeed, and which tools are necessary will help
lessen any anxieties you're bound to endure.

I began my food-writing career after graduating from journalism school. My first job was in 1976, where, as editor of a
fourteen-page weekly "Lifestyles" section of a Canadian newspaper, I pulled recipes off the wire and slotted them between
feature articles and wedding announcements. From there I
became the editor of a city restaurant magazine. Later in my
career I became a full-time magazine editor and freelance food
writer. I have written restaurant and cookbook reviews, recipes,
cover stories, profiles, advice-based essays, and opinion pieces.
For the last three years, I've judged a national cookbook award.
My general career as an editor and writer for newspapers, magazines, books, and Web sites has spanned almost thirty years,
giving me a valuable well of experience from which to draw.

For several years, I have been teaching food-writing workshops for the Writing Salon in San Francisco. Since 2000, I have
chaired an annual food writing conference at Book Passage in
Corte Madera, California, where I teach and also invite
acclaimed food writers, editors, and agents to speak. I also
teach food writing for the University of California Extension.

The material in this book comes from my own experience,
my research, and from telephone interviews with the wise ones.

Almost every quote in this book was the result of a personal interview. Occasionally I quote from previously published material, indicated by "said." I've also quoted a few times from speakers at conferences or on a radio program. To help you keep track of who's who, a list in the back identifies interviewees by last name.

How to Use This Book

Writing specifically about food, as opposed to writing in general, is the focus of *Will Write for Food*. This is not a basic book on writing. Sections such as memoir and fiction focus on the use of food as a vehicle, and do not address the entire subject of how to write in that form. Many excellent books will give you comprehensive information in those areas. You will find them listed within the chapters and in the appendix.

I prefer that you read the chapters consecutively, of course, but you may also open to any chapter. Each is designed to be as complete in itself as possible, but sometimes you will want information that lurks in other sections. References will be provided.

Each chapter ends with writing suggestions designed to put what you have learned to immediate use. The usefulness of any one exercise may not seem apparent, but if you complete at least one in each chapter, you will find new points of entry into your head. You'll uncover new material, open vaults of memory, and access your passion. If you already write, these exercises will expand the way you find and process material and test whether your current skills are still producing satisfactory results.

It's normal to have resistance to writing suggestions and to turn the page. Find it in yourself to examine your reasons not to write. The exercises are short, fun, and not very time consuming. The goal is to write, so why not get started? I hope that's why you bought this book in the first place. Trust yourself.

Food writing is a tough field with fierce competition. I aim not to frighten you to the point of discouragement but to inspire you to act on a lifelong dream, or to move forward as a writer. You deserve inside information, resources, and support. It's so much easier than moving forward all alone.

Don't stop with my book. Find others who will guide you by joining industry groups or volunteering. And most importantly, make time every day to write. Don't give up. Persistence is half the battle. Besides, you need written work to show the editors who are actively looking for you. Give them something to read.

Please let me know if this book has helped you. Write to me through my Web site, http://www.diannej.com.

1

What, Exactly, Is Food Writing?

A recipe for fettuccine with prosciutto, cream, and nutmeg. The history of tea. A first-person adventure in Chinatowns around the world. Where to get the best deli sandwiches. A guide to macrobiotic cooking. Food writing wanders over dozens of subjects; the storytellers and their craft are what bring it together.

Hundreds of people publish books and articles on food, some writing for the first time. One of them could be you. It's easier to choose what to write about if you understand why you want to write about food in the first place. Says freelancer David Leite, "People get this warm glow when they say, 'I want to become a food writer.' It becomes this romanticized overarching career." What's your reason to write about food?

- ❧ You'd like to tell your life story and pass down recipes to family members.
- ❧ You're a caterer or chef whose customers have asked for recipes.

- ➤ You're fascinated by the history of a certain food and want to research it.
- ➤ You want to write a cookbook based on expertise you've developed.
- ➤ You can't find a cookbook that deals with your child's allergies, and you know other parents could use one.
- ➤ You want to capture the cuisine of a country and people you love.

Whatever motivates you, food writing has a requirement that makes it irresistible: you like food, and you get to eat and write about it. What's better than that?

If you have the desire, perseverance, and writing skills, you can join the ranks. This book shows you how. It explores food writing in all its sensuous and practical glory, with insights from the best writers in the business, practical information on how to succeed, and most of all, what tools you need to pursue your passion.

Today is a great time to be a food writer, full of opportunities. While at its most basic, food writing covers recipes and restaurant reviews, it also includes:

- ➤ Reference works
- ➤ Food history
- ➤ Travel-related stories about food
- ➤ First-person storytelling
- ➤ Food themes in fiction
- ➤ Reporting and news stories
- ➤ Nutritional emphasis
- ➤ Science writing

This first chapter explores nonfiction narrative for newspapers, magazines, and books as a starting point to define food writing. I asked some of the most creative minds in the field to tell me what good food writing means to them. Is it simply good writing? Or is the most important element that it makes readers hungry, helps them experience pleasure, activates their senses, and evokes images of a certain place and time?

Good Writing Is the Essence

I believe good writing is the main determining factor of good food writing, and I set out to see what others had to say. Former *Saveur* editor in chief Colman Andrews put it bluntly: "If you're not capable of being a good writer, you can't be a good food writer. It's about clarity of expression, style, voice, accuracy, knowledge of structure and rhythm of language. The idea that food writing is a separate discipline is false."

Freelancer David Leite agrees. "While the best food writing is evocative, has an unmistakable voice and an immutable sense of place, it does all the things good writing can do. Some people can write about changing motor oil with as much sensuality as eating a peach. It's how you use the language, how you communicate."

I'm a big admirer of Calvin Trillin. He has written about food for decades in the *New Yorker* and now occasionally writes travel pieces for *Gourmet*. He adamantly refuses to describe his work as food writing. He calls it "writing about eating," and doesn't distinguish it from any other nonfiction. He insists he is not a cook, has no culinary knowledge, and does not rate food. "It's probably fair to call me an amateur," he cracks.

To further make his case, Trillin told me he does not describe food in anything he writes. I found it hard to believe. How could someone write about food without adjectives? I dashed to my bookshelf and reviewed several of his essays. Here's the furthest he will go, from his 1974 book, *American Fried: Adventures of a Happy Eater:* "Being in a traveling trade myself, I know the problem of asking someone in a strange city for the best restaurant in town and being led to some purple palace that serves 'Continental cuisine' and has as its chief creative employee a menu-writer rather than a chef. I have sat in those places, an innocent wayfarer, reading a three-paragraph description of what the trout is wrapped in, how long it has been sautéed, what province its sauce comes from, and what it is likely to sound like sizzling on my platter—a description lacking only the information that before the poor beast went through that process it had been frozen for eight and a half months." For Trillin, the most important part of the craft is "careful writing, making sure every word is the right word." He says he learned this from reading A. J. Liebling, a *New Yorker* writer and author of *Between Meals: An Appetite for Paris,* an acclaimed 1959 account of eating well in Paris.

As in other fine writing, there's lots of room for creativity within the form, say two award-winning freelancers. *Vogue* columnist and author Jeffrey Steingarten says his short stories take the form of "flashbacks and flash forwards." *Bon Appétit* columnist and contributing editor Alan Richman says food writing provides more opportunity for free expression than most other forms of journalism. "When it's a review or critique of food, the experience is subjective, so you can say whatever you want. You can be mean, funny, or profound," he explains. "When it's a piece about a head of lettuce or a new shop or a restaurant opening, you're writing about a subject that's been covered thousands of times, and you have the opportunity to seek out a new angle. The repetitive nature of food writing should encourage creativity, not stifle it."

What All Food Writing Has in Common

Some say there's something specific about food writing, that it must, at minimum, stimulate the senses and make you hungry. "You get to make a primal appeal to an appetite that is neither intellectual nor social. It's the 'amphibian brain,'" says former *New York Times* food columnist and essayist Molly O'Neill. "Writers need to leverage the seduction of the senses in a clever, controlled, highly conscious way." Antonia Allegra, founder of the Symposium for Professional Food Writers at the Greenbrier, in West Virginia, says food writing spurs her to action. "It's writing that makes me want to either taste, cook, or look at food. It drives me food crazy and gets all those senses going."

Some believe food writing is all about consumption. "The primary requisite for writing well about food is a good appetite," writes Liebling. "Without this, it is impossible to accumulate, within the allotted span, enough experience of eating to have anything worth setting down. Each day brings only two opportunities for fieldwork, and they are not to be wasted minimizing the intake of cholesterol."

And then there's the factor of overall pleasure and enjoyment. Says Darra Goldstein, editor of the national magazine *Gastronomica*, "Some food writing is almost utopian. Communicating pleasure and enjoyment is a part of that."

Food writing often evokes a place or memory, or the immediacy of a moment. Judith Jones, a vice president and senior editor at Knopf who has edited such legends as Julia Child and James Beard, says food writing "describes taste, textures, flavors, and smells, and gives a food experience a larger context by writing about a more common experience, drawing on something universal that speaks to everyone." She points to an essay by M. F. K. Fisher, whom she also edited, titled "P is for Peas," where the author and her family pick peas in the vineyards of Switzerland. Here's a sentence:

> I dashed up and down the steep terraces with the baskets, and my mother would groan and then hum happily when another one appeared, and below I could hear my father and our friends cursing just as happily at their wry backs and their aching thighs, while the peas came off their stems and into the baskets with a small sound audible in that still high air, so many hundred feet above the distant and completely silent Leman.

Yes, this is food writing, because peas are the subject. But there's so much more: a scene, a terrain, ambiance, and relationships, all vividly drawn. You are there with her on the hillside, watching the scene.

Former *Town & Country* magazine's food and wine editor James Villas, another classic food writer, excels at capturing the moment. Here's the opening line of his essay titled "The Unsung Sardine," from *Villas at Table: A Passion for Food and Drink:* "At the fashionable Brasserie Lipp on the Boulevard St.-Germain in Paris, a svelte young French socialite sits in the front room chatting with her companion, sipping a *vin blanc cassis,* and checking out the crowd. When the black-tie waiter approaches to take orders, she doesn't hesitate. *'Les sardines beurre,'* she directs, *'suivies par la sole meunière.'* Sardines and sautéed sole, simple and uncomplicated, perfect for a light dinner." Villas takes a fly-on-the-wall approach. He puts you in the restaurant with him, gives you a chair at his table, and lets you take in the scene. Many travel-writing pieces use this style to draw readers in.

AN EDITOR WHO CULTIVATES BRILLIANT FOOD WRITERS

Judith Jones, vice president and senior editor of Knopf, has influenced American culinary culture for decades by publishing gifted food writers, including some of my favorites: Julia Child, M. F. K. Fisher, Edna Lewis, and Laurie Colwin. When I asked Jones how she came to work with them, she said modestly, "You follow your instincts, the things that you love. If you feel strongly about a book, the rationalization is that there must be others like you who want it. I thought if I wanted to know that much about food, there were others like me."

Here's more about these writers and how Jones became involved with them:

Julia Child: In 1960, Jones received a manuscript for what would become *Mastering the Art of French Cooking.* "The first choice had been Houghton Mifflin, but when the editor there reviewed the manuscript, her reaction was: Why would any American want to know this much about French cooking?" Jones had recently returned from living in Paris for three-and-a-half years, and had been hired at Knopf as a French editor to deal with translations. She lobbied to become the editor of Child's book and Alfred Knopf gave her a chance. The rest is history.

M. F. K. Fisher: Jones became friends with Fisher over years of mailing her galleys of Knopf books. Fisher was already known, and Jones wanted her to endorse Knopf books. In the 1960s, Jones visited California with her husband Evan, a distinguished food writer in his own right. Fisher invited them to her home in St. Helena for lunch. "It was so hot we ate in the cellar," recalls Jones. Fisher made a "Provençal lunch, cold salads and other things. She owed one more book to her current publisher, then we did a book together." *Among Friends* came first in 1971, followed by *A Considerable Town* in 1978, *Sister Age* in 1983, and *As They Were* in 1982.

W. H. Auden once said he could not think of anyone in the United States who wrote better prose than Fisher, but because she chose food as her subject, her audience was extremely limited. Perhaps, but she is probably America's best-known food writer, with a continuing fan base that enjoys her sensuous, humorous, and beautifully sad voice.

Fisher's most quoted essay is the foreword to *The Gastronomical Me*, which begins: "People ask me: Why do you write about food, and eating and drinking? Why don't you write about the struggle for power and security, and about love, the way others do? . . . The easiest answer is to say that, like most other humans, I am hungry."

> I tell about myself, and how I ate bread on a lasting hill-
> side, or drank red wine in a room now blown to bits, and
> it happens without my willing it that I am telling too much
> about the people with me then, and their other deeper
> needs for love and happiness.

Edna Lewis: In the 1970s, Lewis had a restaurant in New York frequented by the likes of Truman Capote and Tennessee Williams. Jones was intrigued. "I could see right away that she had a story about her whole relationship with food, her family, that she was part of the American experience," Jones remembers. "She had a beautiful way of talking about food. She was an instinctive cook. I said, 'Write your own book, your own experience, and let's do it together.'"

The result was the classic *The Taste of Country Cooking*, published in 1976. You'd never know Lewis owned a New York restaurant. This book goes back to her roots and celebrates how her family prepared and enjoyed American food in a rural Virginia town founded by freed slaves. Dignified and knowledgeable, she expresses her joy of fresh, natural tastes, capturing a simpler time of living off the land, where vegetables came from a garden, meat from a smokehouse, fruit from orchards, and canned jams and condiments from the previous summer.

In her foreword, Lewis explains why she wrote *The Taste of Country Cooking:* "Whenever I go back to visit my sisters and brothers, we relive old times, remembering the past. And when we share again in gathering wild strawberries, canning, rendering lard, finding walnuts, picking persimmons, making fruit-cake, I realize how much the bond that held us had to do with food. Since we are the last of the original families, with no children to remember and carry on, I decided that I wanted to write down just exactly how we did things when I was growing up in Freetown that seemed to make life so rewarding."

Laurie Colwin: Primarily a fiction writer whose themes were love and family, Colwin attracted an ardent following by word of mouth. In her novels, her characters are domestic sensualists who like to cook humble but deeply satisfying dishes. She wrote two simple and unpretentious books about cooking and food, *Home Cooking: A Writer in the Kitchen* and *More Home Cooking: A Writer Returns to the Kitchen*. Reading her makes you feel as though she is your favorite bighearted, funny friend, instructing you with love on how to entertain, and confiding about how much it delights her to cook and eat with friends and family.

Jones was a fan. Over lunch with the editor of *Gourmet*, Jones suggested that Laurie Colwin would be a strong new voice for the magazine, writing about food. "I had read all her stories, and they always had food in them, so I said, 'I bet she would be good.'"

Colwin wrote *Home Cooking* and *More Home Cooking* with Jones. In *Home Cooking*, she writes about her cozy home in New York, where she fed people plain, old-fashioned food such as roast chicken, string beans, lemon cake, and coffee. "One of the delights of life is eating with friends; second to that is talking about eating," starts a passage in *Home Cooking*'s foreword. "And for an unsurpassed double whammy, there is talking about eating while you are eating with friends." Colwin died prematurely of heart failure in 1992. All her books remain in print.

Other award-winning authors Jones has edited are James Beard, Marion Cunningham, Marcella Hazan, Ken Horn, Madhur Jaffrey, Irene Kuo, Joan Nathan, Claudia Roden, and Nina Simonds.

Writing about the Senses

As you've read in some of the examples I've provided, food writing is often all about the senses: touch, smell, sound, appearance, and taste. Many newcomers think this means all they have to do is write about how food tastes. When I hand out a list of adjectives (see page 122) to new students in my classes, it always thrills them. Seasoned food writers work many senses into a single paragraph, while putting them in context. Here's an erotic passage from Ruth Reichl in *Comfort Me with Apples:* "He kissed me and said, 'Close your eyes and open your mouth.' I sniffed the air; it smelled like a cross between violets and berries, with just a touch of citrus [smell].

My mouth closed around something very small and quite soft [touch], the size of a little grape but with a scratchy surface [appearance]. 'Do you like it?' he asked anxiously. I tasted spring [taste]. 'They're fraises de bois from France!' He slipped another one in my mouth."

Smell is the most important sense, because most of what you taste comes from smelling it first. That's why you can't taste food when you have a cold. Jean-Anthelme Brillat-Savarin, a lawyer and gastronome, figured it out in his 1825 book, *The Physiology of Taste.* "For my part I am not only convinced that without the cooperation of smell there can be no complete degustation, but I am also tempted to believe that smell and taste are in fact but a single sense, whose laboratory is the mouth and whose chimney is the nose; or to be more precise, in which the mouth performs the degustation of tactile bodies, and the nose the degustation of gases." (Brillat-Savarin was the author of the famous comment, "Tell me what you eat and I will tell you what you are.")

Identifying odors and tastes is elusive, and writing about them is just as difficult. Writes Diane Ackerman, in *A Natural History of the Senses,* "Smells coat us, swirl around us, enter our bodies, emanate from us. We live in a constant wash of them. Still, when we try to describe a smell, words fail us like the fabrications they are." Most writers convey a flavor or aroma by using analogy, where something is "like" something else. But it's tricky. "You could say basil tastes a little like mint," proposes Colman Andrews. "What if you've never tasted mint?"

It's easy to get carried away with adjectives when writing about the senses because adjectives are a perfect way to describe them. Too many will weaken writing, making you sound sentimental. Darra Goldstein suggests reading M. F. K. Fisher, who uses "one perfect adjective that somehow manages to encompass a whole range of sensation, or something atmospheric that allows you to understand what the sensation was." She gives this example from a *New Yorker* essay: "It was reward enough to sit in the almost empty room, chaste rococo in the slanting June sunlight, with the generous tub of pure delight between us, Mother purring there, the vodka seeping slyly through our veins, and real wood strawberries to come, to make us feel like children again and not near-gods." Rococo is anything but chaste, says Goldstein. "It's over the top, but Fisher manages to convey the sense of childlike innocence she goes on to describe in the sentence by means of this single adjective."

While taste and smell are critical to food writing, so is touch. Touch informs the reader about the ripeness of a cantaloupe, or how to judge a steak's doneness. Steingarten believes we should monitor other physical sensations as well, such as the sense of locomotion in stirring, where you detect physical changes and sensitivity to temperature as a sauce thickens. Chef and author Anthony Bourdain explores touch in *A Cook's Tour: In Search of the Perfect Meal:* "I had to learn to use bits of bread, pinching the food between the two—and only two—fingers and the thumb of the right hand, the digits protected by a layer of folded bread. . . . Abdul (was) tearing the white centers from each little triangle of bread, creating an ersatz pocket. . . I called him on it, accused him playfully of cheating while I struggled with the thick, not easily folded hunks."

Then there's the visual aspect. Some writers excel at writing about the physical features of food. In *An Omelet and a Glass of Wine,* Elizabeth David describes sugar-coated coriander and caraway seeds, "bright as shiny tiddlywinks." In *Between Meals,* Liebling wrote that the haricot verts he was served "resembled decomposed whiskers from a theatrical-costume beard." While these examples instantly bring images to mind, note that one sounds positive while one does not. Notice how the similes are more sophisticated than mere adjectives.

David, a British writer who educated first England and then the world on Mediterranean food, writes in a sensuous, stimulating, and intellectual style. Here she focuses on sight, scent, and taste: "Now there are signs of autumn on the leaves of some of the almond trees. They have turned a frail, transparent auburn, and this morning when I awoke I devoured two of the very first tangerines of the season. In the dawn their scent was piercing and their taste was sharp."

Writers Jane and Michael Stern provide an elegant example combining touch and visual writing in *Gourmet,* where they describe the ultimate apple pie. You can see their minds going into slow motion to describe the experience: "The crust is as crunchy as a butter cookie, so brittle that it cracks audibly when you press it with your fork; grains of cinnamon sugar bounce off the surface as it shatters. The bottom crust is softer than the top, but browned and still breakable. Where the top and bottom meet, there's a knotty cord of dough that becomes impregnated with enough fruit filling to make it chewy. Inside is a dense apple pack of firm Ida Red crescents bound in syrupy juice." The specificity of the words, combined with active verbs such as bounce, crack, and shatter, makes this description so powerful.

Some writers think the least important sense is sound. But consider how it enlivens the experience in Alan Richman's colorful *Bon Appétit* essay, "The Great Texas Barbecue Secret": "Because the meat is seldom pricked during cooking, the fat accumulates, sizzling and bubbling. Slice, and the drama unfolds. Think of a bursting water pipe. Better yet, imagine a Brahman bull exploding from the gate at a rodeo."

Describing your perceptions is difficult to get right. Most beginning writers tend to overdo it. In the worst case, says *Los Angeles Times* writer Russ Parsons, it can be cloying, gratuitous, and prurient. "The idea is not to be flashy but elegant. You want to use enough sensual language that you get across your pleasure and your involvement with the topic, but don't want to come across as overblown, which reads as cheap and unconvincing. Write it and keep going over it, taking out as much as you possibly can and leaving the essence."

So how do you become skilled in describing the senses? Molly O'Neill advises beginning writers to live by their senses for a while. She kept a taste journal for ten years. "Every time I tasted something I wrote about it. Now I have a large anthology of the experience of taste," she explains. She uses the journal to feed an "unconscious kind of database that exists beneath the realm of consciousness, looking for what will trigger it to come to the surface."

Perhaps the best way to access the senses is not to take them for granted. I like the way Richman and the Sterns slow down to describe each moment as it unfolded. Editor Judith Jones advises writers to use the senses as a starting point, the evocative element, and then go on to the larger theme or context.

Getting Passion Across

Just like the senses, passion is an essential part of food writing but difficult to get across. Strong feelings can mislead. It's easier to tell readers about your enthusiasm by stating it outright than by revealing it through the words you choose. The classic writing rule of "show, don't tell" applies here, where your job is to show your devotion rather than to tell the reader about it. It's challenging. When you turn a camera on people to get to their passion, says Andrews, they freeze up, use big words, and become stilted, especially when they're very emotional about a subject. "You can't just open a vein and let it flow out. If you're very passionate about some wonderful dish, you have to tame your passion to write about it, [or] it will probably come across sounding stupid."

O'Neill shows both emotion and restraint with this lead for a recipe column in the *New York Times:* "There should be soup all the time, but especially in the winter. Like the steam that fogs windows as a caldron simmers, soup gives the body a sense of safety and satisfaction." Passion is what makes writing come alive, says O'Neill. "The writing says, 'I really have something to tell you.' It's an act of will versus a compulsiveness to share, to examine, and to tell a story. It has fresh language and accuracy. It propels the writer like a life force. It's not a commodity, but a state of mind. With enough practice one learns to work with it."

When you're in the midst of feeling this kind of fervor as

you write, it's a beautiful thing. Goldstein says passion overtakes her and won't ever let her go. Even when she was writing her dissertation and working as a professor, she had to write about food because she was thinking about it all the time. That's because passion is really a compulsion, explains Jones, conveyed in a sense of urgency.

Intensity comes and goes, like being in and out of love, says freelancer David Leite. "At times I'm on a holy tear," he admits. "It's just coming out. I'm channeling something. As quickly as it came, one day I wake up and it's gone. I have to accept that. The only way to get it back on a regular basis is to sit down and write every day." Sometimes he writes for six hours and it's only the last sentence of the day that delights him, he says. But when that happens, "It's enough to float me, to give me energy to pick up and start writing again tomorrow." The bottom line about passion, he says, is to take advantage of it when it's there, because there's no regular way to get it.

Obsession can be a by-product, and in that case, "Jeffrey Steingarten is the king of obsession, the ultimate foodie in the history of the world," says Richman. He means that as a compliment. Many of the people interviewed for this chapter admire the obsessive way Steingarten takes on a subject. Here's an example from Steingarten's first book, *The Man Who Ate Everything,* in his essay on choucroutes:

Whenever I travel to France, I like to hit the ground eating, but my urgency on this trip was even more intense than usual—a brief week in Alsace was barely long enough to sample the fourteen authentic choucroutes. I had passed a sleepless night and morning on the trip to Strasbourg—two plane flights and an endless wait for airport connections—while my wife slumbered beside me like a puppy. Anticipating that I would lose consciousness as soon as we rented our car, my instructions to her had been the model of clarity: Drive directly from the airport to Itternheim on the forlorn outskirts of Strasbourg, avoid the twofold snare of ineffable scenery and medieval churches. Park at the Hotel-Restaurant au Boeuf and make a reservation for lunch. Enjoy yourself very quietly for the next two hours. Wake me at 1:00 p.m. for our first steaming plate of true choucroute.

Jones, editor of, *The Man Who Ate Everything,* says Steingarten is equally at home whether tasting baguettes at a contest or fishing for tuna, as he "becomes the average man who has passion but makes the same gaffes and laughs at his own compulsiveness." Steingarten is hilarious when he uses himself as a scapegoat. When I asked him about humor, Steingarten says it's not necessary to be funny all the time. "Some writers aren't funny in every sentence but you know you're going to end up laughing," he says.

Obsessiveness can lead to being in love with your subject, which occasionally means including too much information in a piece. Even Steingarten admits he needs editing. "I'm not about to chastise Anna Wintour (editor in chief of *Vogue*) about not finding something interesting," he says. "I will change it a little and she'll read it over. People don't realize she reads every word twice." For more on how to edit your own work, see page 94 in chapter 4.

The Role of Voice

Great writers, including food writers, spend years perfecting their voice. Voice combines writing style and point of view. It is also called style. *The Elements of Style,* an essential handbook for writers, refers to voice simply as "the sound a writer's words make on paper." It's what makes you authentic. It conveys your personality, flair, and originality. "Voice exists to make the piece more readable, to make it more enjoyable, to explain or illuminate difficult concepts without seeming dry," explains editor Andrews. "People can explain a difficult subject and because they write conversationally, it comes across better."

You can't invent a voice, most say. I once asked a writing coach at a conference how I could write in a voice as lyrical as Molly O'Neill's. He suggested an exercise where I copy O'Neill's style by parodying it, which would give me insight into how she pulls it off. But editor Judith Jones disagrees, "Woe unto a writer who tries to imitate another writer's voice," she cautions. "It's not something borrowed or imitated, it is you. It describes how you actually feel. It's what makes the writer individual." She's right. I have my own voice, and my job is to make it come out clearly. The same goes for you. Don't try to copy the writing of those you admire.

O'Neill says, "Voice is a guide in a landscape, the guide in a journey. Voice holds a reader's hand and says, 'Come on, this is going to be fun, it's okay to do, we've got a lot of serious things to look at here and I'm going to help you.' As long as voice is clear and consistent, the reader will respond. The reader has to know where you're coming from and how it's going to affect them."

Voice helps readers form an image of the writer. To put it in modern business parlance, it's as though you were creating a brand. It's possible to write a story without using much voice, particularly in newspapers, where news stories are more likely to be straightforward. When I wrote my first essay after years of newswriting, I was startled by my own voice. I wondered if I was revealing too much of my personality. For readers to get the most out of a story, they should understand who you are. Your voice gives the narrative unity and strength, says Goldstein. "Writers starting out are afraid to put their voice in there. They think, 'What if people criticize it or don't like it?' Without it, your writing can be a little pallid, and sounds like everyone else's writing. Voice makes you sound sure of yourself." So don't worry about being "writerly," because it makes your work more serious and boring. Write the way you speak.

Your writing expresses your uniqueness. "Voice is the sound, rhythm, and point-of-view that unequivocally evokes the writer," writes David Leite on http://www.egullet.org, the Web site of the Egullet Society for Culinary Arts and Letters. "You know it when you read it." He suggests reading passages by Jeffery Steingarten, Calvin Trillin, Tony Bourdain, M. F. K. Fischer, and Ruth Reichl. You can hear each author's voice in your head as you read. "And more importantly, you can never confuse or interchange them. Bourdain is not Steingarten, who is not Trillin, who is not Reichl."

"Voice is often misunderstood," explains former *Los Angeles Times* food editor Russ Parsons. People usually think they must reveal their inner secrets and it's a deeply personal matter. But voice is not about you. "It's the rhythm of language, writerly tricks, the choice of words."

Maybe the way to use the writing coach's advice is to find your own voice by exaggerating it. Amanda Hesser, author of the memoir *Looking for Mr. Latte: A Food Lover's Courtship, With Recipes,* said she exaggerated both her own characteristics and her boyfriend's to make their voices more clear, and she did so without worrying that the story was becoming fictional. "She was the bumbling, snobby food person who needed to be put in her place; he was muse and hero," she explains on the Leite's Culinaria Web site at http://www.leitesculinaria.com.

The best food writers capture the authentic emotion of the moment, the tone of what's going on at the time, and what they feel physically. If you have trouble finding your voice, consult list of descriptions as a starting point (see page 19). Ask a few friends to describe your voice to you. Often they're better at it than you are, because you might think of your voice as "just you," and therefore not describable.

Other ways to make your voice stronger in writing include your choice of language and cultural references. Examine your word choices and play with them. Do you use big words, for example, or reference movies or music? Your voice can show age, geographic location, gender, or even your religious persuasion. Here's how restaurant critic Jonathan Gold opens a review: "If you grew up eating hot dogs in the swinging San Fernando Valley '70s, your family probably had allegiances to the Hot Dog Show or Flooky's or the Wiener Factory, which were as inarguable, as inevitable, as the question of Orthodox, Conservative or Reform." Without his ever explicitly saying so, you can assume he's Jewish, grew up in Los Angeles, and probably is in his forties now. Without a strong voice, you risk becoming a superficial narrator.

WRITERS DESCRIBE THEIR OWN VOICES

Darra Goldstein, author and editor of *Gastronomica: The Journal of Food and Culture:* My voice changes when I write for different publications. For an essay in *Gourmet,* I had a kind of cheerful, playful voice that underlies subject. For my editor letter in *Gastronomica,* I feel compelled to sound intellectual. Now I'm working on a scholarly article. I have to restrain the impetuous voice. It's not appropriate for the audience.

Colman Andrews, author and former editor in chief of *Saveur* magazine: It varies a lot according to the story. When I don't have lots of words, I keep myself out of the story, or do so in subtle ways. A lot has been autobiographical, where voice has to be in it as much as possible. Sometimes it depends on the intensity with which you let your voice be heard, or it has to do with the appropriate publication.

Alan Richman, editor-at-large of *Bon Appétit* magazine: I'm a diffident, cranky, New York guy who walks into a restaurant and waits to see how he's going to be abused. I'm a passive-aggressive guy who gets the last word. I am someone to whom things happen. Writers should take a passive role so readers feel represented.

Russ Parsons food columnist for the *Los Angeles Times:* By nature I'm kind of a smart-ass. I try to score as many points off myself as other people when I'm writing in the first person. It's important to be self-deprecating, not self-aggrandizing. I pay a lot of attention to rhythm, sentence length, and structure.

Jeffrey Steingarten, author and *Vogue* magazine food critic: Obsessive, possibilities to humor.

Calvin Trillin, book author, freelance writer, and columnist:
Genial glutton.

Judith Jones, author and Knopf vice president and senior editor:
I focus on how I feel, how I think. That's what makes it individual.

Molly O'Neill, book author, freelance writer, and former food columnist for the *New York Times Sunday Magazine:* Poetic writing has to be balanced by precision, clarity, [and the] tension between humor and gravity. You only have one voice but it has many different expressions. My piece for the *New Yorker* is different than a news story for the *New York Times* or a memoir about my family. All are particular parts of my voice. I have more range in longer form.

David Leite, freelance writer and publisher of the Leite's Culinaria Web site: I write the way I speak, influenced through a lifetime of hearing my mother's humor. I can be a little wicked at times. I turned to humor in adolescence. I developed that person and it came out on the page.

DESCRIBE YOUR OWN VOICE

Writing becomes stronger when you know who you are. If you decide you are sarcastic, for example, then you have a tool with which to assess your writing to ensure your voice comes across that way. Go through the following list and pick the top five adjectives that you think describe you and your voice. If you have trouble, ask friends to select some adjectives for you.

- Reassuring
- Humble
- Vulnerable
- Believable
- Mysterious
- Knowledgeable
- Approachable
- Relaxed
- Competent
- Knowing

- Enthusiastic
- Calm
- Workmanlike
- Funny
- Matter-of-fact
- Sarcastic
- Sardonic
- Avuncular
- Reserved
- Ironic
- Spare
- Poetic
- Provocative
- Sensuous

- Bemused
- Tart
- Lyrical
- Wry
- Defiant
- Self-effacing
- Welcoming
- Playful
- Sensitive
- Incisive
- Curious
- Intellectual
- Aggressive

Writing Exercises

1. This exercise will make your writing livelier. It shows you how to use simile and metaphor instead of adjectives, how to substitute generic nouns, and how to use varying sentence length to your advantage.

   Write a long paragraph about eating a favorite piece of fruit, using all the senses. Use a simile and a metaphor in your paragraph. (A simile tells the reader what something is like, such as "The grapes were like a string of tiny black pearls." A metaphor directly compares one thing to another, as in "I picked one of the shiny jewels, dusky with the Napa soil, and held it in the palm of my hand, trying to feel its weight.")

   When you're done, go back over the paragraph, and look for generic nouns, substituting concrete ones for them. For example, if you're writing about workers on a farm, you might replace the word "people" with the word "farmhands." Once you've made some replacements, go over your work once more and look at your sentence structure. Are you in a rut, with sentences all of one length? Adjust them to make some short and some long.

Right away, you'll see a stronger, more distinct voice emerge in your writing. Elizabeth Lyon, author of *A Writer's Guide to Nonfiction*, led a class on this practical exercise at a writer's conference seminar I attended.

2. More ways to use simile and metaphor: Fill in the blanks by comparing the following foods to nonedible objects such as wet newspaper or diesel oil. Write a long sentence. Instead of "The cheese was as ripe as a locker room," write "The cheese was as ripe as a locker room of thirty sweaty soccer players disrobing after a game."

   The cheese was as ripe as. . .
   The donut smelled stale, like a. . .
   The roast beef sandwich tasted as though. . .

3. David Leite told me about an exercise for the senses he learned when he studied acting. Every day for a week, the actor holds an imaginary familiar object in his or her hands—in David's case, an ordinary coffee mug. Each day he smelled, looked at, and tasted imaginary coffee. He did this exercise for five minutes a day for one week. It's a great way to slow down, study one thing, and capture its essence. Record your observations to see whether you are stuck using one particular descriptive device, such as adjectives. Mix it up by using cultural references one day or similes the next.

4. Develop your writing ability to show rather than tell. Choose a favorite food. Write two paragraphs explaining why you love it. Get your passion across without sentences starting with "I just can't get enough of. . . ." If

you love licorice, show your devotion by writing about the lengths to which you will go procure it, for example, or how often you consume it.

2

Characteristics of a Food Writer

I f you want to be a food writer, you're probably already passionate about food and eating, and perhaps cooking as well. That's where it begins. Almost all the writers interviewed for this book talked about passion, or else exuded passion, no matter how many years they had been on the job. If your friends think you're odd because you love to talk about food, take heart. You're on the right path.

Knopf vice president and senior editor Judith Jones, who has edited such superstars as Julia Child and James Beard, says she's "absolutely convinced" people love food because they are born with a food-loving gene. "I saw that in my own family, I was always curious and asked questions, loved food, whereas my sister couldn't care less," she recalls. "You can develop taste, but passion is certainly a genetic thing, like a good ear for music."

Many food writers I've met are enthusiastic, intense, and energetic in an obsessive kind of way, and love nothing more than immersing themselves in research. And who can blame them? After all, if you get paid to write about a day in the life of a bing cherry farmer, the history of *tres leches* cakes, or a restaurant roundup in Rome, it's hard not to throw yourself into the task.

Based on interviews with food writers and editors, I've made a list of characteristics. Some play off each other. For example, it's easy to be a fastidious researcher when you're passionate about your subject. It's easy to be knowledgeable about your subject if you've done your research. It's easy to be energetic if you're passionate. See how these traits come together?

Some characteristics can be learned. When I studied how to become a newspaper reporter in journalism school, I learned how to research anything and how to persist until I got the interviews I needed for stories. Those skills have served me well all through my career. Few writers have all the traits I've listed below. You don't need every single one to succeed. Certain characteristics may predispose you to be good at certain types of food writing. Researchers like historical writing and longer stories. Skeptics make good restaurant reviewers. Attention to detail, persistence, and curiosity are terrific characteristics for any kind of food writing, but particularly for recipe developers. In chapter 5, you'll learn why developing recipes requires making and testing them over and over. You've got to be persistent and curious about why your braised lamb turns out different each time.

Here's my list of characteristics. As you read, consider how many of these describe you. (If you don't mind marking up book pages, check them off.) You need to see if you are suited to the task, just as some people become firemen because it suits their personality, values, and interests. Some of these identifications may be no-brainers, but others will deserve more thought. Many are interrelated. There's no magic number to tick off. Only you can decide whether you have the skills and determination to write about food.

- *Passionate:* People who love food are an eager, enthusiastic bunch, and it carries over when they write. A huge appetite for joy and appreciation fuels food writers, says former *New York Times Sunday Magazine* writer and cookbook author Molly O'Neill. It pushes them to communicate pleasurable and enjoyable experiences their readers have never had. "Passion is really a compulsion, conveyed in a sense of urgency," says Jones. "This is what makes writing come alive."

Passion usually involves the pleasure experienced by writers and readers, but not always. I felt passionate about being a board member of a food bank, which led to a long essay on feeding the hungry in *Gastronomica* magazine. I wanted my readers to feel outrage, compassion for the less fortunate, and compunction to act, even if it was just to donate food or money. I felt intensely dedicated to my goal of communicating how our country feeds hungry people. My job was to get emotion onto the page, so readers would want to jump into in the story and continue all the way through.

Some of the best writers remain passionate despite years on the job. Alan Richman, editor at large for *Bon Appétit,* says when on an assignment to find and eat food, he becomes "crazy with happiness when things taste so good," perhaps in part because it's not that common. You'll learn more about restaurant reviewing in chapter 4.

➡ *Enthusiastic researchers:* You can never have too much information on a subject before you begin writing about it. Food writers are always asking questions. As fastidious readers and researchers, it's common to have an obsessive personality, and think every aspect of, say, a goat cheese producer's life, is fascinating. By the time they have done enough work on the subject to justify writing about it, they burst with information. *Los Angeles Times* food columnist Russ Parsons admits, "When I'm researching a story, I go completely berserk. I may have 300 pages of research and photocopies for a 1,500-word article. I want to know everything, to have total saturation in every aspect of the subject."

Saturation is a starting point for the article. Your next job is to sift through the information and decide what's compelling and necessary. That depends on the angle of the story, who your readers are and what they want to read, your word count, and your structure. More about this a bit later, when I discuss the importance of being focused (page 27).

Research doesn't necessarily mean spending hours in a dingy library pouring over dusty tomes. It can be much more exotic. Food writers are constantly on the go—traveling, finding familiar foods in new and unusual places, tasting the way people in another country prepare a familiar food, and bringing new flavors to readers, says Toni Allegra, head of the Symposium for Professional Food Writers.

Cooking is another part of research. It's easier to write well about some subjects if you cook, advises *Gastronomica* editor Darra Goldstein, as it helps you understand your subject. If your research involves historical cooking methods or recipes, for example, try the methods or make the recipes. Describing it is not enough, because cooking is an important part of your understanding of the food and how the context of cooking works into your story. You must be willing to make or eat whatever is necessary in the name of research.

In recipe writing, research might mean looking up the origin of a dish, understanding the chemistry of how it works, or comparing recipes to see how others made the dish.

➻ *Energetic:* You can't be running around the world, transcribing notes, endlessly looking up information, and interviewing without being energetic. O'Neill, for example, says she works seven days per week, twelve hours per day. Not everyone works that hard, and it's not like you won't succeed if you don't. But O'Neill's seemingly boundless energy might be one of the reasons for her success.

And as I mentioned earlier, passion is the best fuel for working long hours or pushing yourself to get the story, chapter, or recipe done. On days where you're so immersed in your work that the hours fly by, you know you've chosen a great profession. Enthusiasm keeps you interested, keeps you asking questions, keeps you engaged and challenged. It's the same in any competitive industry.

➻ *Focused:* When you find a topic endlessly fascinating, it gets hard to decide what to leave in and what to leave out. You need focus. I have this problem occasionally. While researching a story on table etiquette, for example, I ended up on the floor in a bookstore, enthralled by out-dated books on how to supervise servants doing meal preparation. I liked the quaint notions so much that I mentioned some to my editor, who reminded me that I was writing about today's social graces and asked if I had the right sources for the story. Oops.

Fortunately, word counts will rein you in. Outlines are a good tool as well. The thing to understand is that people don't have to know everything, just what's most impor-tant. The more you add, the larger the subject becomes, and soon it's about everything and not something in particular.

➻ *Skeptical:* Research often includes the ability to approach information with healthy skepticism. Ernest Hemingway, who often wrote about food in his novels, said in a 1958 interview in the *Paris Review,* "The most essential gift for a good writer is a built-in, shockproof, shit detector. This is the writer's radar and all great writers have it."

It's not that you have to spend months trying to verify information and sources, but you shouldn't just rely on what other people have written unless you know that they themselves are good sources or experts. Origins of customs or events are particularly suspect in food writing, says Goldstein, because even when wrong, they become myths perpetuated as common knowledge.

I just read in the food section of a daily paper that Julia Child dropped a chicken on the floor during a television show, picked it up, and said it's fine to serve because no one will know. I've seen that episode. She was transferring a potato-based dish from the stove onto a plate and dropped some of it on the stove-top. No chickens were involved, but the writer of the newspaper story just took what she read somewhere and ran with it. In a perfect situation, she would have been suspicious of that outrageous-sounding story, and she would have found a way to check it out.

Editors and writers can tell when others don't do their homework. Parsons, the former editor of the *Los Angeles Times'* food section, says there's lots of writing that wouldn't be regarded as research, such as the passing along of secondhand information, as in the chicken story above. But you can't pull off something accurate without testing it yourself. Or without researching it yourself. An author I worked with spent hours in the library verifying assertions some famous people had made about themselves, such as "I was the first to" or "I won an award for." Most of the time, she discovered, these people had exaggerated.

• *Fearless:* Research requires fearlessness. It's easier to be fearless if, once again, you're so enthusiastic that you plunge into things. Food writers must "taste things they don't want to taste, talk to someone they don't want to talk to, and get themselves wedged into a situation to get the information, to learn," says freelance writer David Leite.

Anthony Bourdain is the king of fearlessness. He traveled around the world for his book *A Cook's Tour* and for a television show, doing extreme eating, a term he disavows. "It's really important to be a good guest, because the table is the best reflection of a nation and fastest way into that culture," he counsels. "You have to be willing to put yourself in a situation and let things happen. You can't be squeamish or hesitant. It might require that you match your hosts shot for shot with vodka laced with bear bile. Now is not the time to say 'I'm a vegetarian' or 'I'm lactose intolerant.'"

"It's a common flaw to be contemptuous of the subject or afraid of the nasty bits like dirt, strange food, unfamiliar experiences, or to feel jaded," he continues. "Fear of the other makes a lot of food and travel writers bad writers. Get people to talk about eating in Mexico— they complain about the water, think they might get sick, and they don't want to eat raw vegetables."

You have to be the kind of person who wants whatever it is so badly that you go for it. Bourdain knew there would be consequences to his extreme eating around the globe, and if you've read *A Cook's Tour,* you know that he was quite ill sometimes. But it didn't keep him from eating a still-beating snake heart, or downing street food in Southeast Asia.

Sometimes fearlessness is about getting up the nerve to contact people you hold in high esteem. I had that challenge writing this book, and I'm here to tell you that two people I worshipped from afar and feared calling turned out to be polite, accessible, prompt, and interested in helping me. What would have happened if I never got up the nerve to contact them? Not only would the book be the poorer for it, but I wouldn't have the rosy glow I have right now from remembering our interactions. They made my day, my week, my year!

I have three pieces of advice that might help you get difficult tasks done. If you have to make a phone call, do it first thing in the morning, as soon as you get to your desk. That way you won't stew over it all day long and keep procrastinating. Act "as if." That means behaving as though you are a superconfident, warm, witty person who would be fun to talk with, even if you're nervous as hell and don't believe it. Ask yourself, "What's the worst that could happen?" Often, fear of what will happen is blown out of proportion compared to the consequences.

➻ *Inquisitive:* Food writers share endless curiosity and culinary adventurism. They like to wander around hoping to stumble upon something curious or magnificent, such as finding four new kinds of melon at a French street market or meeting a master bread baker at a party and talking for hours. Richman says he has been called a culinary anthropologist because of the amount of research he unearths while working on his stories. If you're not curious enough, says Leite, "You're not going to get to the next sentence, and you're not going to discover the next thing to write about."

➻ *Persistent:* Hand-in-hand with curiosity is the ability to be relentless. Former *New York Times* restaurant critic Mimi Sheraton writes in her memoir, *Eating My Words,* that she went to a restaurant twelve times until she was sure how she felt about it. Luckily, the *Times* picked up the bill. Even if the work seems tedious, such as pouring through tons of information to find a few facts, or asking so many questions you run the risk of sounding thick, the best food writers keep going until they get what they want.

➻ *Knowledgeable about the subject:* When they're ready to write, the best food writers know the subject matter inside out. This strategy increases confidence and helps provide credibility if you're not an expert on a certain food or ingredient. If you're not an expert, suggests Colman Andrews, editor in chief of *Saveur,* "The next best thing is to learn about it and take the reader along with you as you go." This takes guts, because you must sound like you know what you're talking about. People have done it. Laura Werlin took this approach with her first book about cheese (see page 145).

I've done it myself. I pitched a story to a national magazine about how to serve cheese plates at a dinner party. I had served cheese casually but wanted to learn more. I read enough from books to write a pitch letter, then skimmed six books. By the time I started writing, I knew what I was talking about. I felt comfortable with this technique because the article was short. I made my major points, filled them in, and I was done.

You might structure a story by playing the neophyte and taking the reader on a journey as you become more knowledgeable. Jeffrey Steingarten favors this technique in his *Vogue* essays. It soon becomes clear, however, that he has researched the subject thoroughly and cleverly leads you down a path.

➻ *Professional:* Beginning writers are sometimes perceived as lazy, or as dabblers. People think there are special rules for food writing, that it's not as demanding as other kinds of writing, says Andrews. "Because food writing is kind of trivial or unimportant, they think they don't have to be as accurate, because they're not writing about the president, they're writing about Wolfgang Puck."

I'm glad he's honest enough to say so. In my own experience, when I tell people outside the profession that I write and edit on the subject of food, I get a curious look, as in "Is that really a profession?" Some people also think food writing is a hobby and an excuse to eat and travel well. Close. It's actually a *profession* where you get to eat and travel well, if you're doing it right.

The standards for being a professional food writer are not rocket science. Always:

1. Be polite in your transactions, particularly when asking for help, and thank people who have helped you.

2. Be thorough and accurate: particularly when spelling names and stating titles.
3. Make deadlines and provide exactly what you've said you were going to write, or what you've agreed to write; cooperate with your editor to the best of your ability.
4. Avoid hissy fits or prima donna behavior (if you want more assignments).

➤ *Nostalgia for the past:* When I wrote my first food-themed essay, it was about my mother and her cooking. Eventually I learned I was not alone in writing about food and memory. It's common to want to write about your family, particularly the person who taught you how to cook. This desire parallels the way people start out in fiction writing, working from autobiographical information. It's what you know. The information is easily accessible because it's right there in your brain.

When I teach, students tell me of their desire to write nostalgic memories. I've heard it so often I've decided it's a normal part of the process. Sure, start with your recollections. Practice setting the scene, putting the story in context, and adding a few recipes. Starting is different from publishing. If publishing is your goal, you must say something new. I actually did get the essay about my mother published in an international magazine. It focused on her inability, as an immigrant, to master Western foods like sandwiches, spaghetti, and meat and potatoes. It was funny and bittersweet, but most important, it had an angle that made my story different from the same old thing editors see repeatedly: Most editors don't see a lot of memoir pieces about having a mother who was an Iraqi Jew from China who cooked funny Western foods.

Magazine editor Goldstein says she sees too many story pitches "for the good old days, the grandmother, the sentimentality for everything done by hand lovingly. We all had childhoods and we all look back lovingly, but I'm more interested in the edgy stuff, things that help us understand more about ourselves or who we are." Bill LeBlond, editorial director of Chronicle Books, once told a crowd at a cookbook proposals seminar that if he had to read one more book proposal from people who learned about cooking at their grandmothers' knee, he would throw up.

I'm not trying to dissuade you from writing about your family. If you know how to shape your writing, it's certainly possible to write a cookbook, memoir, or essay focusing on a family theme. Take, for example, *In Nonna's Kitchen: Recipes and Traditions from Italy's Grandmothers* by Carol Field, which succeeds for a couple of reasons. It's about Italian food, and Americans are obsessed with Italian cooking. Field is an accomplished cookbook writer, and it was not her first book. And it's about several grandmothers who have spent their lives guarding their culinary heritage, not just about one grandmother who cooked for Field. *Monsoon Diary: A Memoir with Recipes,* by Shoba Narayan, chronicles family rituals and love of food, but also discusses her trouble adjusting to an arranged marriage and shatters stereotypes of immigrant life. Her funny, sparkling narrative doesn't hurt either. It might have something to do with her masters in journalism from Columbia, where she was awarded a Pulitzer fellowship.

I'm not trying to depress you, but I'm not the cheerleader type who says anyone can do it. These two writers paid their dues to get to where they are today. They work very hard on their writing, and so must you.

- **Ethical:** Along the lines of persistent visits to restaurants (à la Mimi Sheraton) is the issue of ethics. Food writers must have a strong sense of who they are and whom they represent. They get offered many free things, particularly food and travel. The best writers pay their own way or, if they're lucky, a publication pays their way. Otherwise, a writer might feel indebted to a restaurant or tourist association, and be less likely to write that the fish was overcooked or that a food festival was boring. Inevitably, food writers get to know other people in the business, such as chefs and public relations people, and sticky situations can result. A food writer's job is to be honest. Reviewer Richman explains that good food writing is "not press trips to Tuscany, not free meals at restaurants, and not the adoration of famous chefs where you sit around saying 'yum yum' to everything put in front of you."

➻ *Careful:* When I asked experienced food writers what they dislike most about other food writing, the number one complaint was the use of too many adjectives, clichés, and flowery metaphors, where, instead of crafting beautiful sentences, writers rely too much on strings of adverbs and adjectives to move the story along. That means avoiding writing sentences like "The huge artichoke on the garnet dinner plate was a sage-colored flower waiting to be devoured, its leaves pointing skyward, concealing the hidden treasure within." Metaphors compare by saying a thing is something else, such as "the artichoke was a sage-colored flower." I'm not telling the reader anything new. "Hidden treasure within" is a cliché because it's not original. And while I'm critiquing, "was" doesn't carry the sentence forward with strength or interest.

Veteran writer O'Neill keeps rampant and vague adjectives at bay by evolving her taste vocabulary, even after decades as a food writer. Her main tool is a taste diary she kept for ten years. One of her mentors suggested using such a diary so that later, if she was writing about a raspberry, she could go back and consult her earlier impressions.

Generic descriptions are just as bad as overwrought ones. Here's an example I found just now when I picked up a national food magazine and turned to a recipe.

"These beans are fantastic served with grilled chicken and rice. And if you have some nice chicken stock on hand, you can use it instead of water to cook the beans." Why are the beans fantastic? Do they complement the chicken and rice a certain way, and if so, how? Texture? Flavor? What is "nice" chicken stock? There's no way to know.

While vague language won't ruin the recipe, a more specific introduction helps the reader imagine making the dish and serving it. Suppose the beans, with their dark red color, provided colorful contrast to the white rice, or the stock was deeply flavored. Specific writing is always preferable. Allegra suggests you learn to use a tool like Rodale's *Synonym Finder* to find the right words, because "you can only say 'delicious' so many times." To help you along, I've listed useful adjectives on page 122.

Writing about food isn't just about describing flavor and smell, anyway. Food may be the subject of a story, but the point of the story can reside in recounting, reporting, and finding the right details, as well as in the history, associations, implications, and of course, the context of the story itself.

According to O'Neill, another way writers can go wrong is when they write advertisements for themselves rather than guide the reader on a journey. Further, some writers get confused between knowledge for the sake of empowerment and knowledge for the sake of showing off. I've read lots of showy writing. It's the self-satisfied I'm-sitting-here-eating-truffles-on-the-balcony-of-a-terribly-expensive-hotel-in-Capri-and-you're-not approach. This type of writing implies the writer thinks he's excruciatingly important, which in turn implies his readers are not. Insulting your readers does not endear you to them.

All the writers interviewed here write in the first person, but they pull it off because of their experience, writing style, solid reporting, and research. They separate the narrator from themselves—the writer—so they are not building a story based on confession. They don't say "I" in every sentence. Even though the writing involves them, it's not about them. It's about engaging readers in a great story. Steingarten always writes in the first person as a "naïve narrator" who knows less than the author. But he doesn't believe he has to be consistent. He tries different styles in the same piece, such as using a conversational tone and then a businesslike tone, and has tried switching from first person to second person (speaking to the reader as "you," as in "you walk into a bar. . . ").

Related to this focus is too much navel-gazing. When I was a magazine editor I found many of my writers' first drafts filled with minutiae, particularly in the beginning of the article. I call this the "deep dive," where writers move quickly into the small details. They get so involved in the story they lose perspective. "You need a sense of levity and relief," advises O'Neill. "If you just go around being what you think, you become a caricature of yourself. A writer is a prophet, standing on the mountain screaming. Once you're no longer a siren, you are no longer really a writer." Whoa.

Writing Exercises

1. Write a paragraph about your passion for a certain food. Use *show, not tell*; show your passion instead of telling readers ways that you are passionate. Show would be, "I meant to stop myself after the first five handfuls, but before I knew it, I looked down and saw an empty, grease-stained cardboard bowl, with a few shiny kernels sticking to the bottom." Tell would be, "I really love popcorn."

2. Write two paragraphs about your favorite dish, using no adjectives. This is not just a description, but details about

different ways you've made the dish, where you've eaten it, or who joined you at the table. At first the writing will look stark and spare. Now go back and add specific adjectives to make the story sparkle. Limit yourself to three.

3. Go back over your paragraphs from exercise 2 and change any generic nouns to specific ones. For example, change "room" to "kitchen" or "meat" to "duck breast." How do you like the result?

3

Getting Started

I f you've always wanted to write about food as a career, how do you get started? What qualifications do you need? How do people move up the food chain to become food writers?

Fortunately, lots of answers exist. Above all, you must enjoy learning. That's what keeps the best food writers growing and moving forward. They're interested in many subjects, not just their area of expertise. You probably have the same kind of enthusiasm about food, so the next step is to back it up with knowledge. If you're feeling intimidated about your qualifications, this chapter will show you how to pump up your background and skills before you ever write a word. Credibility is an important part of getting a writing job and being taken seriously. The more you have to offer in terms of knowledge and experience, the more likely you are to succeed.

Part of learning about food writing is finding out what jobs exist, what appeals to you, and how others began their careers. One day you'll have a story about how you got started. Learning how to do it will make you more confident. All you need is a plan.

What Types of Jobs Can a Food Writer Have?

Food writers write all kinds of things: cookbooks, news, restaurant reviews, feature articles, travel guides, recipe development and more. When I tell people I'm a food writer, their mouths water as they imagine my glorious life of eating. They imagine I hold court in expensive restaurants every night, get baskets of fine wines and pâtés delivered to my office, have chefs fawning over me, hold elaborate dinner parties, jet to Italy on assignment to do a story on pasta. . . . Well, no. That's not my life. It could be someone else's in the food-writing world, though, if it was ratcheted down a notch—perhaps that of a top author or food personality who writes for the biggest, glossiest magazines with big budgets and expense accounts.

No two food writers do exactly the same job. We are a tough bunch to categorize. Many people do a little of everything, as you'll see in the "Week/Day in the Life" stories on pages 41– 48. I am a food writer for newspapers and magazines, but that's not all I do. I coach people who want to write food-based books and freelance articles; edit proposals and manuscripts; conduct research on agents for clients; and teach.

When the International Association of Culinary Professionals (IACP) asks its members for profile information, they request a limit of five primary professional activities. Under the category of writer, subcategories include freelance writer, magazine writer, newspaper writer, restaurant critic, syndicated columnist, cookbook author, menu and recipe developer, and recipe tester. Here's a breakdown of the IACP categories, so you can see what kind of work food writers do and how much the jobs overlap:

Freelance writer: Most food writers are freelancers, writing for magazines and newspapers. The advantage of working for yourself is working when you want, as much as you want, from your own home and kitchen. Here's the hard part about it: Most write as a sideline to something else because pay for food writing is notoriously low. An IACP survey estimates that many food writers make around $32,000 per year. So in addition to writing, freelance food writers might also cater, work in restaurants, become private chefs, attend cooking school, develop and test recipes for companies, take people on food tours abroad, or teach cooking classes. Writing for corporations pays better—writing press releases, Web site copy, developing recipes and curricula for chefs—but those jobs usually go to experienced cookbook authors who have paid their dues. For an example, see page 45.

Some freelancers work full-time, but most do not. Full-time staff jobs are even more rare. When you see stories in newspapers and magazines, the full-time employees—editors, senior editors, assistant editors—have written some of them in addition to doing their regular jobs.

Syndicated writer: Usually a self-employed freelance writer, this person writes a regular column that a syndication sends to many newspapers around the country. Most freelancers, however, write a story that is published in one place.

A WEEK IN THE LIFE OF A RESTAURANT REVIEWER

Laura Taxel is a full-time freelance food writer and restaurant reviewer in Cleveland, Ohio, and the author of *Cleveland Ethnic Eats 2004: The Guide to Authentic Ethnic Eats in Northeastern Ohio.* To give you an idea of what the life of a food writer entails, I asked her to write to me, diary style, about what she accomplishes in a busy week. Here is her report.

Monday: I had to finish a *Cleveland Plain Dealer* feature about a woman from the Dominican Republic who hosts Caribbean ghost dinners, complete with fried plantains and a professional specter investigator, in a converted nineteenth-century warehouse reputed to be haunted. She did her best getting her recipes down on paper for me but I had to question her closely and rewrite them. Before I finished, it was time to get out of sweats—how I love having a home office—shower, and head out to lunch with a radio reporter who's interviewing me for a series on how the restaurant business impacts the local economy. Made a quick stop on the way home at the grocery store so Barney [Taxel's husband] would have something for dinner, as I would be out for the monthly gathering of Les Dames d'Escoffier International (LDEI).

Tuesday: Started the day at the dermatologist. I wanted to talk rash but he was determined to get personalized dining-out recommendations first. At lunch, as guest speaker at a college alumni luncheon, I told stories about Ohio restaurants, the people who run them, and the extraordinary food they serve. Then I sold and signed copies of my book, *Cleveland Ethnic Eats*. Dinner was at a new restaurant on the other side of town. I'll be including it in the next edition, which I update every year. I tasted many things for the first time—rice and lentil patties called *idli*, fried lentil doughnuts, and *dosai*, which are crispy, paper-thin, rice-flour crepes.

Wednesday: A research morning. Did some background reading for a story about traditional winter holiday foods and the meanings they hold for people. Then had two phone interviews—one with a food historian and the other a local woman who's made wassail and plum pudding for thirty years.

Spent the remainder of the day trying to come up with a way to organize all the material I've gathered for the holiday piece, with two frustrating hours of false starts and nothing to show for it. I'd been invited to a VIP reception for the opening of a new Brazilian steakhouse but decided I needed a quiet night at home. It was a good opportunity to get some work done because my husband was out, but I talked myself out of it. Made an omelet with eggs and feta from the farmers' market, threw together a salad with greens from the garden—simple and scrumptious—read, and went to bed early.

Thursday: Spent most of the day at my desk. Finished an article for Continental Airlines' magazine and emailed it off, then caught up with invoicing and filing. I planned to work on an assignment for *Cleveland* magazine this week, an anatomy of a perfect sandwich and the ten most interesting ones in town. But yesterday my editor called to say he'd changed the run date for the piece . . . again. So I used the time to craft a couple of story pitches. One was for a regional travel publication about the Grand River Valley Ice Wine Festival to be held next March. The other, for a national food magazine, is about a renowned Cleveland chef. His restaurant's been named one of America's best. He has become one of the country's few cheese finishers, importing raw milk varieties from Europe and overseeing their aging in his own cooler.

Had a fabulous dinner at a restaurant I'll be featuring in my monthly column, Letters from the Table, in *Northern Ohio Live* magazine. The kitchen deserves the hype it's been receiving. Everything "Slim" (my husband's nom de plume) and I ate—from soft-shell crab in honey-mustard dressing to skewered scallops with chervil oil and celery root puree, and crispy duck breast, seared foie gras and grit cake—lived up to its promise.

Friday: My car had a repair appointment at the dealership, so I ganged up a bunch of other chores at places along the way. My dentist wanted restaurant recommendations while he cleaned my teeth. I visited a Korean grocery store to gather the facts for an entry in *Cleveland Ethnic Eats*. Chatted with the owner to the extent it's possible when neither speaks the other's language. We both did a great deal of friendly head-nodding, smiling, pointing, and handshaking. I might include his store as a stop on the

Elderhostel ethnic food tour I'll be leading next month. Late in the afternoon, I met with a nonprofit to help plan a fund-raising event that will showcase local female chefs.

Would you like to change places? Taxel has been a food writer for twenty-five years, working up to this kind of career. When I told her that her job sounded like a dream, she answered, "My work isn't a fantasy, it's quite real: Lots of fun, simultaneously demanding and difficult, and poorly compensated. How's that for bringing it back to earth?"

Cookbook author: While these self-employed writers concentrate on writing cookbooks, they also write freelance articles. Some might develop recipes for industry as well, for food retailers, food manufacturers—any company that might take out an ad, produce a newsletter, magazine, or book, or put recipes on its Web site. Cookbook authors are paid an advance to work on their books, which might take anywhere from one to six years, depending on how many recipes they develop and where they travel to do their research. Cookbook authors who are well known with a significant fan base and publishing history may command an advance large enough to put off other jobs while writing the book, but this is rare. Almost all will have to continue taking on other sorts of work, because the advance will not support them.

A Day in the Life of a Recipe Developer and Writer

Greg Patent, based in Missoula, Montana, is a cookbook author and freelance writer. He has written for *Saveur, Fine Cooking, Food & Wine, Woman's Day, Family Circle,* and *Bon Appétit,* and contributes regularly to Cooking Light. His cookbook, *Baking in America: Contemporary and Traditional*

Favorites from the Past 200 Years, won the 2003 James Beard Award. Here's an e-mail he sent to catch me up on what he's been doing.

> I just finished a piece for IACP Food Forum—1,200 words on how I'm going about my next cookbook on baking with immigrants. I also did seven recipes and text for *Real Simple* magazine, which pays quite well.
>
> And I'm doing eight holiday desserts for *Food & Wine.* They're actually writing the story to focus on me as a baker and flying me to New York for one day for a photo shoot. Then, the very next day after I return, they're sending out the Lee brothers (well-known food writers who write for *Travel & Leisure* and the *New York Times* and [who are] just now finishing up a cookbook on Southern food for Norton) to watch me bake at home and interview me for the story.
>
> The whole thing is so wild. But I feel honored that the magazine is going to such lengths to promote my work. Right now I'm in the middle of testing the eight recipes (none from any of my books) and need to finish in about a week.
>
> Whew! I'm exhausted just writing the above.

Isn't it fun to imagine you could have a lifestyle this glamorous? Greg's culinary career began back in 1982, when he became a full-time spokesperson for Cuisinart, Inc. He is working on his fifth book.

Menu consultant, recipe developer, and tester: Freelancers may also be recipe developers and testers, working for corporations who might want recipes featuring a particular product, such as soy sauce or cheddar cheese. Menu consultants work directly for restaurants and usually have a background in the restaurant industry. If not, they are wordsmiths who write or check menus. "Developer" and "tester" are often interchangeable terms.

Restaurant reviewer: Restaurant reviewers at daily papers can be full-time employees, but most papers rely on freelancers. Sometimes the editor of the section will be a restaurant reviewer as well, or the full-time writers will do all kinds of feature writing in addition to reviewing restaurants. (For more on restaurant reviewing, see chapter 5.)

Newspaper writer: When staff writers exist, often they have migrated from another section of the newspaper. Kim Severson, now an award-winning food reporter for the *New York Times,* moved into food from regular reporting. It's rare to have a top reporter and investigative writer devoted to food. Other reporters migrate from the sports or business departments, or become restaurant reviewers after writing movie or book reviews. *New York Times* restaurant critic Frank Bruni previously headed the *Times'* European bureau office. If you want to work on a newspaper as a full-time writer whose beat is food, you may have to become a journalist first.

A DAY IN THE LIFE OF A NEWSPAPER WRITER

To give you an idea of how a full-time food writer does her job, I called **Kim Severson** and asked her about her week ahead when she worked at the *San Francisco Chronicle.* Here's what she said:

> I get into work around nine a.m. and hit the ground running. There might be small mechanical things to do, such as fact-check an address for a restaurant and make sure the hours are correct. I might function as an editor and read over other writers' stories, or do last-minute edits of my stories.
>
> Meanwhile, I'm thinking about the next six stories I need

to set up interviews for and write. Over the weekend I covered the opening of Tracy Des Jardin's new taco stand and I'm on deadline to write that story. I need to cover Alice Water's effort to make gardening and preparing school lunch part of the curriculum in Berkeley schools. I'm also finishing a review of the Tandoor Kitchen, which was actually pretty good.

Tomorrow there's the weekly food staff meeting that runs one and a half hours. On Thursdays some of the staff and interns from the California Culinary Academy cook lunch in our new test kitchen and we talk about the recipes.

My inbox is crammed with 100 e-mails. Sizzler has a new ad campaign. Krispy Kreme wants to come by to pitch its new donut store in the area. A dozen new restaurants are opening and all want coverage in the paper.

Someone has delivered a box of Slim Fast with 50 percent less sugar and they want us to sample it as a new product. Michael Bauer (executive editor of the food and wine sections) brought in some Bronx grapes he found at a market. He tried them at Chez Panisse and wanted us to taste them.

I also follow diet and nutrition news, so I get a huge number of e-mail news alerts from organizations such as the U.S. Department of Agriculture (USDA). There's a hearing on a state senate bill on banning junk food in schools. Today there's a USDA dietary guidelines press conference on the foods that will inform the food pyramid. I may run out [to attend it] but I doubt it.

You never know when an editor on the news desk will see a story come in over the wire and want me to follow it. I'll drop everything and write it for tomorrow's paper.

I never know what the day is going to be like when I walk in. Most people in the news business want this kind of rhythm.

Severson is an award-winning journalist who worked as a reporter at other newspapers before crossing over into the food department. At the *San Francisco Chronicle,* she won many awards and two Pulitzer nominations. Her breaking stories on trans fat led to her book, *The Trans Fat Solution: Cooking and Shopping to Eliminate the Deadliest Fat from Your Diet.*

What You Need to Break In

How did food writers like Taxel, Patent, and Severson get where they are now? Did they work in restaurants, or get degrees from places like the Culinary Institute of America? No. Of the dozen or so top writers I interviewed for the earlier chapters, all said they didn't think a food background was essential, because the bottom line is whether you know how to write, interview, research, report, and develop stories. Only author Molly O'Neill said she "doesn't even look at those who don't have a food background" when she hires freelancers to do research or write for her. "I want somebody who has worked in restaurants, catered, traveled, or who went through a ten-year apprenticeship. That's what it takes to have taste." However, she allows there's always the exception to the rule. A. J. Liebling, the *New Yorker* writer and book author, had no background in food, but, according to O'Neill, had a "great capacity for joy and appreciation, and he learned."

Some in the food writing business even think too much of a food background is a liability. "It's important to be open, to research, to not accept the norm, to explore and discover new findings and research thoroughly," says Knopf cookbook editor Judith Jones. "Sometimes if you think you know too much, it's limiting." Others believe it helps to come into the field from an entirely different background. "Some of the best don't necessarily start with food, they end up with food," says *Gastronomica* editor Darra Goldstein. "Bringing a certain approach to life, or intellectual activity to food, can make for an interesting mix." Jeffrey Steingarten was an attorney before becoming a food writer for *Vogue*. But more importantly, he was a funny guy, having honed his humor writing at the *Harvard Lampoon*.

What are the best ways to break in? The easiest is if you are already a published writer and choose to change your focus. I started out as a general newspaper reporter and later edited magazines about automobiles, computers, and city life. I knew how to write, research, interview, and get published. The hard part was gaining enough knowledge to write about food and earning credibility as a food writer.

The second easiest is if you break in from the food world as a knowledgeable cooking professional, food historian, culinary school graduate, food retailer, or food producer. Being a food celebrity is another excellent way to become a writer, if that happens to be you. Amanda Hesser wrote her first book, *The Cook and the Gardener: A Year of Recipes and Writings from the French Countryside,* after cooking in France in a chateau with a live-in gardener. That was before the *New York Times* hired her. Certainly, the book added to her desirability.

How to Get an Education

What if you're not already a writer or someone with a background in food? You can still succeed by getting an education. Even people with writing or food-industry credentials have to fill in the gaps. No suffering is required. Studying, when it comes to food writing, is a pleasurable act. You like to eat, don't you? And you like to read good food writing, right? All you need to know is what to study, how to find classes, and how to network. But let's start at the beginning. One of the first things you need to know is how to become discriminating about food.

Taste, taste, taste: When I embarked on a food writing career I felt intimidated by writers who seemed to know everything about food, including how it should taste. I wondered how I would learn this skill. The answer, fortunately, was to do something I did already anyway. "Taste, taste, taste," says Goldstein. It's impossible to be discriminating if your palate isn't developed.

"Eating a lot is the first thing," agrees *Los Angeles Times* food editor Russ Parsons. But eat with an open mind. "People try to fit food into categories—it is this, it isn't that," he warns. "They compare it to how it fits their preconceptions. The point of view of the novice can be overdone. You can only play the fool so often until people ask themselves why they are reading your work."

There's no such thing as being right or wrong about how food tastes, says *Saveur* magazine editor in chief Colman Andrews. "You need to know something about your subject matter, but it's pretty much understood by the reader that if you're commenting on a dish, you're offering an opinion, not a cold hard fact. Some people have a more experienced or sophisticated palate. When you taste a $200 bottle of wine and you don't like it, I hope you have the courage to say that. When the chef's specialty is brought out like a religious relic and you don't like it, you're still the boss."

What if you don't like certain foods? Andrews says that's fine, because it's impossible to argue with the way people react to food and flavor. The issue is what you tell the reader. Let's say you hate caviar, he says. "That's fine as long as you're not saying no one should eat caviar because it's too salty and pops in your mouth."

In *The Man Who Ate Everything*, Jeffrey Steingarten decided the same day he was appointed food critic for *Vogue* that he should get rid of his food phobias—such as Korean food, anchovies, Indian desserts, and lard—by eating all the things he didn't like to see if his opinion might change. "Scientists tell us that aversions fade away when we eat moderate doses of the hated foods at moderate intervals, especially if the food is complex and new to us," he theorized at the beginning of his book. To his surprise, he liked almost everything except blue food. "In just six months," he writes, "I succeeded in purging myself of nearly all repulsions and preferences, in becoming a more perfect omnivore." He goes on to say that he eventually attained such a Zen-like state that all the food on the menu at a Parisian restaurant looked appetizing, making him unable to order dinner. You'll read more about developing the palate and how to approach individual tastes in chapter 5.

The companion to developing a discriminating palate is reading for knowledge, not just pleasure. This process takes time, kind of like studying Buddhism—you never stop learning and trying to improve. It's easy to overlook this commitment. Reading some articles, you may think that you could write something just as good right now. Depending on what you read, it's possible, but unlikely. I enjoy Caroline Bates's restaurant reviews in *Gourmet* and admit to fantasizing about what it would be like to write reviews for this top food magazine. When I read Jeremiah Towers's memoir I was startled to learn that in the 1970s, Bates reviewed Chez Panisse while Towers worked there as a chef. Bates has been a restaurant reviewer for more than three decades! Of course. Why would *Gourmet* hire an amateur? She paid her dues, and so must you, depending on how far you want to go.

How Some Food Writers Got Their Start

Colman Andrews, former editor in chief of *Saveur* magazine, used the pseudonym Persona to write restaurant reviews in Los Angeles for an underground newspaper called the *Staff,* and then moved on to the *Los Angeles Free Press.* "Persona was an imaginary person who wrote very flamboyantly, used food puns and had been everywhere and done everything," he recalls.

Author **Molly O'Neill** worked as a chef for ten years and studied cooking at La Varenne École de Cuisine in Paris. She co-founded a restaurant in Northampton, Massachussetts, then moved on to run restaurants in Provincetown and Boston. While a chef in Massachusetts, she got a call from an editor from the *Boston Globe* daily newspaper, asking if she would write a story. The editor of the city magazine there read the published story and called her.

"He told me that if I wanted to be a real writer, I'd come work for him," says O'Neill. "I was young and stupid, so I did. Fortunately, he was a brilliant editor and working for him was one of the luckiest things that ever happened to me. Writing about food was my reward for writing about business, cops and robbers, and news. He taught me how to be a reporter and how to write cleanly and on deadline. He was supportive and he was a merciless critic."

At some point O'Neill wrote a letter to M. F. K. Fisher and "asked her if she would help." Fisher said yes. "So I went to Sonoma and, for about ten years, I went back every year to visit and to work on my writing."

I found this so astonishing that I asked if she thought a beginner could write the same kind of letter today. "The fun part of food—the grassrootsness of it, the small townness of it, the discovery of it, the sense of Wild Westness of it—is over," she replied. "There's less tolerance for learning curves, less room for serendipity. Training figures larger than chance. Having said all that, if you are talented and willing to work like a galley slave, you can find out a lot about yourself and how the world works by making a living in food. And the walls around the highest echelons of the food world ain't all that high."

Russ Parsons had been a sports writer at a newspaper in Albuquerque for ten years and never thought about becoming a food writer, even though he loved to cook. Because the paper was small, he was able to branch out into general feature writing and music writing. One day he got an assignment to write about a woman who was named cooking teacher of the year by *Bon Appétit*. He took her class as part of his research for the story, and found he enjoyed it. He became an "obnoxious hardcore foodie, read voraciously, took more classes, and went to bed with a stack of cookbooks." Friends let him work in their restaurants.

Parsons grew dissatisfied with the way the paper covered food, where copy editors took the "rip and read" approach, ripping stories with no local angle off the wire and running them. He told the editor he wanted to write about food, and got a six-week tryout, editing and writing for the food section. He became the paper's restaurant critic after six months.

Cookbook author and freelancer **Greg Patent** won second prize in the junior division of the Pillsbury Bake-Off when he was a teenager. Instead of pursuing a career in food, he got a PhD in zoology and embarked on an academic path. He made the jump to food writing in 1982, after he became a television cooking teacher as a hobby. Once the daily newspaper in his town of Missoula, Montana, ran a story about Patent's standing as a finalist in a cooking contest, they let him write a local food column.

During her job as chef at the Swallow restaurant in Berkeley, *Gourmet* editor **Ruth Reichl** became a restaurant reviewer for a San Francisco magazine, a gig she got from a customer who was an editor at the publication. She went on to freelance stories for *New York* magazine and eventually was appointed food critic of the magazine's sibling, *New West,* a California regional magazine.

Freelance writer **Alan Richman** started out as a newspaper newswriter, sportswriter, feature writer, and columnist. Later he switched to magazines and got a staff job at *GQ* magazine, writing features, profiles, and a wine column on the side. "The editor in chief asked if I wanted to make it a food-and-wine column instead. " I jumped at the chance, since I'd rather eat than drink." Later he became a freelancer for *GQ, Conde Nast Traveler*, and *Bon Appétit* magazines. He never worked in restaurants nor graduated from a cooking school, yet has won ten national awards for his writing.

Writer **Jeffrey Steingarten**, a former attorney, wrote satire and parodies for the *Harvard Lampoon* while a Harvard law student, and tried out for a job at the *New Yorker* before his appointment as food critic for *Vogue*. He met Anna Wintour in 1979, years before she became editor in chief of *Vogue*, because he knew her husband a bit. Wintour became editor of *Home and Garden* magazine, now *HG*. She asked several writers, including Steingarten, to try out for a new, more serious column about food. The assignment was microwaved fish, 800 to 1,200 words.

"I said I didn't even know how to microwave," he recalls. "She said, 'We'll get you a microwave.' I said I can't have just one, as there are several manufacturers, and different features and power levels. She said, 'How many did you need?' I said twelve. She paused. She said, 'Well, okay, we'll get you twelve microwaves.' In the end I only got three because the fuses started going." Steingarten turned in 4,200 words. The magazine printed about 4,000. "The pattern was set," he says. "I turned the assignment into a first-person adventure, not perfectly well, but that's what I've been doing ever since, making some jokes along the way." Later Wintour went to *Vogue*, and Steingarten followed shortly thereafter.

Asked if there was a slight difference between an attorney's salary and a full-time columnist's, Steingarten admitted he should have saved more. When negotiating his salary, he asked if Wintour would pay him "as much as a New York plumber makes annually." He got it the next year.

Writer **Calvin Trillin** was a successful freelance writer, working for national magazines, before he began writing about food for *Life* magazine in the early 1970s. Later Trillin traveled around the country for fifteen years for a *New Yorker* series called U.S. Journal, writing a 3,000-word feature article every three weeks. When he got "worn down on reporting," he wrote lighter pieces for comic relief, covering topics such as Cincinnati people arguing about chili, or making the rounds at the Breaux Bridge Crawfish Festival.

"I had neither the credentials for nor any interest in inspecting, say, a serving of Veal Orloff for the purpose of announcing to the world how it measured up to what dog-show types call the standards of the breed," he writes in his foreword to *The Tummy Trilogy*. "I wrote about eating rather than food, and I wrote as a reporter who was enjoying his work rather than as an expert."

Laura Taxel was a general freelance writer when she sent a humorous essay about barbecuing to a local magazine. The editor said she could use a piece with lots of advice instead. Taxel gathered information from friends and the Kingsford Charcoal Company and turned in a rewritten article. "The editor liked the results so much I ended up with a monthly cooking column that lasted almost three years, and so began a career."

Inspired by M. F. K. Fisher, **Amanda Hesser** decided to become a food writer and began by studying cooking in Europe. Later she worked for La Varenne École de Cuisine in France for two years, testing dozens of recipes for a book by Anne Willan. She met the school's gardener, who inspired her first book. In New York, she freelanced before being hired as an editor and writer for the *New York Times*.

As for **me**, I had been the editor of a fourteen-page women's section of a newspaper, filling it with recipes from the paper's wire service, plus wedding and feature articles. The publisher of a city restaurant magazine, who wanted a new editor, approached me for the job and I accepted. In this new job I visited restaurants and wrote features about chefs and restaurants. What's not to love?

Even though it sounds daunting, if you can pay your dues by tasting, reading about, and cooking food, it doesn't get any better than that. Doing so just fuels your passion.

"You will embark upon an educated journey," explains freelance writer David Leite. "As you go along, there will come
these 'aha' moments where you put together all these bits and
you can talk intelligently about a rack of lamb or two types of
apple. You realize you've moved to another level."

To increase your knowledge, read food writing, whether
books of nonfiction or fiction, magazines, newspaper food
sections—anything you can get your hands on that interests
you. Here are my suggestions:

Read great books: Like tasting, reading is a pleasurable way to
increase your knowledge. If you don't like to read, you will find
it difficult to write. Below is a list of books compiled from recommendations from people I've interviewed for this book, plus
my own suggestions. It reflects the work of authors who are
primarily literary nonfiction food writers, not recipe writers
(see more about great cookbook writers in chapter 6). I have
not included books by anyone interviewed within these pages.
Please assume that whatever they've written is magnificent or I
wouldn't have /bothered.

This first list is of classic narrative writing. Some of these
books are hard to find and some are out of print. You may
have to special-order from bookstores, contact libraries, and
peruse used book sites or used bookstores. But it will be worth
your time. You can cook from these books but they offer so
much more than just the subjects of food and cooking. You'll
find beautifully drawn portraits of people's lives and times.

- James Beard, *Delights and Prejudices,* 1964. An erudite memoir with recipes from a great American gastronome.
- Jean-Anthelme Brillat-Savarin, *The Physiology of
  Taste: Or Meditations on Transcendental Gastronomy,* first published in France in 1825. Lively
  and amusing meditations, examinations, and discussions on food, cooking, and eating. Try to find the
  version translated by M. F. K. Fisher.

- Samuel Chamberlain, *Clementine in the Kitchen,* first published in 1943. A cook introduces Americans to the charms of French cooking.
- Laurie Colwin, *Home Cooking: A Writer in the Kitchen* and *More Home Cooking: A Writer Returns to the Kitchen.* Novelist Colwin, who died in 1992, wrote two memoirs that are a mix of warm conversations, practical advice, and recipes.
- Elizabeth David. Try *South Wind Through the Kitchen: The Best of Elizabeth David,* a collection of her best writing and recipes compiled from nine books written between 1955 and 1977. You'll find long sentences, and sensuous depth and detail about food and ingredients.
- Roy Andries De Groot, *Auberge of the Flowering Hearth,* a 1937 adventure about his visit to a mysterious French inn in a hidden valley. Also see *In Search of the Perfect Meal: A Collection of the Best Food Writing of Roy Andries de Groot,* a collection of essays by this gifted writer and gourmand.
- M. F. K. Fisher: She wrote narratives about food as a metaphor for life, with an exacting, sensuous vocabulary, and sharp wit. Her style was new in an America accustomed to recipes and instruction. *The Art of Eating* condenses her first five books from 1937–1949 into one volume. It includes *How to Cook a Wolf, Consider the Oyster,* and *The Gastronomical Me.*
- Patience Gray, *Honey from a Weed,* 1987. Lyrical portraits of Mediterranean places where the author has lived and cooked.
- Edna Lewis, *The Taste of Country Cooking,* 1976. A joyful and evocative memoir of American country cooking from the granddaughter of a slave.
- A. J. Liebling, *Between Meals: An Appetite for Paris,* 1959. A *New Yorker* writer reports on eating in the now-vanished Paris of the 1930s.

- Harold McGee, *On Food and Cooking: The Science and Lore of the Kitchen,* 2004. So much more than a reference book, combining culinary lore with scientific explanations.
- Angelo Pellegrini, *The Unprejudiced Palate: Classic Thoughts on Food and the Good Life,* 1948. A charming look at the good life of food, wine, and cooking from a passionate Italian-American cook and gardener.
- Waverly Root: *Eating in America: A History,* 1994. With Richard de Rochemont, this former journalist chronicles an erudite and fresh history of American food and eating customs.
- Jim Villas, *Between Bites: Memoirs of a Hungry Hedonist,* 2002, a memoir of discovering his palate in France in the 1960s.
- Joseph Wechsberg, *Blue Trout and Black Truffles: The Peregrinations of an Epicure,* 1953, devoted to the eating-places and vineyards of France.

If you prefer to sample many authors and styles of food writing at once, here's a list of suggested compilations:

- *The Best Food Writing* anthologies, an annual collection featuring many of the writers interviewed for this book.
- *Through the Kitchen Window: Women Explore the Intimate Meanings of Food and Cooking,* 1997. It's out of print but still one of my favorites.
- *A Slice of Life: Contemporary Writers on Food,* 2003. A banquet of accomplished food writers on the nature of food, language, and the adaptability of social customs.
- *The Wilder Shores of Gastronomy: Twenty Years of the Best Food Writing,* 2002, from the journal *Petits Propos Culinaires.* A collection of essays that includes many written by writers in this chapter. The

journal began in 1979 and has been out of print for many years.

⟶ *The Penguin Book of Food and Drink*, 1998, celebrates a century of gastronomic writing, including humorist S. J. Perelman's "Farewell, My Lovely Appetizer." (Many food writers, including Jeffrey Steingarten and Alan Richman, revere Perelman's writing style, most of which is not directly about food writing.)

⟶ *Endless Feasts: Sixty Years of Writing from Gourmet*, 2002. A banquet of food and travel writing, profiles and memories, with an introduction by Ruth Reichl.

Read great magazines and newspapers: Read the national food magazines, such as *Gourmet, Food & Wine, Cook's Illustrated, Fine Cooking, Cooking Light, Saveur,* and *Gastronomica* to keep up on trends and as a continuing form of education. Read newspaper food sections online, particularly those in the *New York Times, Washington Post, San Francisco Chronicle,* and *Chicago Tribune.*

Study cooking: As long as you're willing to read, why not study? Take cooking lessons through adult education classes, a community college, retail stores, or privately. Many professional cooking schools hold weekend classes for the public. Cookbook writers sometimes hold private cooking classes in their homes.

Or work in a restaurant for a while. Russ Parsons, as a general newspaper reporter, wrote a story on a cooking teacher, and by taking her class realized he wanted to learn more. He took more classes, began assisting her, then friends let him work in their restaurants at no pay. "After I really immersed myself, I felt comfortable writing about food," he says. Working in restaurants isn't for everyone, but you'll get to see chefs in action, see how the back of the restaurant functions, and learn techniques and tricks cooks use to get dishes to the table on time. Perhaps a restaurant would let you watch, rather than cook.

You don't even have to leave the house to study cooking and food. You can learn a tremendous amount from television today. Watch cooking shows and shows about food. My favorites are the old-timers—Jacques Pépin, Julia Child, and Martin Yan—but you can't go wrong on the Food Network. For high drama, there's always *Iron Chef.*

Study food writing: Go to food-writing symposiums and conferences. The oldest is the Symposium for Professional Food Writers at the Greenbrier in West Virginia. Book Passage, the largest independant bookstore in the San Francisco Bay Area, offers Food Writing for Beginners, an annual February weekend conference with speakers. (Disclosure: I am the chair.) If you live in New York, the French Culinary Institute offers a food journalism course by writer Alan Richman. Mediabistro.com lists a variety of food-writing courses on both coasts. L'Academie de Cuisine in Gaithersburg, Maryland, offers food-writing workshops periodically, as does the Culinary Institute of America at its St. Helena, California, and Hyde Park, New York, campuses.

Continuing-education classes sharpen your writing skills. Look for classes in your community on nonfiction writing, memoir, personal essay, writing for the senses, or other subjects that apply to food writing. Or sign up for an online class. *Writer's Digest,* publisher of the eponymous magazine and writing books, holds classes and conferences. Shaw Guides (http://www.shawguides.com) lists hundreds of writing classes around the country. Gotham Writers' Workshop offers ten-week online classes in nonfiction writing.

Get a degree in journalism or food studies: New York University is the only school in the United States with a food studies degree program. Most universities take a more interdisciplinary approach to food studies and offer classes through departments that include anthropology, psychology, and nutrition.

Take English classes to improve your writing, and English literature classes to immerse yourself in good writing. If you're not satisfied with classes offered at colleges and universities near you, get your education online (see Cruise the Web on page 62).

Internships are one of the big benefits of studying at a college or university. During my studies as a journalism student I landed two internships: one at a city magazine, and another at a national magazine. The first internship resulted in a cover story (totally rewritten by the editor in chief, but hey, no one had to know). Freelancer Mary Margaret Pack worked as an intern at the *San Francisco Chronicle* while a student at the California Culinary Academy. By the time she graduated, she had a handful of feature stories to show as credentials for future freelancing queries. Both these internships came about because of arrangements the school made with publications.

During college studies in journalism, *The Cake Mix Doctor* author Anne Byrn interned at her hometown newspaper every summer and Christmas break, where she formed relationships with people in the food section. Her coup at the paper was scooping the story of Elvis's death. Living in the South, that was a big deal. She was a junior in college. "It was a Sunday night," she recalls. "That was my shift. There was no one else to write the story."

Travel: Experience firsthand how food is sold, how it tastes, and how people prepare food in their own countries. Watch food preparers in markets and on the street. If possible, meet home cooks and watch them in the kitchen. Visit the night markets of Asia and farmers' markets in Europe. Rent a place with a kitchen and try cooking something unfamiliar. Go to big and small restaurants to taste the local food. Take culinary vacations led by experienced cooks and chefs and get to know them (for more information on what types of trips are available, see page 291). Buy cookbooks about the food of places you've visited.

Network: If you are a cooking teacher, entrepreneur, or other food professional, join the International Association of Culinary Professionals so you can attend the annual conference and receive the directory of members. To meet other people interested in food, join the American Institute of Wine & Food, or local groups where you can meet people with similar interests. Attend food-based events in your community.

Byrn says she can't emphasize enough how networking has aided her career. While in college she majored in home economics in addition to journalism. When she graduated she heard about a job from a home economics networking group she had joined. Some of its members were food writers. The opening was for a food writer at the *Atlanta Journal.* She got the job in 1978 and worked there until 1993, at which point she became the section editor.

Believe you will move forward, and be patient: "Sometimes when you throw yourself into the moment you find out you are more learned than you think," says Leite. "Past experience can suddenly coalesce and you know more than you thought you did." On the other hand, it will take a long time because food writing is a skill that must be practiced over and over. You must spend an extraordinary amount of time learning about food and writing, says O'Neill, just as you would spend years learning how to play the piano well. But persevere and most likely it will pay off in the end.

CRUISE THE WEB

Web sites focusing on food:
➡ Food Newsgroups, a huge list of groups where people talk with each other about their passions, be they chocolate, sushi, or vegetarian cooking:
http://www.foodweb.com/w.w.bites/foodnewsgroups.html

- The Cook's Thesaurus, a cooking encyclopedia of cooking tools and ingredients: http://www.foodsubs.com/
- EG Forums, from the Egullet Society for Culinary Arts and Letters. Forums for schmoozing with other foodies. Includes interviews with food writers and cooking classes: http://forums.egullet.org/
- Food writer David Leite's Culinaria Web site: http://www.leitesculinaria.com
- Food writer Bruce Cole's site features his own articles and a great list of links: http://www.sautewednesday.com/
- The Food Network's official Web site: http://www.foodtv.com
- Food Reference, a Web site for food history, trivia, and quotes: http://foodreference.com

Recreational cooking classes:
- Star Chefs: http://www.starchefs.com
- The Guide to Recreational Cooking & Wine Schools: http://cookforfun.shawguides.com/

Online cooking class:
- The Culinary Institute of America: http://www.ciaprochef.com.

Classes on food writing:
- Symposium for Professional Food Writers at the Greenbrier: http://www.greenbrier.com/foodwriters/
- Food Writing Conference, Book Passage, California: http://bookpassage.com (click on the "Classes & Conferences" link)
- The French Culinary Institute's "The Craft of Food Writing": http://frenchculinary.com/subpages/amateur/foodWriting.html
- Media Bistro: http://www.mediabistro.com/courses/cache/menu_1.asp

Food studies:
- ◆ Department of Nutrition, Food Studies, and Public Health at New York University: http://www.nyu.edu/education/nutrition/NFSR/ASFS.htm
- ◆ Association for the Study of Food and Society: http://www.food-culture.org

Food magazines:
- ◆ *Food & Wine:* http://www.foodandwine.com
- ◆ *Bon Appétit* and *Gourmet:* http://www.epicurious.com
- ◆ Saveur: http://www.saveur.com/
- ◆ *Fine Cooking:* http://www.taunton.com/finecooking/index.asp
- ◆ *Cooking Light:* http://www.cookinglight.com/cooking/
- ◆ *Cooks Illustrated:* http://www.cooksillustrated.com/
- ◆ *Gastronomica:* http://www.gastronomica.org/

Newspaper food sections:
- ◆ Gourmet Spot: http://www.gourmetspot.com/newspapers.htm

Online cookbook stores:
- ◆ Jessica's Biscuit eCookbooks: http://www.ecookbooks.com/index.html
- ◆ Foodbooks.Com: http://www.foodbooks.com/
- ◆ Cookbooks We Love: http://www.cookbookswelove.com/

Online writing classes:
- ◆ http://writersonlineworkshops.com
- ◆ Shaw's Guides: http://writing.shawguides.com/
- ◆ Writing Classes.Com and Gotham Writers' Workshop: http://www.writingclasses.com/

Online English classes:
- ◆ Virtual University: http://www.vu.org/
- ◆ Virtual Student: http://www.virtualstudent.com/

Associations:

➥ International Association of Culinary Professionals:
http://www.iacp.com/

➥ American Institute of Wine & Food: http://www.aiwf.org

Writing Exercises

1. Make a plan of five things you can do to move your knowledge base forward and get closer to writing about food. For example, buy a magazine subscription; take a cooking class; join a chat room. What are the things you need to do to succeed? Give yourself a deadline for accomplishing these five tasks.

2. Investigate two of your favorite food writers. Read as much as you can about them to discover how they started out. If they have written books, this information might be in a foreword or introduction. "Google" them to find interviews or profiles. Write a short report on how each of them got where they are today.

3. Read one of the books on the list on page 56–59. Choose a style of book you might like to write. Write a 250-word book report on what you enjoyed about the book most. Evaluate the author's writing technique, subject matter, structure, and whether the book held your interest. Identify the beginning, middle, and end by writing a sentence about each part.

Becoming a Successful Freelance Writer

Writing for newspapers and magazines satisfies many desires. It's a way to entertain and inform while unleashing your creativity and passion onto the printed page. It's such a thrill to see your own work in print. I'm still not tired of it, even though it's been almost thirty years since my first piece ran in a daily newspaper.

Writing articles can be a long and frustrating process if you don't know how to get to a published story—and even if you do. Months can pass—even a year sometimes—before a story you've pitched to an editor appears. Editors are busier than ever these days, sometimes sorting through nearly 200 story idea queries per month. Your job is to come up with a story idea an editor can't resist, get the go ahead, write the story, get paid, and then do it all over again. I'm going to tell you how. As a newspaper and magazine editor, I've evaluated and accepted work from writers for most of my career. Since 1996, I've been on the other side as a freelance writer as well.

In this chapter I'll give you insider information on how editors assess a story. In addition, editors and award-winning food writers will offer advice on how to come up with, shape, position, pitch, pursue, and write your story idea, no matter what kind of publication you target or what type of writing you prefer. You'll learn about pay and even some strategies for how to increase it—no small task when it comes to food writing. And you'll get a short primer on tax deductions, so start saving your receipts now.

While this chapter does not cover restaurant reviewing specifically (which is discussed in chapter 5), it will provide valuable information on how to target and pitch a publication.

How to Come Up with Story Ideas

What should you write about? Your brain should be constantly generating ideas based on what's going on in your life and what you read. "You've got to be like a lint brush," says writer Barry Estabrook, a contributing editor for *Gourmet* and founding editor of *Eating Well* magazine. "Ideas are cheap. Execution is harder. People tend to get too attached to a single idea. Come up with so many that you don't get obsessed with any one."

Notice he didn't say to write one story and then find a home for it? Many beginning writers take this path and don't succeed. The problem is that every publication wants a story written just for them. Since yours was written for you, you'll have to convince an editor that it's right for the publication's specific style, voice, and readers. That's why editors reject almost 95 percent of ideas and stories.

So back up and give your brain fodder for ideas. Here's how:

- ➭ Read food sections of newspapers. Keep a pen and paper handy and write down any ideas that come into your head. Tear out articles typical of those you'd like to write, either in subject or format.
- ➭ Do the same with food magazines, general magazines, and trade publications. This time, check writers' bylines against the mastheads of magazines

to see what kind of stories freelancers write for each
publication.

- Visit bookstores to see what's new in the cookbook
section.
- Notice trends in restaurants and food shops.
- Watch food shows.
- Visit farmers' markets and specialty food markets
and producers.
- Spend an hour with your cookbooks, looking for
subjects you could turn into articles because of your
own passion.
- Look at your own life for ideas. If you just went
through a kitchen remodeling, or you're planning a
trip to a cooking school in Morocco, you might have
a story.
- Figure out what kind of stories you're best at
writing, based on your personality. For example, I'm
a practical person who loves to explain how something works, or to help people get better at a task,
so I'm attracted to service or how-to stories.

The act of wondering led me to write many articles that were
published in an international magazine aimed at supermarket
shoppers, published by Sunset. I put myself in the shoes of
readers, both in the market and at home. *What can you make
with those yellow premade logs of polenta, and are they actually edible?* I wondered. That led to a story and recipes for a
Busy Cook column, followed by wondering what to do with
a can of tuna besides make a sandwich, and what to do with
a box of frozen spinach. Next came how-to stories based on
other questions I had, like secrets of a great buffet, how to
order wine at a restaurant, and how to plan a cheese course for
a dinner party.

Freelance writing tends to fall into two categories: general
writing and specialized writing. General writing covers all
aspects of food. If you find everything about food exciting,
from cooking to farming to travel to history, you're probably a

generalist. Specialists, on the other hand, write mostly about one subject in many incarnations. I met someone recently who is obsessed with bacon. He wants to establish a Web site, newsletter, and blog, leading to acres of written material on how much he loves cured pork. Later, when he pitches story ideas to editors, he can direct them to his writing, even if none of it has been traditionally published.

Writing as a specialist can be a strategic way to build your business. Barry Estabrook, a generalist and founding editor of *Eating Well,* established his expertise as a writer on seafood when he became a freelance writer. Previously, he had worked as a commercial fisherman, was familiar with the seafood business, and developed a keen interest in the controversy between fishing and conservation. After reading about an escape of farmed salmon in Maine waters, he wrote an article on farmed salmon for *Gourmet.* The editor of an environmental magazine saw the piece and assigned him a story on overfished sea bass. Another editor at the environmental magazine asked him to review a book about wild salmon depletion. A fisherman saw Estabrook's salmon article and invited him to spend a few days aboard a commercial fishing vessel. That adventure turned into an article he pitched and sold to *Gourmet.* The fishermen on the boat told him about scallop divers they knew in Maine. He sold the story idea about scallop divers to *Gourmet.* See how naturally Estabrook continued his freelance career? Granted, he is a veteran of the food-writing community, but the story still makes a point: as his stories built on each other, they further established his credibility. If Estabrook writes a seafood-based book next, he will be even more sought after as an expert freelance writer.

What Kind of Story Should You Write?

Coming up with story ideas is the first step. Shaping them into certain article conventions is the second. Here are some of the most popular for freelance writing:

Recipe: For many food publications, recipe-based stories are a huge focus. *Cooking Light,* for example, prints around eighty recipes per issue, with almost all contributed by freelancers. Most of these stories comprise a short introduction followed by three to five recipes. The feature article might include small bits of side information on technique, a guide to choosing an unfamiliar ingredient, and information about its history, where to buy it, or how to serve it. Think of a theme that helps readers plan, such as low-effort or low-fat dinners; or one that inspires them, such as Greek food for a party or slow-roasted stews for winter nights.

In the case of *Cooking Light,* you would want to avoid esoteric ingredients and keep the method straightforward. Before you submit a piece that includes recipes, familiarize yourself with the publication's editorial style. Don't call for asafetida, for example, if you don't see esoteric ingredients in any recipes.

"Recipes need to feel like they're coming from a cook with a style or profile of her own. We're not looking for generic recipes you can find anywhere else," said Sarah Jay, managing editor of *Fine Cooking.* "We definitely want our authors to have opinions about the method, ingredients, et cetera, yet they should also be flexible enough to change it if we're not getting a result that we like."

To write about seasonal cooking, keep in mind that national magazines have long lead times. *Cooking Pleasures* has a one-year lead time. For most magazines, you might have to pitch a story more than six months in advance, so a story on indoor grilling during winter would be pitched to a national magazine in late summer. Newspapers, on the other hand, think a few weeks ahead.

Most food publications have test kitchens where people will make your recipes to ensure that they work. Often editors can judge recipes just from looking at your story idea. If you've read chapter 7 on recipe writing, you'll be in good shape.

Trend: Usually articles on trends are reported, meaning you interview and quote experts and sources, and come to conclusions based on their expertise. Some include statistics. Trends from other print sources sometimes lead to great queries for food-based publications. If you subscribe to nutrition and health newsletters, for example, you might reshape the trend stories and pitch them to food publications with a health focus. If you see positive research on elderberry's power as a defense against colds and flu, for example, you might dream up a few recipes for how to use the extract and syrup and send a query to a health-oriented publication such as *Delicious Living* or *Health* magazine.

Guide: Here you'll educate readers on how to make choices about a particular subject, such as how to buy organic, select winter greens, or brew exotic teas. Travel guides help readers find restaurants and specialty foods in a region.

News: In news reporting, you would interview several people and piece together their comments for an article on a breaking development. Most news reporting appears in newspapers rather than magazines, because it is a specialized skill requiring journalism. Examples would be breaking stories about mercury levels in fish or California's new rule banning foie gras.

Personality profile: Based on an interview with one person, such as a chef, restaurateur, food producer, retailer, or food personality, the focus is on an interviewee who has achieved recognition, made a significant contribution, or performs unusual work. *Food & Wine* has a regular column called Profile that meets this criterion.

Interview: Similar to a personality profile, interviews take the form of questions and answers that follow an introduction and brief biography of the interviewee.

Roundup: Usually a comparison or list, roundups help readers choose from a group, such as five kinds of Indian spices, or ten great Italian restaurants. If you're attracted to the idea of a roundup, find a publication with "Ten Best" kinds of titles.

How-to: Teach readers how to solve a problem or do something better. These articles can be technique based, such as how to make great mashed potatoes, how to find vegan restaurants in New York, or how to choose the right kitchen equipment. How-to or service stories are organized in a logical, instructional order, anticipating how readers think about a given task and the questions they might ask while thinking about it.

Human interest: These are stories about warmhearted people who do good deeds, such as soup kitchen cooks who feed 350 homeless people every day, or a group that sells baked goods for a cause.

Historical background: Pique an editor's interest by combining history with other forms listed here, such as destination or service writing.

Cookbook review: If your target publications include reviews, find out how they assign them. A magazine might get dozens of books every month from publishers, choose which ones to review, and hand them out to reviewers. If you find a small publication that publishes reviews, you could try writing one based on a cookbook you've purchased, and submit it. Use previously published reviews as models for how to shape your story. Be careful how you criticize—very few cookbooks are all good or all bad, and publishers are more likely to publish positive reviews than negative ones.

Destination and travel: Food-based travel pieces might take you to a food festival, a region known for artisan foods, or a city famous for its restaurants. You don't even have to go anywhere, says *Los Angeles Times* columnist Russ Parsons. "Write about what's going on in your backyard. Don't be embarrassed by your limitations." He quotes a songwriter friend who wrote, "Some people can go around the world and not see anything, other people can go around the block and see the whole world."

First-person essay: Personal stories are the top choice of many writers but not the priority of most publications. Most editors are flooded with personal experience articles. Usually they don't publish more than one article per issue, if they publish any at all.

That doesn't mean it's impossible to get published, just that you have lots of competitors. Here's how to increase your chance of success: the number one way is to write about an experience that relates to readers and their lives. What universal theme resonates for them? If it's just about what happened to you, then the response from editors can be "So what?"

When it comes to subject matter, you have lots of choices. Perhaps you:

- achieved a goal, such as graduating from cooking school or cooking a special feast
- just returned from a fabulous food-based vacation (in a sidebar, give readers ideas on how to duplicate it)
- have a funny cooking, eating, or traveling experience, or one that should be avoided
- had a life-changing or inspirational experience that will help readers cope with a challenge in their lives
- did something for the first time, such as served as an apprentice in a restaurant
- went to an event, such as a wine auction or family reunion with amazing food, or a food festival
- are obsessed with a favorite food, or have a favorite story about food
- cook unusual holiday dishes
- volunteer in the food world
- like to garden, hunt, or camp, or have some other hobby that could involve food

A few places that take first-person essays are *Newsweek*'s "My Turn" column, the *New York Times Sunday Magazine*,

Safeway Select, the *San Francisco Chronicle Sunday Magazine,* and *Woman's Day, Family Circle,* and *Slow* magazines. *Saveur* sometimes publishes a "Memories" column. In addition, magazines particular to some subjects, such as camping or gardening, are good prospects.

Regardless of the style or topic of your story, you must have a clear and imaginative focus, a fresh angle, and a slant appropriate to the publication. News and trends are always good. "You can't just repeat what other people have written," says *Gastronomica* editor Darra Goldstein. "Try and find your own new angle to it, your own discovery, instead of the same thing recycled many times." Sometimes it's enough to put a fresh take on a non-original idea. Said Jeanne McManus, former food editor of the *Washington Post,* in an interview, "I like pieces that broaden the discussion about food, that surprise you in that they take something—an ingredient, a technique—something that we think we all know about and slightly change forever the way I, the reader, think about it."

How to Target and Position Your Story

Your next step is critical, and one that many freelance writers fail to do: zoom in on a publication that's most likely to publish your story. Targeting means systematically finding the most realistic and appropriate place. Let's say I'd like to write a local story about the growing Vietnamese food scene in my town. Notice that my story idea is not a topic, but a trend. "Magazines are really of the moment, not a compendium or a definitive thing like a book or encyclopedia," said Martha Homlberg, editor in chief and publisher of *Fine Cooking,* during an International Association of Culinary Professionals (IACP) annual conference. "We don't want the whole thing, we want a slice. Not the topic. It's what you do with that topic."

The topic of the story would be "Vietnamese food." If that's as far as I got, an editor would be likely to say, "So what?" The subject of Vietnamese food is not specific or intrinsically interesting by itself. If I change it to say that many markets and restaurants have opened in a particular neighborhood, however, now I have a trend story, one with news value that should be published.

The next question I'd ask myself is, "Who cares about this story?" The newspaper for that neighborhood might care, as might an alternative weekly and the daily newspaper. All are local, a key point. A national magazine would not want the story, because it focuses on a small region.

The other part of targeting involves identifying an audience. This sounds obvious but I can't tell you how many story ideas I rejected when I was an editor because the writers didn't understand the magazine's reader base. If you want to write about food for children, target magazines aimed at parents. If you like exotic, expensive vacations, focus on magazines with upper-income, traveling readers. It's not hard to figure out who reads the magazine if you review the content in a few issues, including the ads. Try the library for a complete listing of publications called the *Reader's Guide to Periodic Literature*. Sometimes a magazine's Web site will list reader demographics under advertising information. Which publications interest you and share your values? In many cases you are the target audience and would therefore be good at coming up with appropriate story ideas.

Once you identify a publication, find up to a year's worth of issues and search for stories similar to your idea. This is harder than it seems, as some publications are not available in libraries and don't put their content online. Also, many industry magazines are free to qualified subscribers, which might not be you. Canvass friends and others who might keep the publications you need to review. Visit big newsstands. Respond to free offers for sample issues.

In the case of the Vietnamese food story, you'd look through the neighborhood newspaper to see whether it has published stories on food-based businesses, and if so, what kind. If you find none, you'd move to the weekly and focus on restaurants because the readership is more likely to eat out than cook. For a daily, again, review past issues to see how they cover local food trends, and reshape your story as necessary. Perhaps there's a first-person essay on searching for the best takeout roast chicken. If so, a story about the best takeout Vietnamese might be too obscure. Follow this same reasoning with any other publication you'd like to pitch.

Speaking as an editor, I can't advise you to send custom pitches on the same subject to various publications at once, unless they have wildly different readers. An airline magazine and a food magazine are not different enough for me. I wouldn't want readers to say, "You know, I think I just saw a similar story in a different magazine." This strategy will not win you any points with editors either.

Be realistic about which publication you target. If you've never been published, don't bother starting with *Gourmet*. Find the smallest publications in your area. Or find a Web site or small newsletter. They may not pay or may pay next to nothing. At this point, you shouldn't care too much, because you need clips to establish your credibility to a bigger publication.

Krista Montgomery, senior food editor of *Cooking Light,* explained how to review food magazines for clues at an IACP annual conference. "See how long pieces are, see what the points of view are and who the authors are," she suggested. "Read the editor's letter, see if the columns have rotating columnists. See which stories are written in-house and which are not by referring to the masthead [list of names at front of the magazine]. See which names [in stories] repeat. Look at whether stories are text or recipe driven. See if the recipes and text are done by the same person—recipes could be done by a chef or a recipe developer."

Once you feel confident your story would fit the publication, list the most important points and subpoints to prepare for your query letter. Put the points in logical order, based on questions readers would ask. Review the sample stories you selected for similarity. Notice the style and voice. Is the writer part of the story or invisible? Does the magazine hold the reader's hand in the instruction, or assume a certain level of expertise? Does the writer sound breezy or authoritative? If it's a trend story, find a statistic to make the trend credible. Do a word count of an example story and plan how many points you can cover in the same amount of space. If your story raises questions, do enough research to answer them. Notice whether the similar story includes sidebars—boxed smaller stories or lists. If so, come up with a few sidebar ideas.

Don't write the story yet. First take a look at what kind of publication is likely to publish it. Then write the pitch.

How to Boil Water: A Lesson in Positioning

Martha Homlberg, former editor in chief and publisher of *Fine Cooking,* shows how food magazines have their own style, voice, and vision. Here's her take on how each pitch letter would slant a story on how to boil water:

Fine Cooking: I've boiled water for years, and I've developed my own method that's fast and produces an even boil. I'll include information on pot selection, the best source of heat, the benefit of using a lid, some do-ahead tips, and I'll give recipes for salted water, acidulated water, and water infused with a bouquet garni. I could do a sidebar on making a bouquet garni.

Cook's Illustrated: Good boiled water is crucial to good cooking, so we decided to experiment to find the best way to boil. I tried aluminum versus stainless, 8-quart versus 12-quart, with a lid, without a lid, gas versus electric, starting with hot versus starting with cold, and our results will surprise you: Cold water and no lid worked best.

Saveur: My Italian grandmother used to boil water for her pasta using the clippings from my grandfather's vineyard as fuel. Her agnolotti was soulful and satisfying, and I'd swear it was the fruity scent of that smoke that made the difference.

Bon Appétit: Boiling water is the focal point of an evening spent with good friends and good food. Charleston couple Bunny and Chad built their Craftsman-style bungalow kitchen with a special boiling bar so friends could gather and sip wine while the water does its magic.

Food and Wine: Enter the world of Trey, chef-owner of the white-hot restaurant of the moment. In his off hours, he craves nothing more than to hang with his friends at the renovated leather factory he shares with his designer girlfriend Giselle. Their casual evenings kick off with green tea martinis made from boiled Icelandic water and served in stemware designed by Giselle.

She's exaggerating to make her point, of course, that editors at each of these magazines have a firm idea of how their magazine differs. One of the main reasons they reject queries is because writers don't create enough of a slant to make the story appropriate. Another is because writers pitch a subject—boiling water—rather than a slant on boiling water. With Homlberg's clever examples, it's easy to see the difference.

Finding the Right Markets

Another way to decide who wants your story is to understand which kind of publication to target, what's realistic, and how to approach them.

National food magazines: Everyone wants to be published in one of the big food magazines. It's difficult to get a feature article accepted, though, unless you have written a cookbook, own a popular restaurant, have your own television show, are a well-known cooking-school teacher, have written for big magazines or newspapers, or apprenticed under a celebrity chef. Some magazines, such as *Cook's Illustrated* and *Taste of Home,* take no freelance articles at all.

That's fine. You can be realistic. Let editors get to know and trust you by writing short pieces. Look at departments in the front of food magazines and come up with an idea for a 250- to 500-word short, newsy piece. The Good Living section of *Gourmet* features finds such as a local specialty food producer. The News & Notes section of *Food & Wine* has 80- to 100-word pieces about a dinner series at a museum and a dispatch from abroad. Saveur Fare in *Saveur* might profile a producer, a food festival, and a bakery. *Bon Appétit's* Starters department has short creative pieces as well.

While departments are usually collections of short work by different writers, columns are usually written by one person and provide clues on subjects the editors think are important enough to appear regularly. *Food & Wine* always has travel, restaurants, wine, and entertaining columns. *Bon Appétit* has regular writing on technique, healthy cooking, and restaurant recipes. *Eating Well's* departments include two on nutrition.

Gastronomica, a quarterly magazine published by University of California Press, breaks away from the pack. It takes no advertising and includes none of the usual food photography. Editor Darra Goldstein says she welcomes articles from any field touching on the history, production, uses, and depictions of food. It's certainly easier to crack than the big glossy food magazines, unless you're only interested in recipe-based stories. For more details, see http://www.gastronomica.org.

Regional magazines: The biggest cover several states, such as *Southern Living* and *Sunset,* two magazines owned by Time-Life. Both *Southern Living* and *Sunset* take freelanced food and travel pieces and recipe-based articles. State magazines don't necessarily do much food writing at all. *Texas Monthly* is an exception.

Trade publications in the food and beverage industry: Seafood Business, Restaurant and Institutions, Food Arts, Pig International (no kidding), and *Natural Foods Merchandiser* are a few of the food-industry trade magazines that cater to specific audiences such as food service operations, restaurant management, and retailers and wholesalers. Many well-established freelancers work for these publications because they pay better than those oriented to consumers. If you are a chef, a caterer, or have worked in food service or production, industry publications could be an ideal outlet for you, as story ideas will come easily.

To learn more, get a free one-year subscription to some food and beverage publications at www.localcareer.com/seekers/publications.cfn and study them for opportunities. There's even a thorough book on the subject: *Writing for Trade Magazines: How to Boost Your Income by $200 to $500 per Week,* by Kendall Hanson.

National travel magazines: Many travel features in these magazines include information about restaurants and dining as part of a destination. For example, *National Geographic Traveler* publishes articles such as "Confessions of a Cheese Smuggler." In a department in *Islands* magazine, you might see a piece on "Anguilla, a wine and food lovers' getaway."

Women's magazines: Check the women's magazines for those with recipe sections, such as *Martha Stewart Living, Oprah, Family Circle, Yoga Journal, Health,* and *Woman's Day.* Some carry nutrition and diet-based advice articles as well. Chances are good that you need to be a published writer to start at these national magazines.

Food sections of daily papers: I'd like to be optimistic about selling articles other than restaurant reviews, but I'm not. Newspapers take less and less freelance work. Most dailies are part of big chains like Knight Ridder or Cox News Service. The chains swap employee stories between newspapers, so food section editors have lots of stories from which to choose.

The food section has a tight budget anyway, with most of it designated for buying food, maintaining the test kitchen, recipe testing, food styling for in-house photography, culinary demonstrations, and professional development for staff members, says Heather McPherson, food editor of the *Orlando Sentinel* and president of the Association of Food Journalists. She fills a four-page section each week by writing her own stories and subscribing to the United Press Syndicate for a seven-day menu planner and King Features Syndicate for wine columns from the *San Francisco Chronicle*. "We take very little freelance because budgets in newspapers across the country are shrinking," says McPherson. "You make the most with what money you have. I won't pay someone to do something I can do."

Aim for a local angle for newspapers. Here's a tip from *Washington Post* former food editor Jeanne McManus: "I like pieces that show the pulse of the city in which we publish the food section, pieces about people doing real things in the world of food."

Weekly papers: Usually these are alternative papers written with attitude for people in their twenties and thirties who go to clubs and restaurants. You'll always find restaurant reviews, but the question is whether there's a budget to do other food writing. Weeklies usually work a few days to one week ahead.

Virginia Wood is food editor of the *Austin Chronicle*. She says she fills two and a half pages per week with restaurant reviews, profiles, company stories, and cookbook reviews. Her assignments go to seven regular freelancers. Wood said two of these freelancers were working chefs she'd known around Austin who changed careers and were interested in food writing. Two writers who were also trained chefs approached her with good ideas or impressive clips. A restaurateur suggested a mutual friend as the wine writer. The final writer is the spouse of one of her *Chronicle* colleagues. "I didn't go looking for people with food service backgrounds, but five out of seven of us have spent years in the kitchen, which I think informs our writing in important ways," she concludes.

Other weekly papers are community based and might be good prospects for first-time writers. Freelancer and cookbook author Peggy Knickerbocker started out at San Francisco's *Nob Hill Gazette*—"some silly thing about Thanksgiving," she recalls—and *North Beach Now,* with a story on the oldest cappuccino machine in the Italian neighborhood. From there she used her clips to approach the *San Francisco Examiner,* where she wrote a piece on cooking for people with AIDS.

City magazines: These tend to focus on restaurant reviews and capsule reviews to please their advertisers. Occasionally they profile specialty-food producers, such as an old-time candy bar manufacturer, or a piece on organic farms open to the public. They might have stories profiling local food people, or roundup pieces on where to get the best sandwich or coffee. Most produce an annual "Best Restaurants" cover story. The most sophisticated and most often copied city magazine is *New York.*

General and association magazines and newsletters: National magazines such as those of insurance companies, the American Automobile Association, and the American Association of Retired People are hard to crack, as are airline magazines. But all take food stories. Newsletters are a good option if you're starting out. They don't pay much, but you'd be surprised by what they accept. Rural electrical cooperative newsletters often contain recipes (check your local library for a list of these).

The Web: I've tried, but I can't find good markets for food writing on Web sites other than restaurant reviewing (see chapter 5). Passionate individuals write most food-based Web sites as a way of self-expression. Most do not take contributions. Freelancer Sam Gugino writes about wine and food for Msn.com, a Web site that can take its pick of writers. Slate.com runs the odd food story, usually trend based. Forbes.com has wine and spirit stories done mostly by one writer.

Other freelancing opportunities: Contribute to anthologies, guidebooks, and reference guides. Look for opportunities based on what you know. Cooking school teacher and writer Thy Tran wrote the cooking chapter in *How to Fix (Just About) Everything.* For the book *Asia in the San Francisco Bay Area: A Cultural Travel Guide,* she wrote a chapter on the San Jose Vietnamese Community.

Write Your Query Letter

Now that you have chosen your target market and publication, and refined your story idea, your job is to spin the subject to fit the publication and write a one-page query letter explaining your idea and why you are the best person to write the story.

Target the editor who receives query letters. If the publication does not list a food editor on its masthead, call the editorial department. Whoever answers the phone can help you. Usually it's an editorial assistant or associate editor, and part of their job is to field questions from writers. Don't be shy. You want to know a couple of things: to whom should you pitch your story, and whether it should it be sent on paper or in an e-mail. Get the correct spelling of the editor's name and confirm his or her title.

Editors are flooded with query letters and reject almost all of them. When I was an editor my rejection rate was around 95 percent. In most cases I gave the letters to the editorial assistant, who typed a standard rejection letter that I then signed. Every once in a while, a query was good enough to merit a personal rejection note. Here's why queries fail:

- Generic story idea, not targeted
- Too long
- Unfocused
- Badly written
- Just an introduction, no story idea. "If someone says

'I'd like to work for you, contact me if you're interested,' I'll never contact them," said *Fine Cooking* publisher Homlberg. Like most editors, she doesn't have time. She might put your letter and writing samples into a file, and mean to get back to them, but she probably won't.

Ideally, query letters are one page long. Here are the elements:

The hook: Grab your editor's attention with the same kind of lead paragraph you'd write for the story. Your first few sentences must demonstrate that you can write and that you understand the audience's mission and readers. Here's one from freelancer Janet Fletcher: "Everybody knows that broccoli is a great cancer fighter. But too many people overlook its cousins. . . that have comparable health benefits and underutilized potential in the kitchen. Kale of many kinds, kohlrabi, broccoli romanesco, and broccoli rabe are among (those) that deserve a wider audience."

If you reference a story or department, it shows you read the magazine and have thought about a story that is right for them. Editors will pay attention.

The pitch: Explain your story idea in just a few sentences. If you can't, it's a sign you haven't thought it through closely enough. "The more specifics you can give, the better," said Montgomery at the IACP conference. For a story with recipes, "Say where you see the recipes going, give me some titles. You don't have to have all the recipes, just some suggestions." State the length, whether it will fit in a particular section, give a working title and a summary. If you have thought of other elements such as sidebars and tip boxes, mention them.

Your credentials: State why you are qualified to write the story. The best reason would be that you have written stories like this before. If you have been published on an entirely different subject in an unrelated field, don't mention it, as editors will not see that experience as relevant. If you've never been published, bring up relevant work experience or personal experience. If you've already done some interviews, or have been granted access to a prestigious profile subject, these facts might compensate for lack of writing experience.

The close: Thank the editor and say you look forward to hearing back. If you are leaving the country within a month, and need to hear by then if you should do a story on Turkish spice markets, say so.

Multiple story queries might increase your chance of getting published if you pitch two or three ideas of one paragraph each. For one national magazine, I pitched three stories. They had just accepted one idea from another writer, didn't like the second, but wanted the third. For another magazine, I pitched two articles and the editor wanted both. The challenge is to be concise.

If you send a surface-mail query, include a postage-paid postcard with which the editor can respond quickly. This will increase your chances of getting any response at all.

To send an e-mail query, put a few key words in the subject line with the word "Query." Don't send clips as attachments. Editors have grown tired of big files that download slowly or arrive in formats they can't open. Wait for the editor to ask for clips. If articles are online—even on your own Web site—put links in the body of the e-mail and make the editor's life easier.

You could follow all the advice I've given here, but if you send a badly written query with typos, or you have spelled the editor's name wrong, you'll turn the editor off and reduce your chance of being taken seriously.

SAMPLE QUERY

Here's a letter I wrote to *Sante* magazine, which accepted and ran the story.

Dear Mr. Costantino:

Recently your magazine featured a short article in the First Press section called "Cooking Up the Perfect Proposal." While it was an excellent primer on how to write a proposal, many chefs don't write them. Instead, they work with a writer who writes the proposal and the book by interviewing the chef and developing recipes.

I propose an article that would help chefs decide if writing a cookbook is for them. It would discuss whether to collaborate with a writer, the difference between ghostwriters and collaborators, how to find a writer, how the process works, and what it costs. I will interview some of the best ghostwriters and collaborators, top agents, and a few chefs who have worked with writers. I will also discuss the pros and cons of writing a book alone, and interview chefs who have done so.

I am a freelance food journalist and former magazine editor who has written for such publications as *Gastronomica*, the *San Francisco Chronicle*, *Safeway Select*, and *San Francisco Weekly*. I am also chair of the annual Food Writing for Beginners conference in Corte Madera, California.

I look forward to your response with interest.

Sincerely,
Dianne Jacob

Get a Response

You sent off the query. Now you wait. Typical responses range from two to eight weeks, regardless of whether you sent your query by surface or e-mail.

When you've waited an appropriate amount of time, send a follow-up one-paragraph letter or e-mail. Be polite and professional. Ask if the editor has received the query. Name the date you originally sent it. Attach a copy of the query. End with a sentence like "I look forward to hearing from you shortly."

E-mail is terrific for follow-ups. I locate the original e-mail in my files and send it as a forward, then drop in the same paragraph I described above. The editor sees the original query again, with the original date. Sometimes editors respond with some version of "I need more time." If I don't hear back, I e-mail again, with a shorter note. "Be persistent," said Tina Ujlaki, executive food editor of *Food & Wine,* at IACP. "It takes a lot to get through, and it might mean we just haven't got around to it."

If you still don't hear back, don't phone. Even if you get editors on the phone, they will not know who you are, won't know where they put the query, probably won't have time to look for it, and will have to get back to you.

Waiting for a response can get frustrating. I've waited as long as a year. "After spending about three weeks sending queries and clips with no success, I'd get so depressed I took naps on the floor because if I slept in bed that meant I was really depressed," says freelancer Linda Furiya. But she persisted, and eventually an airline magazine hired her to do a roving feature on city dining. That article led to more assignments.

Some editors are so swamped that they don't bother sending any response at all. You have to be prepared for that outcome. In fact, even established freelance writers complain that they get no response sometimes, so don't get too discouraged if it happens to you. Pitch a new story, or move on to a new publication. You've put in a fair amount of time on the story by now. Don't give up. Refocus.

What if an editor wants your story? She or he will discuss length and deadline, and offer a fee. If you want the job, take it and don't haggle over the money. It's considered impolite to do so before you have proven yourself. Sometimes, if an editor likes the letter but doesn't want the particular story you've pitched, she will ask if you'd be interested in a story she has generated where the writer has not yet been assigned.

Up until now, I've assumed you don't know the editor you're pitching. But there's another way to do it: network. If you meet editors at writer's conferences, industry events, or even by chance, your job is to be memorable enough that editors remember you when you send in a story idea. You don't need a business card, but be sure to get theirs so you can follow up on e-mail. To increase the odds, query them the next day on a subject you brought up in person. Don't wait for six months, trying to get up the nerve. Get it over with. Six months from now, you might as well be a stranger.

Once you have been published, it's your job to try to establish a relationship with your editor. The more comfortable an editor feels with you, and the more you deliver professional stories on deadline, the more assignments you will receive. If editors like one story, they might like more, so keep pitching ideas.

What about Pay?

It sounds silly to start this paragraph with a question like this, but in food writing, it's legitimate: you might have to write for free when you're starting out. Because competition is so intense, and because many publications have a small budget, you might be asked to do so. On the plus side, your story will be published and you'll have a clip. You'll get the experience of working with an editor and working on a story. If you do a good job, you might get an assignment for pay. On the other hand, you won't get paid this time around. If in your gut you feel the editor is taking advantage of you or not taking you seriously, don't sign up for the job.

I have been asked to write for no pay twice, by daily papers. When I submitted a short essay to a large daily paper, an editor called to ask if it could run in a reader response section, with no compensation. I said I was a professional writer and declined. When a different daily paper advertised for a cookbook reviewer, I applied. The food editor said I could pick up the cookbook at the reception desk. When I asked about payment he said there was none other than the book. I declined that job as well. The bottom line is how badly you want to be published, and how long you'll be willing to work for nothing. My advice is to stop working for nothing as soon as you have a few clips. Or barter: One newsletter gives me a free subscription in exchange for two articles a year. That's better than nothing.

I've since learned I can work almost for free by being paid close to nothing. I've received $25 for cookbook reviews, $30 for restaurant reviews in a guidebook, and $150 for a 3,000-word story. My experience is hardly unique, even for the big names. "I always dabbled in food writing as an aside but never planned to become a food writer. I never thought I could make a living as one, as the $50 and $75 I got for most of the food pieces I wrote proved," says *Bon Appétit* editor at large Alan Richman of his early days in the business.

Why is food writing such a badly paid profession? A full-time freelancer put it this way: She asked if, when I was a magazine editor in other fields, I had 100 people standing behind me willing to do my job for nothing. I said no. That's her situation, she explained. If she asks for more money, someone else will step in to fill her place for less, or nothing. Another freelancer wrote this when I told her about my book: "I'd better hurry and get my career more established, because I'm sure that once all those would-bes read your book and follow your advice, the competition will be stiffer than ever."

Even freelance writers at the top of their game don't feel well compensated. When asked about the hardest part of freelancing, Estabrook said, "Money. Even when you're making top rates at magazines and doing books, it's a financial grind. Competition is such that publications aren't really forced to pay more than they do for articles. If you did an article every month for *Gourmet,* you would make $50,000–$60,000 per year, with no medical care. That's a grueling pace you probably couldn't keep up."

Most food writers don't write full-time. They can't afford it. Says Wood of her regular writers at the *Chronicle,* "None makes their living as a freelancer, because it's almost impossible to do so." Again, keep your day job or work part time at other jobs unless your spouse or partner can support you, you have a generous trust fund, or you can arrange to win the lottery.

Write Your Story

During a break in a writing class I taught, a student approached me and said she was a terrible writer. I asked her how many drafts she wrote. "One," she answered. Whenever I tell that story to fellow writers, they laugh. Your first draft isn't *supposed* to be good. Anne Lamott calls it a "shitty first draft" in her excellent book on writing, *Bird by Bird: Some Instructions on Writing and Life.*

The first draft is whatever you write to get started. Make it awful, incomplete, and out of order—whatever you want. Then go back over it several times, filling in pieces, shaping and polishing your work. Good writing doesn't flow out in a single piece, fully formed. It needs revision.

Start with a compelling lead paragraph, called a lead: Draw in readers by piquing their interest. Spend a long time getting it right. Here are a few strategies:

- Base it on common experiences everyone understands. Here's a lead from an article in *Bon Appétit:* "As desperately as I wanted to overhaul my seventies nightmare kitchen—it was ugly and claustrophobic, and the oven was held together with grease—I was scared. . . . Was there a way to do the job without losing my money, my mind, and my marriage? Here's what I found out."

- Put readers in the center of the story immediately, a particularly good technique for travel stories. Here's the first sentence of a profile on a European hotelier in *Food & Wine:* "'Lisbon—I love it,' says hotelier Grace Leo-Andrieu, explaining why she decided to open her latest property, the luxurious Bairro Alto, in Portugal's capital."

•• Give a telling anecdote about one person to illustrate the point of your story. An *EatingWell* story on sugar addiction begins: "Long ago, Peg Duvall fell into a trap. As a teenager in the 1950s, Duvall studied diligently and led a life surrounded by high school friends. But she had a hard time relaxing at night."

•• For a how-to piece, hook readers by reassuring them it's going to be worth it. Here's a lead in *Fine Cooking:* "Learning to love beets isn't nearly as hard as you might imagine, because a roasted beet isn't so much a beet as it is a sweet and tender roasted vegetable."

   "I have learned to write about something vivid, like kneading the dough, with little clouds rising into the air," says freelancer Knickerbocker. "Capture your audience with something visual. I position the reader in the moment where I was captivated and then go back and write the story. *Saveur* taught me that."

Follow with a nut graph: Once you've drawn the reader in, explain what you're going to tell them. A nut graph bridges the lead and the rest of the story. It explains the point and tells readers what they will learn. Sometimes leads are so condensed that the nut graph is a sentence ending the first paragraph, as in the kitchen renovation story in the first example.

Near the top, tell readers why they should care, what's in it for them: Readers are busy. This is particularly true in newspapers, where you have to get to the point quickly. Readers want to know if this article will be worth their time. *Fine Cooking* accomplishes this in the first sentence of the beet story.

Hold readers' hands: You know where the story's going, but your readers don't. Drop a trail of bread crumbs all the way through. Reassure readers you're telling them what you said you would, and foreshadow what will come next. Readers don't like to be surprised. Prepare them for a story that takes a turn or covers several points.

If you're writing a recipe-based story, chances are good that you'll write a lead and nut graph, then go right into the recipes. In this example from *Cook's Illustrated,* a nut graph frames the story: "Years ago, in the kitchen of a university apartment, my Taiwanese roommate taught me to create a simple noodle dish that involved no more than boiling the noodles. It was a cheap, quick, meatless meal on which a student tired of Salisbury steak could subsist. Could I create something that recalled that satisfying dish, yet was a bit more substantial—more suited to a weeknight dinner?"

Make sure the body of the story follows a logical path: All stories have a beginning, middle, and end. Before tackling the middle, draft an organizational plan of points you wish to make. Each paragraph's first sentence makes the decision for the rest of the piece. Thoughts should flow in logical order from one topic to the next. Once you have a structure, if you feel more comfortable starting in the middle, go for it.

Strong close: Does your story have one, or does it trail off? In the conclusion, tell readers what you've already told them. If you've relayed an anecdote or created a theme in your lead, circle around to it again in the conclusion.

HOW TO INTERVIEW

�'● When you first contact your interviewee, politely explain the point of your story. Say where it will be published. If you haven't pitched the story yet, say you're calling to get permission to interview the person for a story. Once you have an interviewee's consent, your query letter has more teeth.

Request a convenient time to come by or telephone. Say how much time you'll need. I'm not a big fan of interviews by e-mail. Because people are busy they will answer with the smallest possible sentence and then you're done. There's also no room for the best part, when the two of you spontaneously travel down a new path to new material. I do interviews by phone, on a headset, and type my notes. Some people tape interviews and then transcribe the notes.

➡ Create a list of questions by doing research and eliminating those that will annoy your subject, such as "What's the name of your award-winning cheese again?" Annoying questions are different from dumb questions. If your subject uses a word you don't understand, ask what it means. You're not the expert; you're the information gatherer.

➡ Focus. If you're interviewing Wolfgang Puck because a restaurant magazine wants to know how he runs several establishments at once, don't ask about his technique for making gnocchi.

➡ Ask open-ended questions. Yes or no answers don't tell readers anything. Your interview will be over before you know it and you'll have no story.

➡ Remember that the interview is not about you and is not a conversation. Do not state your opinions or tell stories about the time something similar happened to you. You're not there to entertain or make friends with your subject.

➡ End when you said you would, and thank the interviewee for making time to talk with you. If you need more time, make another appointment. Send a thank-you note when you're done.

Edit Your Own Work

When you think you've drafted the story you want, your next step is to strengthen and shape it. Be ruthless. You might end up deleting half of it, moving paragraphs around, and rewriting the other half. None of this means you can't write. On the contrary, it means you are doing the work of real writers: revising. Here's how:

- Cut any throat clearing, where you have to warm up to get to the story. See if the lead starts a few paragraphs from the top.
- Eliminate repetition by saying what you mean clearly. Don't keep writing the same idea in slightly different ways.
- Write in active versus passive voice. Active voice means someone takes action: "John cut the crusty bread." Passive voice means the action is more removed: "The crusty bread was cut by John." Passive voice flattens your writing.
- Create action by packing your story with verbs. Powerful verbs make your writing more vigorous.
- Adjectives are the curse of food writers. Find one specific word and cut the rest.
- Tighten every sentence, eliminating all other unnecessary words, particularly adverbs such as "very" and "really."
- Cut out tangents or put them in sidebars.
- Use "show, not tell." Don't tell readers you didn't like sitting at the dinner table with your dad. Show them what it was like. Put them there at the table with you.
- Revise by ear. Read your work out loud to feel its rhythm and flow. It sounds silly but it's an invaluable way to eliminate clunky sentences and find parts that need clarification. When you hesitate over a sentence's construction, that's a clue to examine it more closely.
- Put your story away for a few days. When you come back to it you'll be more objective about what to fix and the fixes will be clearer.
- Edit for grammar, punctuation, and spelling. Proofread for typos. I can't emphasize this enough. There's nothing more irritating to editors than a careless mistake. It makes editors worry that you're not as accomplished as you seem. Have someone else read your work to look for errors.

"My process involves a lot of thinking before, during, and after," says freelancer Alan Richman. "It's not about polishing words but polishing the thinking, making things more focused."

What are the hardest things about writing articles? To quote Knickerbocker, "To be a good journalist, take the profession seriously, get the facts right, and present something new and fresh. Combine accuracy with creativity and passion."

BOOKS TO HELP YOU BECOME A BETTER WRITER:

- *On Writing Well: The Classic Guide to Writing Nonfiction,* by William Zinsser
- *Elements of Style,* by William Strunk Jr. and E. B. White
- *Writing Down the Bones: Freeing the Writer Within,* by Natalie Goldberg
- *Bird by Bird: Some Instructions on Writing and Life,* by Anne Lamott.

Dealing with an Editor

Once you submit your story to the editor, you may not hear back right away. Don't panic. Eventually your editor will read it and contact you about changes. Most stories need tweaking. Perhaps you left out critical details, or your lead is buried, or you need more information in certain areas, or the tone is wrong. Being edited is part of the process. Be polite and accept the requests.

If you are having control issues about someone changing your work, get over it. It will happen forever, no matter how long you've been writing. Yes, an editor can make changes you don't like. To object, pick your battle and make a reasoned argument, politely. Most editors, particularly on newspapers, don't even show you what they've done to your story before it is published. After one of my restaurant reviews was printed, I discovered that an editor interjected her own opinion, one contrary to my own. I called her and explained, politely, that my opinion was mine alone. She didn't do that again.

As a Freelancer, What Can You Write Off Your Taxes?

If you become a food writer, can you now write off all meals, research, and travel? Probably not, unless you can meet certain criteria, according to Tom Geary of San Jose, California, a tax accountant with thirty-five years of experience.

The first test is how much time you spend on food writing. According to the Internal Revenue Service (IRS), if you put in at least 500 hours per year, you have a business. If it's less than that, you have a hobby.

No deductions are allowed for hobbies unless your hobby makes a profit. In that case, you can deduct expenses up to the same amount as your hobby's expenses. If you took a loss, where food writing earned you $2,750 but you spent $3,500 on food, travel, classes, and office expenses, you could deduct only $750 of the expenses. These expenses constitute a miscellaneous deduction and may be subject to further restrictions.

If you have a food writing business that takes up more than 500 hours per year, you may qualify for some tax deductions. Here are test questions the IRS might ask to determine whether your business qualifies, according to Geary:

1. Do you keep records documenting your writing and research? Doing so would indicate you have a serious business. Let's say you wrote a restaurant review. You

need more than the credit card receipt to show as evidence. Keep notes on the meal, a sample menu, a map, a parking receipt, and a sample draft. For recipe development, keep versions of each recipe, with notes on how you worked.

2. Do you have the expertise to run a profitable business, and have you hired experts to help you in areas where you are not an expert? If so, you may write off whatever expenses are ordinary and necessary for performance of your business. Let's say you took a weeklong cooking class in Venice. You received a syllabus, kept notes, took photographs and researched restaurants, markets, and food purveyors, thus establishing a true business purpose for your trip: your desire to increase your knowledge and expertise of Italian food, thereby improving your marketability.

3. Is it reasonable to expect a profit? The more you can show you are in business to make a profit (a big challenge with food writing), the more legitimate your write-offs become. Here are a few examples:

    •◆ You want to travel to Turkey and write articles about your food explorations there. Querying editors before you leave indicates you are looking for profit-generating opportunities. Querying editors afterward might indicate you are looking for ways to write off your vacation. It doesn't matter if the editors reject the articles. What matters is your intent and record-keeping prowess.

    •◆ Let's say a newspaper paid you $75 for three recipes. The cost of groceries came to $100. While you didn't make a profit, expenses might be deductible if you argue that you are paying your dues, gradually increasing your exposure and experience to increase your marketability.

➡ You want to write a book on choosing kitchen equipment. Your purchase of kitchen equipment might be deductible if you can show that you also bought similar books for research purposes, wrote a book proposal, interviewed kitchen-shop retailers, and looked for an agent. Even so, since they are capital expenses, the deduction might occur over the life of the equipment as opposed to a full deduction on the year of the purpose.

Once you meet the above criteria for a business, you qualify for the right to deduct ordinary and necessary expenses for a self-employed business person, such as telephone bills, office supplies, and membership fees. I suggest you keep detailed files of your work-related papers, including copies of your notes, plus all bills and receipts.

Many food writers also cater, develop recipes, and teach cooking classes. The good news is these pursuits are interrelated and can be considered one business with interrelated expenses. Therefore the Venice cooking class may make you a better caterer and recipe developer, in addition to increasing your knowledge as a food writer.

This is a cursory discussion only. For more details, consult a professional tax preparer.

Three Ways to Make Decent Money

As I've said before, generally speaking food writing doesn't pay. But freelance work can pay a little more if you recycle the same article to other publications. Most publications buy first North American serial rights, where the publisher has the right to publish your work first. It does not authorize their right to publish your work elsewhere, such as in another publication or on a

Web site. After that you're free to sell it again, preferably to noncompeting markets both here and abroad. For example, a piece you wrote on spa cuisine in Mexico might fit a travel magazine whose focus is more on travel and less on food. A piece on coriander might first appear in a magazine focusing on herbs, and then in a more general publication.

By adding and subtracting according to the needs of other publications, you can publish a similar story many times—and get paid each time. Just apply what you learned earlier about targeting and positioning. Do not disclose that the article was previously published. Magazines don't care unless you're going to make it a problem for them when they see your article in a competitor's publication just as their publication goes to press.

The second kind of freelancing that pays is commercial writing, or writing for companies rather than publications. Janet Fletcher, a *San Francisco Chronicle* food writer, got into commercial writing serendipitously. She was pitching companies to become commercial sponsors for her new newsletter when one company offered her regular work. Her newsletter turned into a mini-magazine for a supermarket chain with seasonal stories, recipes, and product information. That job continued for about three years. Fletcher went on to write advertorials and special advertising sections that appeared in food magazines, and for ten years, wrote the newsletter of the American Institute for Wine and Food.

Now, after around twenty-five years of food writing, almost half of Fletcher's income comes from commercial work. She writes Web site copy and develops recipes for corporations and commodity boards. The nonprofit boards, such as the Almond Board and the Beef Council, hire her to write text aimed at professional chefs. For the Culinary Institute of America, she writes material for conferences.

In this kind of writing, you're usually "pitching a product or a place or a service," says Fletcher, "but it's a soft sell with an editorial feel to it." Commercial writing has its downside. Most of your work doesn't appear with your byline, so it's harder to build your portfolio. But if you're a reliable writer with good ideas who knows how to keep clients, you can succeed. "Find a need and fill it," Fletcher advises. "Look for companies whose Web sites are not very good, or who don't have marketing materials and need them. Approach independent public relations firms."

Patti Londre, head of her own marketing and public relations firm, hires experienced freelance food writers for all kinds of commercial writing: press releases, brochures, Web site content, ghost-written first person pieces, press-kit materials, label information, scripts for videos, pitch letters, research papers, and speeches. "We have paid as low as $45 per hour and as high as $100 per hour—that was for hard-hitting media pitching," she says. "We also pay by the project, such as $150 per recipe plus groceries. We shop price a little bit but we're more interested in who can deliver what we're looking for."

Writing for trade publications is the third way to make money. These publications have a narrow focus, though, and you must know enough about the industry and have enough contacts to generate the right story ideas.

Some say syndication is a great way to make money. If you are an established writer, you can query a syndication service about submitting articles for distribution to major daily newspapers, community weeklies, newsletters, and Web sites across the United States and around the world. If the service accepts you, it takes 40 to 50 percent of sales. Sales are based on how many newspapers purchase your story or column and how much they pay. These days, with reduced budgets and access to lots of free or inexpensive copy, newspapers are no longer a great market for syndication. In fact, one cookbook author told me he was only able to sell his column to one newspaper, which then demanded he also sell them all rights to print it. The syndicate will send payment if and when publications pick up your article or column.

In conclusion, editors like writers they trust who pitch well-defined ideas, understand what the publication wants, turn in stories on time, and form a good relationship. If you can follow these rules, you'll always be in print. Then there's the role of passion, my theme from earlier chapters. Says Knicker-bocker, "I don't think I've ever written something that has been an assignment that didn't come from me. [Otherwise] I haven't been able to write well about it. It's always something that has moved me very deeply, where I just have to get something off my chest and have to write the story. Someone's going to buy it. They're going to feel the vibrancy and the clarity.

"I kind of can't believe my life worked out the way it has," she says, "that I get to write and be paid for it."

For More Information on Freelancing:

Books:
- *Starting Your Career as a Freelance Writer*, by Moira Anderson Allen
- *Secrets of a Freelance Writer: How to Make $85,000 a Year*, by Robert W. Bly
- *This Business of Writing*, by Gregg Levoy.

Web sites:
- The International Food, Wine and Travel Writers Association Web site: http://www.ifwtwa.org. If you get ten print or Web travel articles published in a year, you can join.
- Travel Source, the North American Association of Travel and Lifestyle Editors Web site: http://www.traveljourno/com
- Web site of *Writer's Market* books and magazine: http://www.writersmarket.com
- Writer's Weekly, a freelance writing e-zine: http://www.writersweekly.co
- *Writer's Digest* Web site: http://www.writersdigest.com
- For information about grants and contests, see http://www.fundsforwriters.com.

➥ For market information for freelance writers, see http://www.woodenhorsepublishing.com.

Syndication sites:
➥ United Features: http://www.unitedfeatures.com. See submission guidelines on home page.
➥ King Features: http://www.kingfeatures.com/subg.htm. Accepts column submissions. See submission guidelines.
➥ Copley News Source: http://www.copleynews.com/. See submission guidelines on home page.

Writing Exercises

1. I find how-to stories the easiest to write, maybe because I like to help people. Now you try it. Make a list of ten how-to headlines of stories you can write with your eyes closed. Perhaps you're an expert on piecrusts and your article would be about technique. Your headline will not be "All About Piecrusts." Instead, it will focus on how you are an expert giving out advice. "How to Make a Winning Piecrust Every Time" is a more specific, and more exciting, alternative. After you've written your list of ten headlines, pick one and make a list of the steps involved. Now you have the middle of a story. Once you write the beginning and the end, the first draft will be complete.

2. Recycling stories based on the same subject and research is a terrific use of your time and a way to generate better income. Think up three stories based on one subject written for a general consumer publication, then adapt them for an industry newsletter and a magazine aimed at

mothers. Write a lead for each kind of story based on what the readership wants to know.

I'll give you some examples. A lead for a how-to story on food safety for a general consumer publication targets readers who prepare food without thinking too much about bacteria, and has a general lead about keeping the kitchen sanitary when cooking. A lead for a story for an industry publication tackles an interview with a government official discussing new labeling guidelines for meat. A lead for a publication aimed at mothers begins with the story of a child eating leftovers that have gone bad, and then discusses ways a mother might protect her family from ingesting the wrong foods. For each lead idea, I visualized the target audience and slanted the subject directly to them, addressing what might concern or interest them.

3. If you have not been published, come up with a story idea based on your own personal experience, and craft a query letter. A well-crafted query letter might be enough to sway an editor. Here's a sample story idea: "Since I returned to work after having a baby, I've had to plan ahead and buy cupboards full of canned and packaged food. My article will draw upon my experiences of sampling prepared baby food such as crackers and cereal. It will recommend the top five products for busy mothers, based on taste, ingredients, and value."

Secrets of Restaurant Reviewing

What could be better than going from restaurant to restaurant, eating exquisite food with friends, and then writing about it? Being a restaurant reviewer has to be one of the most glamorous jobs in the world. You dine for free at the best places in town, and restaurateurs and chefs fawn over you. Right?

Yes and no. Some of these assumptions are true. You may often eat excellent, cutting-edge, and exotic food that would have strained your pocketbook in the past. But you'll also eat lots of mediocre and bad food, sample foods you might not like, go out more than you want, and work harder than you imagine. You might gain weight as well, but as Susan Reigler, restaurant critic for the *Louisville Courier-Journal* says, "Clothes always come in larger sizes."

The first secret you'll discover is that reviewing involves mediocre food as well as the good stuff. "No one sees you eating bad sushi sixty miles away from home on a Saturday night," admits Tom Sietsema, restaurant critic for the *Washington Post*. The Phantom Gourmet (http://www.phantomgourmet.com), a New England TV personality and critic who writes four reviews per week online, concurs. "For all the dinners that begin with ephemeral tastes of contemporary manna and end with culinary orgasms, there are three mediocre and at least one really bad meal," he complains. Some reviewers I interviewed told me about just plain bad food, and even rotten food that gives them food poisoning. But who feels sorry for them?

You might notice that not much is published about mediocre and bad food. Most publications keep negative reviews to a minimum, unless the place is famous, expensive, or new and opened to great fanfare. Most editors and writers believe it's best to tell readers about places that excite them and give them a reason to go out, rather than telling them where not to go.

The second secret is that reviewing is difficult and time-consuming, even if all you do is write reviews. You may go out several evenings in a week. As a freelancer, I went out three to four nights per week to write one review per week for a weekly paper. Dara Moskowitz, food writer for *City Pages* in Minneapolis, goes out almost every night, as does Michael Bauer, executive food and wine editor and restaurant critic for the *San Francisco Chronicle,* who writes two reviews per week. Sietsema, reviewer for the *Washington Post,* heads out every day for lunch, sometimes breakfast, and sometimes two dinners if he's on deadline. He keeps detailed calendars because he makes upward of sixty reservations per month.

The main reason for multiple trips is to go back to see if your experience was consistent, and to sample more food. One review may require two or three visits per week. On top of that, you have to keep from being recognized (more on this on page 126). You can make it easier on yourself if you plan ahead and space out restaurant visits. Reigler, a full-time critic, says she plans up to three months in advance and might visit one restaurant twice over several weeks.

The third secret is that once you get an assignment, you're on your own. There's little chance of on-the-job training. If you're like other novices, you'll surely have a lot of questions. Even if you've already begun reviewing, you'll learn something new. I'm going to share with you the questions that came up for me when I started reviewing, along with insights and tips from some of the best reviewers in the country. There is more information on the Web site of the Association of Food Journalists (AFJ), http://www.afjonline.com/, which lists a code of ethics and critic's guidelines. The AFJ, by the way, gives annual awards to the best critics in the country. Sietsema and Bauer, both interviewed in this chapter, are multiple winners.

As you read, you'll learn about the complex issues behind reviewing, particularly ethics, that make this field endlessly fascinating. You'll discover practical ways to get your first assignment. You'll also find inside information and candid stories about how reviewers began their careers.

How Is It Done?

First, as a reviewer, you have to choose where to go. At daily papers, the old "newsworthy" standard applies, explains Russ Parsons, former food editor of the *Los Angeles Times*. Questions he asks himself include: "Is there a reason people should know about this restaurant? Are people talking about it and want to know about it? Is it unknown and very good? Is it hyped and not so good? Does it in some way reflect something important about the community?"

If you're a freelancer, you might select restaurants on your own. Most of the time I have decided which one to visit. Says the Phantom Gourmet, "Every new restaurant likes to claim it's pushing the envelope, but part of my job is to know whether what they are doing is truly new or just a new veneer on something that was already passé ten years ago."

To decide on restaurants, you have to be out and on the lookout, scoping out your town for interesting new places to add variety to your reviews by price, location, or cuisine. Or you may have heard that a restaurant has changed chefs or made a major menu revision. Friends and associates will send you tips. Perhaps you want to go to an established place the publication hasn't reviewed for a while. Sometimes the editor wants a particular restaurant reviewed, or the paper expanded into a new county and the editor wants coverage there. Or you might propose a roundup of a particular type of restaurant, such as those with good bars.

As a freelancer, you probably won't have an assignment for your first review, so you'll have to write on spec and then submit it. (That means editors are under no obligation to run the piece or pay you, if they don't like it.) Make sure you read your target publication thoroughly and know what sorts of restaurants are critiqued. Don't pick a coffee shop frequented by seniors if the paper wants only hip, expensive places in certain parts of town. Don't write a 2,500-word review if they top out at 350 words. Your safest choice for a review will be a new restaurant, at least two months old. But don't sweat it too much—the point is to impress an editor, who might give you an assignment for a new article if he or she doesn't want that one but sees promise in your writing.

If you're going to a fancy place, find out about the restaurant and chef, perhaps where the chef worked in the past, and who designed the restaurant, if design is relevant. Sometimes you can find old reviews in other publications that mention the chef. Search for the chef's name on the Web. Sometimes your publication will have received a press release from a restaurant's marketing department, but most of the time you have to figure it out yourself. Try to get a menu. Representing a potential customer, call to ask about the chef's specialties and most popular dishes. If it's pan-Asian cuisine, for example, and the specialty is grilled ahi steak with ponzu sauce, you now have the opportunity to research the cuisine and how the dish is made, and then you'll feel more confident about judging it. While you're on the phone, find out directions, hours, and how to dress, if it's upscale.

Your next decision is when to go. Reviews of dinner are standard, unless the restaurant relies on its biggest crowd at lunch. Monday and Tuesday are the most frequent chef's nights off. Friday and Saturday nights put the most stress on the kitchen. (These are things to consider for your own research, but that readers don't need to be told.) You can go for lunch and dinner, but not just for lunch.

As for how many people to take, there's no right answer. Reviewing can be distracting. It's hard to taste, observe, and simultaneously participate in the conversation around the table. When you go alone, it's easier to soak up atmosphere, experience, and energy level. On the other hand, you may hate dining alone, and the downside is that you can't sample very much food. You could try taking one person who understands that you're working. Old friends or colleagues may let you concentrate and feel comfortable about not talking when you need to think. Most important is to choose people who will eat anything, and who will not take offense at rabbit in cream sauce, offal, or ducks' tongues during dim sum. Make sure they understand that you might ask them to order particular dishes, not necessarily the menu items they'd like most, so that you can sample a variety.

The best reviewers visit each restaurant at least two times, often three. If you go just once, you won't know enough to make decisions. Service, food quality, and atmosphere vary. One night service might be exceptional, and another night your waiter may be off having a cigarette while you're waiting for the bill. Going multiple times helps you understand and more accurately gauge the spirit of the place. Another reason to go back is to taste more food. Sometimes you'll taste the risotto Milanese twice to see if it has improved or if it really is as spectacular as it was the first time. Or you decide you need more dishes to get a balance between grilled, baked, sautéed, and roasted dishes.

By now you're probably breaking out in a sweat, anticipating your next credit card statement. Cost can be a problem. Will you be reimbursed? The short answer is: it depends. If you send two unsolicited reviews to a newspaper, you foot the bill. If you've been given an assignment, you'll probably be paid something. Later in this chapter you'll read more specifics about finances and payment.

Once you get to the restaurant, you'll have a number of questions to ask yourself. I've compiled an extensive list below, based on my own experience, interviews with reviewers, and information from the Association of Food Journalists. All questions may not be relevant, and some are more important than others. Questions about food are always paramount.

Restaurant Checklist

• *At the beginning:* How are you treated when you make a reservation over the phone and when you arrive at the door? Do you feel welcomed? Perhaps you can arrive a few minutes early and take in the scene. How full is the restaurant? Are diners enjoying themselves? Are diners getting similar-looking food and service at each table?

• *The service:* A good staff elevates eating to dining. Your waiter should be knowledgeable about the food and willing to find answers to questions you have or solutions to problems. Is your waiter attentive, overly chatty, or someone with an attitude? Do servers wait until you're finished before removing your plate, or do they let plates gather on the table? Does the waiter check in a few times? Are you told if your food is delayed? While you can complain to see how the waiter responds, your main job is to keep a low profile and not attract attention to yourself. How is the service at other tables? Do they get their food before you do, if seated at the same time or later?

• *The menu:* Use it to examine the philosophy of the chef and restaurant. It's a good way to understand chefs' intentions, how courses flow, which flavors are important, whether seasonality is an issue, and the way they put flavors and colors together. Notice how categories are balanced. Is the menu pretentious, with too many foreign words not explained? Are the prices reasonable, given the surroundings and service? If it's an upscale restaurant, it might present a new menu every day, so you might not want to focus exclusively on particular dishes because they might disappear. If it's a corner family place, the menu may not have changed for years.

➻ *Evaluate the wine list:* Are the prices reasonable, compared to the price of the food and other wine lists? Does the selection and presentation enhance the theme of the restaurant? Does a waiter or sommelier help you select? Are they knowledgeable about the wines?

➻ *Ordering the food:* Taste as much food as possible, particularly signature dishes. Often the menu will list which dishes are most popular, or the waiter will point them out if prompted. Bring guests and taste their food. Choose a variety of dishes and courses, based on cooking techniques, ingredients, and styles.

➻ *Tasting the food:* What is your gut reaction? Are flavors balanced and integrated? Is the dish exciting, fresh or made with quality ingredients? Is it oversalted? Is there too much cream or vinegar, or too little spice? Is it the right temperature? Is the food visually appealing and properly cooked? Does typically unappetizing food look good here?

➻ *The ambiance:* En route to the restroom, walk slowly and evaluate the view or the dining room. How does the setting and style compare to other restaurants of its kind? Are the tables large enough and not crammed together, and are the seats comfortable? Is it too noisy, or the music intrusive? What about the clientele? Does the restaurant appeal to a certain type, such as hipsters, couples, or business folks? Would you take friends or family there to celebrate a birthday?

➤ **When you leave:** How hard is it to get the check, and does someone acknowledge you when you leave? When you're out the door, what is your overall impression? Ask yourself whether you look forward to going back, why or why not, and whether you found dishes you can't wait to try again. What were the strongest and weakest aspects of the evening?

You're probably wondering how to remember it all. You can't, at first. Even the best critics had trouble initially. Bauer says he had the overwhelming feeling that he had to know everything, get it all down, and know every ingredient in a dish and react. "The first two years I was a basket case," he admits. "I didn't take notes—I had to remember. Talk about not having fun. I practically had an ulcer." Fortunately, his anxiety didn't last. Now he can have a good time and recall what's most important. "You don't have to remember every nuance of every dish," he advises. "Learn what you need to know. Let the other stuff go."

It's a good idea to take notes, but not at the table, because you won't want the restaurant staff to discover you. A notepad small enough to fit in your purse or pocket is a great place to assemble your impressions, preferably in a restroom stall. Or record your thoughts in a tape recorder after leaving the restaurant, perhaps in your car. Steal the menu if you can fold it up in your pocket or purse. If it's only paper, don't feel guilty. Later it will come in handy when you can't remember the name or ingredients of a particular dish, or when you want to evaluate the types of food presented. If you don't have a menu, some restaurants list dishes on their Web sites. Or have a friend call to ask for a faxed menu, but don't count on it if the restaurant is busy or too small to have a fax machine.

PUBLICATIONS TO SOLICIT FOR RESTAURANT REVIEWS

You don't have to review for your daily paper, and you probably can't start there anyway. Lots of alternatives exist, once you start looking:

- Weekly (alternative) and free newspapers
- Some national food magazines, particularly *Gourmet*
- Regional magazines
- City magazines
- Travel guidebooks
- City tourist information
- Zagat Survey guide (written by enthusiasts)
- Theater programs
- Airline magazines
- Online guides such as CitySearch, or message boards and chats, such as Chowhound.com (See more about Web sites on page 136.)

Study these sources to see how reviews are written in terms of style, structure, length, and content. Look at the publication's masthead to see if the critic is on staff or a freelancer. Contact the appropriate editor to find out how he or she acquires reviews. Perhaps they are assigned, or perhaps they will take written queries or writing samples.

Or, write your own city guide. Seymour Britchky, Alan Richman's favorite critic, wrote *Restaurants of New York* in 1990. If you can find this guidebook you'll enjoy his hard-boiled writing style.

What Is the Goal?

Your job is straightforward: Point people in the direction of high-quality, brightly flavored fresh food, and paint a vivid picture so they can decide whether to go. You help consumers make informed decisions about where to eat. As a result, you may encourage them to try something new, educate them about new foods or cooking techniques, or inspire them to visit a new neighborhood. Most readers, however, will read your review for entertainment or information value, and may never visit the restaurant. That's okay.

Your goal is not to suggest how the chef might improve the food, because diners, not chefs, are your readers. If you want to feel superior by bossing chefs around, you won't succeed. Even the most powerful reviewer in America in the 1960s didn't take himself too seriously. "It burdened my conscience to know that the existence or demise of an establishment might depend on the praise or damnation to be found in the [*New York*] *Times,* wrote Craig Claiborne in his memoir, *A Feast Made for Laughter.* "Although I reasoned, correctly, that the judgment of the food critic did not invariably determine whether a restaurant would prosper or suffer mortal decline."

How Do You Write a Good Review?

You set out to be honest, fair, exercise good judgment, and be authoritative and accurate. Honesty is critical because it applies even if your friends love a place but you don't. If you're objective, you'll be less likely to get caught up in the romance, like claims that such-and-such place has been making the best pancakes for fifty years. Does the restaurant follow through on its promise? It's your job to find out.

Honesty applies to how well you know yourself. Says Bauer: "People go to restaurants when they're feeling good, having a celebration, or getting together with friends, but for you, it's your work. You have to divest yourself of negative feelings and go into neutral. You can't crave beef when it's your last visit and you have to order salmon."

You get to know your own prejudices and beliefs. Try to keep your "personal pollution" out of the decision, advises Moskowitz. Bauer doesn't like sweet sauces, for example, and says so if he's reviewing that kind of dish. I hardly ever ate red meat, was sick of chicken, and looked forward to eating fish. But I couldn't say every week, "The fish was good." I ate lamb, rabbit, bacon, and steak—whatever was on the menu. Biases can't get in the way.

Personal beliefs can become a problem if, say, you conclude the food didn't justify the high prices at a steak house. Could it be because you think steak shouldn't cost more than fifteen dollars? If so, reveal your prejudice in the name of fairness. Check yourself by asking why you loved a dish. Is it because you love moussaka, or is it the way the chef prepared it, by doing something special?

Sheraton says there's no cuisine that she hates categorically, and no food that she dislikes except tripe. She might hate a dish's representation, but not the food itself. "I don't think you should have preconceptions or apply previous experiences," she says. You can factor them in afterward.

She's also not the kind of reviewer who cuts the chef a lot of slack. "I'm not so much for explaining the philosophical goals of the chef. I'm not interested in whether the chef will be good some day, and not willing to eat something terrible to finance a chef's development. If a chef wants to serve chocolate on cauliflower, he should make it for himself and taste it, and not serve it to the public to see what they feel about it. I don't like experiments." What you eat at that moment is what you judge.

What about Negative Reviews?

The bottom line is your loyalty is to the consumer, not the restaurant. Think about the people who save up for a meal out, says Sietsema, who can't test-drive a meal and are counting on you to tell them the truth. You have to be negative when you really believe that something was bad. You don't have to be cruel or take cheap shots, though.

There's an unwritten rule in reviewing: Critics are harder on expensive restaurants, because a costly place takes a bigger bite out of readers' wallets. High-profile restaurants can take the hit, compared to a small neighborhood place that will suffer. As *Gourmet* magazine editor Ruth Reichl once said, "When a restaurant charges twenty-five dollars for a bowl of turnip soup, pleasant is not enough."

There's no point trashing a small restaurant in a magazine like *Time Out,* says Carpenter, because the magazine has a Critic's Choice section of capsule reviews, which are positive by default. She also feels it's not worth taking the space for negative reviews unless a fancy restaurant has a huge opening. When a reviewer sends in a negative review, Carpenter will send a staff member to check its accuracy. Amanda Doyle, associate editor of *Where* magazine in St. Louis, says she tries to be subtle when writing about small restaurants. If she had a long wait, for example, she will write, "It's too bad they don't take reservations." Sheraton would never give a negative review to an obscure restaurant. "What's the point of saying don't go to this place that you've never heard of?" she asks. Instead she'd end up not writing the review.

At publications where restaurants are advertisers, you could be told by an editor to soften a negative review because of potential repercussions. Often the publication ends up running no review at all to avoid a situation where the restaurant might pull its ad. In *Where* listings, Doyle says advertisers' capsule reviews represent about a third of all reviews and have first priority. She chooses the remaining two-thirds. Overall, negative reviews have fewer political ramifications in the chat rooms of Web sites such as Egullet.com, because the sites are not dependent on advertising.

What do you do when the food is uneven? Bauer once dealt with this issue by writing that a restaurant made "two dishes well and the rest not so well." Readers told him they went anyway, ordered the items he liked, and left happy. The restaurant met their needs. Sometimes everyone else at the restaurant is enjoying the signature salad with blueberries and pine nuts, but you don't like it. In that case, you say just that and explain why.

I like reviewers who use humor to make a negative review more entertaining. Alan Richman, a witty contributing editor of *Bon Appétit,* loves a line he once read in a review of a Chinese restaurant: "The hot and sour soup only had to be one or the other." Grimes once wrote about an Italian restaurant: "The waiters are a colorful bunch. They seem to be working from a playbook not yet available in English-speaking countries, in which diners are regarded as hopeful applicants rather than customers with the power of the dollar behind them."

Negative reviews can have consequences. Years ago, a friend of Bauer's owned a lunch-only place in Dallas. Bauer thought it would be fine to be friends, because he wouldn't review that kind of restaurant. Then this friend opened a high-profile restaurant, and Bauer had to critique it. "It was a mixed review, not all negative," he recalls. "I felt horrible, even though I was much more careful with the review." His friend never spoke to him again. More recently, Bauer learned that on three occasions, angry restaurateurs hired private investigators to follow him and check into his background after he had given their restaurants less than favorable reviews.

In the end, restaurant reviewing is the most subjective form of criticism in the world today, asserts Richman. "There are no standards for how food tastes. Everything stems from the taste buds and taste memory of the reviewer." Most of the time, a restaurant is neither very good nor very bad. It is somewhere between the two, and your job is to see the shades of grey. Reviewers also wrestle with the issue of whether liking the food is the same as the food being good. It's your job to separate these two things and reconcile them, because you have to have an opinion. This becomes an issue when you get hate mail with readers questioning your analysis. All you can do is pay attention to what you're eating, says Reigler, as in the Buddhist philosophy of mindfulness. Don't eat when you're not hungry and don't eat out of habit.

What Makes a Great Reviewer?

Great reviewers have passion, knowledge, authority, a great writing style, and stamina. They write intelligently, from a frame of reference established through years of loving food. They discern quality, ferret out pretentiousness, acknowledge flavors that don't go together, and can point to why a dish works. They give the reader a feel for the place, its rhythm, and overall vibe. And they keep up their energy level and enthusiasm.

Passion is paramount. Alan Richman still has it after many years of reviewing. He says he can't wait to see what a restaurant has in store for him. "I get a hop in my step," he enthuses.

He's also incredibly knowledgeable. You need a deep understanding of your subject to succeed. You already have experience dining in restaurants, you know and love food, and you probably love cooking. From there, you could increase your skill level by taking cooking classes. To supplement my knowledge, I twice took an eleven-week class in French cooking basics, repeating the course to understand the underlying principles and techniques of formally trained chefs. Joan Zoloth, former reviewer for the *Oakland Tribune,* took cooking classes to understand how a dish was put together long before she became a reviewer. She was just passionate about food.

Reviewers thrive on research about food and trends. Do you devour cookbooks, food dictionaries, journals, and specialty online sites? Do you know the food scene in your town? Do you love to find unfamiliar raw ingredients in specialty groceries? Do you enjoy tasting the food of other regions or countries when you travel? Do you consult authorities when you have a question about tofu skins or a particular braising technique?

Critics understand and appreciate other people's cultures, even if they aren't experts in the cuisine. Education and research are particularly important when reviewing ethnic restaurants, where you learn how to approach an unfamiliar cuisine and what to look for in its elements. Some reviewers take along natives or experts in ethnic cuisine, such as people who have cooked a particular food all their lives, or cookbook authors. I almost tripped up when I wrote my first review of a Cambodian restaurant. I ordered a fish dish that is supposed to be mushy. I thought it had the texture of cat food. Luckily, I didn't write that. Although my editors had requested edginess, I would have gone too far by stating that view, which would have appeared disrespectful and uninformed. Instead, I went to cookbooks and spoke with informed people to become educated.

Cuisines of other countries are more accessible in the United States than ever before, and reviewers have to step up to the plate. Earlier on, someone like *New York Times* food editor Craig Claiborne, who reviewed restaurants in the 1960s, only had to know about French, American, Chinese, and Italian food. As *New York Times* writer William Grimes points out, "Today you're expected to say something authoritative on regional Mexican cuisine and Tibetan food and make distinctions." Fortunately, when you're passionate about food and culture, it's part of the fun to explore new cuisines and culinary traditions.

No matter what challenges critics face, the best ones are excellent writers and storytellers. They know how to show enthusiasm and opinion without resorting to exclamation marks. They keep readers interested and entertained from the first to the last sentence. A well-written review conveys the critic's "sense of adventure as an eater and sense of joy in the experience," says Grimes. He describes his style as knowledgeable, but written with wit and a light hand. "Reviews should be entertaining," he says. "You shouldn't weigh people down with info that becomes a burden for them. Deliver information and lift it with a sense of humor." Grimes isn't just talking the talk. In a review of an Italian restaurant, he writes: "The big-hearted entrees can bring down a weak-kneed diner at fifty yards."

Another reviewer I've enjoyed reading is freelancer Jonathan Gold. In a massive restaurant roundup for *Travel & Leisure,* he writes of a Chicago steak house as "a battered old place under the El with blood-rare strip steaks the size of catcher's mitts, baked potatoes the size of footballs, and the best martinis in the world. Beefy, happy men tuck into huge platters of garbage salad—a time-honored Chicago thing not unlike a great antipasto run through a paper shredder—and croissant-size shrimp with cocktail sauce." Can't you just see it? He's given you evocative visual information on the place, the food, and the diners in two sentences.

Some critics find writing the review harder than going to the restaurant, including the Phantom Gourmet. "Strangely, though, it can also be the most rewarding part," he adds. "Finding just the right word, describing a dish or the atmosphere in just the right way as to convey exactly how something tasted can be frustrating, but when achieved, fulfilling. This process takes nearly as long as the dinner itself."

Most reviews follow a similar format, and when you have to write within this format all the time, it can be challenging: they describe the setting, what's on the menu, the prices, the service, and ambiance. Then they go into the appetizers, entrées, and dessert. The worst are the "bite-by-bite" reviews where people just go through the meal, describing everything they had, says Mary Margaret Pack, food writer and restaurant reviewer for the *Austin Chronicle*. For variety, the *Post*'s Sietsema employs action, such as what people at the next table are saying and whether they're enjoying their food. Critics at alternative newspapers have the most freedom to mix it up by adding personal details. Here's an example from the *San Francisco Bay Guardian*, by Eric Richardson: "Only three things will get me to eat hamburgers anymore. One is the smell of them being barbecued next door by Annette, affectionately known as the neighborhood meat queen." Annette would not appear in a daily paper.

As you can see in the above examples, voice is an important part of reviewing. While it's not something you can fake, it's helpful to define it so your reviews are consistent. When I started out, I read the reviews of writers I admired to let their styles sink in. I tore out pieces I loved, particularly those with beautiful or witty writing, and collected them in a file. Luckily, Gold collected his in a book called *Counter Intelligence: Where to Eat in the Real Los Angeles*. A former music writer for *Rolling Stone,* he wrote reviews of neighborhood places for *LA Weekly* in the 1980s that are funny, irreverent, passionate, insightful, knowledgeable, and filled with witty references. Recently he's come back to the *Weekly* to write more. Between these gigs he left Los Angeles for *Gourmet,* and his voice changed. It was no longer irreverent, but more formal, with a kind of hushed tone. Now he was reviewing fancy, expensive restaurants, writing about truffles and foie gras, and his voice had to be appropriate to the publication.

Sheraton says perhaps it's because she's bossy that her voice is authoritative as a result. Experienced reviewers feel comfortable expressing their own opinions. That means not writing what your friends thought of the food. I once wrote that my girlfriend thought her glass of white wine at a Greek restaurant "tasted like Aqua Velva." Yes, it was witty, but I couldn't have defended her judgment if confronted. I could only defend my own point of view.

Because she's famous, Sheraton is not asked to write in a voice that reflects the publication. Many freelancers make their living this way, however. Compare reviews in an alternative newspaper to those in a daily paper. Each publication has its own style and voice, and the writers conform to those parameters. Often the editor doesn't explain the publication's style at the time of assignment, so it's up to you to figure out what's appropriate. The only way you can do so is by reading the publication first, and then picking the most appropriate adjectives to describe the voice (see pages 19–20 for a list).

Carpenter says *Time Out New York* takes a "sassy, edgy tone" in features. She sends reviews back when they're not written that way. "We definitely have a voice. You have to be familiar with it, be able to pull it off," she says. "It's writing that sounds like you're talking."

What about actually describing the food? The best reviewers use specific language. Three of the laziest adjectives I know are "nice," "wonderful," and "delicious." Most of us have resorted to them at times. They are so vague that readers don't know what you mean, other than something positive. It's harder to develop a taste lexicon, but a developed vocabulary is critical to being a successful food writer. "What surprised me the most is how hard it is," says Pack. "I read other reviews and see people struggling with the same kinds of things I do with the language." Which word makes her cringe most? "Unctuous."

How Well Can You Describe Food?

This list certainly isn't exhaustive, but it gives an idea of specific language. If you want more, read reviews, circle the words you like, and compile your own list.

Taste and Smell:

Acrid	Cooling	Peppery
Bland	Fruity	Perfumed
Buttery	Herbal	Piquant
Bright	Mellow	Robust
Briny	Nutty	

Texture:

Brittle	Foamy	Slippery
Chewy	Gelatinous	Velvety
Crisp	Silky	

Appearance:

Blanketed	Melted	Sprinkled
Caramelized	Mottled	Stuffed
Crumbled	Murky	Syrupy
Crusty	Plump	Tired
Drowned	Sheared	Trembling
Lackluster	Shiny	Wet
Leafy	Smeared	Wimpy
Limp	Spice-dusted	

Sound:

Bubbling	Fizzy	Sizzling
Crackling	Popping	Sputtering

Other favorites:

Alluring	Denuded	Impeccable
Comforting	Depth	Liberal
Complemented	Dispirited	Satisfying

Two loaded words I avoid are "expensive" and "authentic." If a publication rates restaurants by price, such as inexpensive, moderate, and expensive, and gives a range in its rating system, then readers will know what "expensive" means. Otherwise it is undefined, leaving readers to wonder. Using the word "authentic" has pitfalls as well. My husband loves pad thai, and ordered it often when we traveled in Thailand. Each restaurant served the noodles differently, even inside a thin egg omelet once. Which was authentic?

Once you've left the restaurant, if you didn't ask your waiter about certain dishes and you still have questions, it's acceptable to call the restaurant and identify yourself. If you're not sure about the hint of ginger in the tomato sauce, ask about the ingredients. Ask how the chef made the chicken with deep flavorings. He might tell you he brined the meat for two days. (Ruth Reichl wouldn't agree with my suggestion, however. She says the last thing you want is a restaurateur saying, "She didn't know what she was eating, she had to call!")

When you're done with your piece, double-check all dates, name spellings, the address, telephone number, and hours. It's not a pain. It's part of your job, and better than getting a call from an irritated editor who just found out from a reader that you spelled the restaurant owner's name wrong (this happened to me) or inadvertently listed the phone number of a high-powered (and litigious) lawyer instead of the restaurant's.

The last characteristic of a good reviewer is stamina, particularly if you have to eat at the same place a few times in one week, or make conversation. Grimes points out that reviewing with guests at the table is an extremely social activity that takes lots of energy. "You are the host," he says. "You can't sit there silently, chewing." Plus, you have to be resolved to sample the same dishes. "How many crème brûlées have I tasted in the last two years?" moans Moskowitz. "A thousand? But other people have only ordered them five times in their lives, and they're excited about them. What keeps me going is their right to have a good anniversary dinner."

And then, you have to watch your weight. Part of having stamina involves the will to just sample. To quote Jane Stern, who with her husband, Michael, co-authored *RoadFood: The Coast to Coast Guide to 500 of the Best Barbeque Joints. Lobster Shacks, Ice Cream Parlors, Highway Diners, and Much More,* "We take a bite and if it sucks, we don't wait around for it to get better." I taste everything, but don't try to eat it all. That's why God made doggie bags.

How Do I Find That Great Undiscovered Restaurant?

"Finds are hard to come by," admits Sheraton. Sure, people tell you about a great new restaurant they found, but "nine times out of ten it's a terrible place." She asks cabdrivers and waitstaff where they eat. She also walks around town, sees an interesting menu in a window, and checks out the place.

"Once you're known, you'll get all kinds of recommendations," she says. "You don't have to look for people to tell you about restaurants. You have to shut them up."

What about Educating the Palate?

Some reviewers think the ability to taste is an innate skill: people are born loving food and having a strong interest in it. Others think taste comes from experience. "Taste is a matter of experience that varies widely with age, ethnic background, locale and era," says Sheraton. And some think it can be taught. Grimes theorizes that a good palate may have physical aspects and a different arrangement of taste buds that affect the experience of flavors. Cilantro, for example, affects people diffrently: they either love it or hate it.

He says you don't have to be an expert in a cuisine to understand how something should taste. If he likes a sauce, he has a sense of whether it's well made, or whether flavors are discordant or lack proportion. While he is not an authority on Indian food, the last time he reviewed an Indian restaurant, he knew the food was a cut above, "because the flavors were distinctly presented and had a lightness of touch, not muddled flavor."

Bauer took the rare step of formally training his palate early in his career. He met his mentor, cooking instructor and author Madeleine Kamman, while working for a Dallas newspaper. He went to her cooking schools in New Hampshire and France, and then traveled around France with her for three weeks. "She really taught me how to taste sauces," recalls Bauer. "She would say, 'Can't you taste the carrot in that sauce?' We'd break it down. I had some really intense dining experiences."

I took an unusual two-part course at Sur La Table cooking school on developing the palate, where instructors doled out substances in small cups and your job was to identify them by smell and taste. We also learned how subtle changes affect a dish. My biggest surprise was when we squirted lime over canned tuna. It was sublime. Then we repeated the experiment with lemon juice. It tasted awful, even though it's common to squeeze lemon over fish and add it to tuna salad. Try your own blind experiments with different sugars, butters, salts—the possibilities are endless. Don't just taste. Study them, touch and smell them.

What if I Haven't Worked in a Restaurant or Been to Culinary School?

Only a tiny percentage of food writers have experience in the profession. This fact bothers some people in the industry, who ask how reviewers are able to judge food and restaurants without having been a chef or waiter.

Sure, it would help. But it's not critical. A reviewer's job is to advocate for the consumer, to represent the person who's spending the money. Most diners have not been chefs or waiters. They just want to know if they'll have a good dining experience.

Restaurant experience can have its downside. You can't feel sympathetic and take the restaurant's side when something goes wrong, and you might become obsessed with technique and focus too much on how the food should be made, rather than communicating your impressions of the final product and the restaurant.

"An eminent food journalist need be a master chef no more than a connoisseur of Bach need be expected to perform the composer's preludes and fugues with immaculate precision," states James Villas, former editor of *Town and Country,* in a *Gourmet* article about Craig Claiborne, who was known not to be a very accomplished cook.

It's not essential that you cook, either. "Although I do not believe that one has to know how to cook to be a reliable restaurant critic, the knowledge certainly helps a critic to describe food convincingly and explain where it fails or succeeds," writes Mimi Sheraton in her memoir, *Eating My Words: An Appetite for Life.* "It is, however, no more necessary to cook well than for a drama, dance, or art critic to perform or paint."

Must Reviewers Be Anonymous to Be Effective?

Yes. To truly represent readers, no one at the restaurant should know who you are. It's impossible to write an objective review if restaurants know you're coming or recognize you. They will not treat you the same way they treat other diners. You will get special attention, more food, and dishes that have been fussed over.

Some reviewers announce themselves so they can get the best table and service. Grimes thinks this behavior is "scandalous." Others might agree to come back for a free meal. Any of these behaviors signals you can be influenced or bought. Restaurateurs will conclude that because they gave you something, you owe them.

Some people don't agree. Jane and Michael Stern, who travel around the country reviewing roadside restaurants and diners, often identify themselves. They say that while New York reviewers can make or break a restaurant, at tiny out-of-the-way diners, "We could be wearing a sign that says *Gourmet* magazine and they don't care," says Jane Stern. Once they made an appointment to meet a restaurateur and were stood up. He was more excited about the opening day of hunting season. Their situation is atypical, though. Most of the time, you'll be reviewing restaurants in your town.

It's easy to be anonymous when you first start out. Your first year will be fine, because people don't know what you look like, and if you pay cash or use a credit card in someone else's name, you're safe. Eventually, however, you're likely to be recognized because waiters who spotted you once at one restaurant can change jobs and spot you at the new place. When this happens, "You have to play it cool," advises Grimes. "Realistically, the restaurant can't do much except little things, like hover too much, send over too many waiters, or send over too much food." He believes that in the end, restaurants are more likely to shoot themselves in the foot by smothering the reviewer with special treatment.

"Ninety percent of the time I know when I've been recognized," says Bauer. The evening is going well and then he senses a difference. The waitstaff becomes nervous. He asks a guest to "look at the kitchen and see whether there's a knot of people by the door. Often the service and experience are better before they know who you are. Then reviewing becomes a balancing act. If service is still bad, you realize there's no way they can pull it together."

Serious critics take steps to disguise themselves. They make reservations in another name, pay cash, or use credit cards with someone else's name. They call from outside the office because many restaurants now have caller ID. They wait until their guests sit down before arriving at the table, sometimes through a back door. They don't go to functions attended by restaurateurs and chefs, such as a restaurant grand opening, anniversary dinner, or wine tasting, where they could be recognized. Once you start reviewing, you will likely receive invitations to events like these. While they are tempting, decline them.

WEARING DISGUISES

Top reviewers go to great lengths to disguise or alter their looks. Here's how the pros do it:

Ruth Reichl, former restaurant reviewer for the *Los Angeles Times* and the *New York Times* and now editor of *Gourmet* magazine, gets the award for queen of elaborate disguises. A theatrical coach helped her with her first disguise when she moved to New York. The woman told her, "You can't just put on a wig. You have to inhabit it," said Reichl in a radio interview. The woman had Reichl create a backstory for a middle-aged Midwestern woman. Some of Reichl's other disguises were Aunt Betty, a nondescript older woman with lace-up oxfords who was not treated well at restaurants; and Brenda, a big boisterous redhead whom waiters loved and for whom they brought extra food.

Reichl became the people in her disguises. "I had voices for them," she admitted. The newspaper auctioned off the costumes for charity when she left.

Michael Bauer, the *San Francisco Chronicle:* "I'm always changing my look. I wear short or long hair, glasses, a goatee, or a beard. I darken my hair, mousse it so it's curly, or comb it back instead." He thinks wigs don't work because they're so seldom worn that they can always be picked out in a crowd. "Change a little bit so people won't recognize you," he advises. "You can't do a disguise if you feel uncomfortable, because you will draw attention to yourself." He advises not to engage waiters or look them in the eye, and not to gesture with your hands when you talk.

Restaurants want to identify him, though. "I was surprised when someone said they had a picture of me in the kitchen. I think, 'Why don't you just do the best job you can, treat everyone like they're the reviewer, and then you'll have no problems?'"

Mimi Sheraton, formerly of the *New York Times:* She had three wigs in different colors and wore them with innumerable glasses. "I had a friend in the eyeglass business." She also varied her face makeup by alternating heavy lipstick with no makeup at all.

William Grimes, formerly a reviewer at the *New York Times:* "I was advised by a theater person not to put on a mustache. Facial hair is a bad idea because it moves around. From the stage, it's harder to detect. I wear wigs and glasses."

Grimes was surprised to learn how restaurants collaborated to "identify me, stop me and defeat my efforts." The *New York Post* ran a photo of him in the paper's gossip column. It was copied and posted in restaurant kitchens, and Grimes heard that some restaurants offered a bounty of $100 for the waiter who spotted him.

Some people in the food community question whether disguises work. A colleague told me she waited for more than an hour while a professional makeup artist worked on Reichl to disguise her as an old woman. But when she and Reichl entered the restaurant, she could hear diners say, "There goes Ruth Reichl," as they walked by. A 2001 story in *San Francisco* magazine quoted chefs who contended that Bauer is not anonymous. I've talked to restaurant owners and chefs who say they can recognize reviewers based on how much food they order and whether they taste the food of others at their table.

In truth, many critics have been reviewing restaurants in the same city for several years, and perhaps they are recognized more than they would like. But the bottom line is that you won't be taken seriously by food writers, editors—and yes, restaurant owners and chefs—if you announce your presence at restaurants and demand or accept a free meal there, rather than trying to represent the consumer and pay for your meals. In her memoir, Sheraton, whose expenses ran about $95,000 in 1983—her last year at the *Times*—said regarding disguises that "The longer I reviewed restaurants, the more I became convinced that the unknown customer has a completely different experience from either a valued patron or a recognized food critic; for all practical purposes, they might as well be in different restaurants."

What about Top Ten Stories and the Like? Are They Reviews?

Yes. Articles such as "The Ten Best Places to Get a Cheesesteak in Philadelphia" qualify as reviews, because the author is critiquing and making decisions. These pieces are standards of many newspapers and magazines, and good ones to pitch. Usually roundups are positive. They are purely subject based and the point is to tell people about the best places you've discovered or about services they need, such as restaurants that stay open past ten at night.

What if you're doing a piece on the best barbecue joints in Kansas City, and Ken's Rib Joint is famous but the food is awful? It's best to say so, advises Sheridan. Otherwise readers will wonder why you didn't bring it up. "Negatives are invaluable in establishing credibility," Sheraton explains.

I Want to Review. How Can I Get Started?

The first step is to be realistic. You're not going to break into *Gourmet* or even a daily paper right away. Start small and target neighborhood papers. There's no disgrace in being published there. "Editors notice who's writing for the free papers," says Grimes. "If you're any good, you will stick in their minds."

Begin by collecting the local newspapers and magazines in your community. Find them at newsstands, cafés, clubs, coffeehouses, and libraries. Look online to find past reviews. Look through a few months of each publication to see what kind of articles they like. Make a pile of the ones that don't publish reviews and prioritize them, starting with the smallest. Maybe they'd start running reviews if they found someone good.

Let's look at *Time Out New York* as an example. A feature story written by an experienced reviewer runs in the front section. It might be a roundup of several restaurants, with a theme like Cheap Eats. That's not a likely place to start. Writers have to establish themselves as trustworthy beforehand to get an assignment like that. But the dining section has three restaurant opening announcements of 150 words each, tucked into the capsule reviews. Might these be doable? Yes, says Carpenter. She uses new freelancers for these pieces because they are not critiques and are therefore less of a risk. The capsule reviews themselves aren't a good bet. They are pulled from the magazine's annual guidebook, which enlists close to 100 reviewers.

How do you get your foot in the door with an editor? You might call the paper, talk to an editor, and make a personal connection. The editor might give out tips about where to start, as Carpenter did above. But that's unlikely. First, editors don't have time to chat with strangers, and few will encourage someone unknown to submit a review. Second, they don't know what kind of standards you apply to the food you review, and whether you've written false statements that make the publication liable for lawsuits. If they're going to give anyone a trial assignment, it's probably a person they know who has already demonstrated knowledge of food. It's not a great idea to cold-call an editor unless you're lucky and you know someone on the inside who can ask him to take your call or talk with you in person for a few minutes.

The other way to go is to write one or two reviews for your target publication, emulating the paper's style, tone, and word count, just to see how you like the experience. Write to the publication's audience. That might mean avoiding a $100-per-plate restaurant if you don't think the publication's audience can afford it. If you wish, submit your work with a cover letter explaining your passion and qualifications. If you have already been published and can attach clips, you're one step ahead.

Sheraton says that since editors are unlikely to take critiques from an unknown writer, you'll do better to submit a related story. Try a piece about a tasting, a roundup of romantic places for dessert, or a funny article about a restaurant. Check other media around town for ideas, or brainstorm with a friend (see chapter 4). Use other kinds of pieces to prove that you know how to write and are knowledgeable about food.

Carpenter suggests taking classes on food writing so you can hone your skills and meet people in the industry. She has given small assignments on restaurant openings to three or four students she met while speaking to groups. If she likes their work, she will keep assigning. If not, at least they have clips to establish their credibility.

If an editor eventually assigns you a review, it's time to ask practical questions. Find out if the paper will support you if the review is negative. Do they have an opinion about reviewing restaurants that also advertise in the publication?

DAN LEONE'S APPROACH TO REVIEWING

I made it a point to interview **Dan Leone,** author of the Cheap Eats column in the *San Francisco Bay Guardian* alternative weekly since 1993. He takes a view of critiquing somewhat different from the advice presented in this chapter so far. Since he freelances for an alternative weekly, he has license to be more creative. As a published short-story writer, Leone makes the restaurant part of a story that's all about him. Here are excerpts from our conversation:

> My angle is different from most reviewers. I still don't know what's in the food. I've been able to maintain a

column without any actual knowledge of food. I just know what I like.

I've had experiences with food that most critics would be outraged about. But since I'm not a very good cook and my kitchen isn't cleaner than anyone else's, I don't get bent out of shape. If I see a bug flying around, it's no different than at home, so I think the atmosphere is just what I'm after. I focus on other factors, like the circumstances around the meal, including what's going on in my life. My reviews are more about the experience.

Often I don't say too much about the quality of the food. I'm more interested in writing a good piece that takes place in a restaurant and hopefully reflects what people would experience if they went there. I don't wear disguises. Some reviews are so bizarre and off the subject that the restaurant is not necessarily the focus.

More mainstream reviewers do not have the freedom to involve themselves in the story to this extent, or to make the restaurant the background of a first-person piece. Leone succeeds not only because he is a short-story writer, but because his approach is still fresh and different from the competition, even after more than a decade in the saddle.

What about Money?

Ah yes, the eternal question of whether you can get paid for your work. This is an ongoing problem for freelance food writers. If an editor accepts your unsolicited piece, it's possible that the paper will not pay, or that they'll pay next to nothing. Even if you get an assignment, you can be paid next to nothing. If you are writing reviews for a guidebook for your city or an online restaurant guide, the pay might be a whopping $25 to $30 per restaurant. That's not nice, but it's okay. You need published work to trade up to the bigger newspapers and magazines, which should at least pay for your reviews.

Nothing is standard when it comes to reimbursement for meals, despite a Web site guideline from the Association of Food Journalists that reviewers should not have to resort to "personal funds to help pay the bill." That's a subtle way of saying you probably won't be paid enough to cover all expenses plus your writing, even from the dailies.

Time Out New York's annual dining guide reviewers get a flat rate for their write-ups, says Carpenter. The company pays for two appetizers, two entrées, and two desserts, no drinks. Reviewers usually go to a restaurant only once because their pay will not cover more visits, and because of the volume of restaurants covered.

Larger newspapers might be more reasonable. They might pay one amount for the article and a budgeted amount for the meal. Ask lots of questions. Do they pay mileage, transportation fees, and parking? Are tips included in the meal reimbursement? How long will it take to get paid and/or reimbursed? This can be an issue if you get a credit card bill with fifteen restaurant meals on it, and you haven't received your check. Will the paper pay the late fee?

Moskowitz was initially paid $150 by an alternative weekly to write a 2,000-word feature on one restaurant each week. She paid for the food out of that budget. That structure lasted two years, until the paper got more advertising and she became better known.

Pack, who also reviews for an alternative weekly, the *Austin Chronicle,* says she is always reimbursed for her meals and visits a restaurant at least twice, maybe three times. She has also been reimbursed for parking when she has had to use a garage. Like many other papers, the *Chronicle* doesn't pay for alcohol. Pack points out that this policy is a little unfair if you're expected to critique the wine list.

"Making money?" asks Leone rhetorically. "Good luck if you can get it. My weekly column has been my only steady gig. I limit eating out to places I will write about; otherwise, I can't afford it." He receives a lump sum for writing, meals, and expenses. At first the editor offered him a budget for the food, separate from the writing fee. The lump sum works better, says Leone, as the amount he spends on food varies.

My experiences are all over the place. One magazine paid me a $50 flat fee for reviews, including food. A newsletter paid nothing but gave me a free subscription. A guidebook paid $30 flat for two paragraphs per restaurant. A weekly paper paid $0.50 per word, which the editor said was higher than what they paid other writers. They gave a reimbursable budget of $160 for food that did not include alcohol, and paid my mileage. A daily paper paid a flat fee of a couple hundred dollars, from which I deducted the price of three meals. There wasn't much left.

J. P. Anderson, restaurant editor at Chicago Citysearch (http://www.chicago.citysearch.com), says the amount he pays writers for expenses depends on the restaurant. "It could be as little as $15 for a hot dog joint or $250 for an upscale restaurant." Usually reviews are based on one visit, though follow-up visits are sometimes necessary.

So why would anyone in their right mind try to make a living reviewing restaurants? Most freelancers don't. They have other sources of income, such as a side job like catering, or better-paying writing jobs like creating marketing copy for corporations.

"There are fewer restaurant critics in this country than senators," asserts Moskowitz. "It's a luxury spot. Plus, there's no demand and nothing but competition. America needs nurses. Nobody needs more restaurant critics."

So what's the draw? You have to be driven not by money, but by your passion for restaurants and your joy upon discovering great food. Besides the glamour and glory, there are advantages. If you're a great writer, you get noticed. You get better assignments. If you can show you've been published, you might get to deduct a percentage of the cost of a meal from your taxes, plus mileage.

What about Writing for Web Sites?

A good way to break in is by publishing on the Internet. While editors tend to take print more seriously, the Web gives you faster exposure because it's easier to get published online. You'll build up electronic clips for editors, which is terrific, because many editors prefer to be pitched by e-mail. In your query, you can direct them to the Web address where your work resides.

What are a few good Web sites for starting out? On Chowhound (http://www.chowhound.com) message boards, writers discuss topics and give opinions, including restaurant reviews and accounts. To quote the site: "Writing at length is encouraged, and literary flourishes are appreciated by thousands." You won't get paid, but you can use the site as a safe place to try out your writing. Not everyone is a Chowhound fan. Author Calvin Trillin jokes that its message is, "In a just world, I would be the restaurant critic of the *New York Times*. A bunch of phonies are actually doing this, but I am the one who knows."

Egullet (http://www.egullet.com) has forums for writing and gives prizes for its contributors, particularly the Golden Gully award for culinary literature. Citysearch (http://www.citsearch.com) and Sally's Place (http://www.sallys-place.com) are national directories that run restaurant reviews in dozens of cities. Chicago Citysearch's Anderson says he'd be less likely to hire critics who have not been published before, but if their writing samples show promise, he'd certainly consider them. Write a review on Hungry Monster (http://www.hungrymonster .com), a national award-winning site. Some cities have independent sites that review restaurants, such as Sally's Place (http://www.sallys-place.com/) in the San Francisco Bay Area. Solo Web site owners might only publish their own reviews, but you can always start your own site to showcase restaurant reviews you have written. Or create a blog. The good thing about using either of these methods is that, while you won't have print clips, you can point editors to your Web copy so they can read samples of your work.

Restaurant reviewers are often experienced journalists. Often they've worked as writers in other parts of the newspaper, or paid their dues for years in the food section. Other reviewers have English degrees and worked as chefs. But don't be intimidated. It really is possible to succeed. Now that you're privy to the secrets of restaurant reviewing, you're miles ahead of other people starting out. You have the insight and resources to get ahead.

How Some Critics Got Their Start

Tom Sietsema, head reviewer of the *Washington Post,* graduated from a foreign service school and interned with ABC news, where he fell in love with journalism. A friend at the *Washington Post* told him the food critic was looking for an assistant. Since Sietsema had always loved food, he manned phones, tested recipes, and did light research at first.

Gradually, he proved himself. "The *Post* was my cooking school," he says. He left his office at 2:00 or 3:00 PM to shop and cook. Within four years he had tested hundreds of recipes. His boss was critic Phyllis Richman, once identified by *Newsweek* as the most feared woman in Washington. His rise to replace her (after she retired) took a total of eighteen years from the time he started at the newspaper.

Michael Bauer, executive food and wine editor of the *San Francisco Chronicle,* says he has always been in the food business. His father owned a meat market in Kansas. All through college he was a meat cutter in his father's store. Because his dad sold meat to most of the restaurants, he felt strongly about supporting them, so the family ate out every night. This was in the 1960s in a small town in Kansas. From there Bauer got his journalism degree and became a reporter and feature writer at the *Kansas City Star.* He moved on to food editor there and then became the restaurant critic and wine editor at the *Dallas Times Herald.* He joined the *San Francisco Chronicle* in 1986.

Patty Unterman, author of *Patricia Unterman's Food Lover's Guide to San Francisco,* had a graduate degree in journalism and was interested in criticism. "I opened a small restaurant in Berkeley and heard from a friend who had been in my class that *New West* magazine needed a restaurant critic. I wrote a sample review and they hired me." She went on to write reviews for the *San Francisco Chronicle,* and now writes a weekly column on food for the *San Francisco Examiner.*

Ed Levine, author of the guidebook *New York Eats,* says he was a discriminating eater even as a child, but his family never had enough money to go to fancy restaurants. His book celebrates eating in New York, with lists of more than 300 take-out places serving a variety of foods, from hot doughnuts to mozzarella to pad thai. He said he used Patricia Wells's *Food Lover's Guide to Paris* as inspiration.

Darra Moskowitz, food writer for *City Pages,* a Minneapolis-based alternative weekly, started working in kitchens when she was young, and always wanted to be a writer. She got her first break when an editor noticed the quality of her writing in a book review (she had worked on it for two weeks) and gave her more assignments. Eventually, Moskowitz made her way into food writing. She also worked for Microsoft Sidewalk when it launched, writing 50- to 100-word capsule reviews.

William Grimes was a copy editor at *Esquire* in New York, and freelanced on the side. After his reviews were published in the *Village Voice,* he drifted over to the *New York Times* as a full-time writer, working for the Sunday magazine and other parts of the paper. Later he moved into food writing and then restaurant reviewing, succeeding Ruth Reichl. "I had written book reviews and knew what reviews were supposed to do. I was confident that I had something to say," he says.

Dan Leone, Cheap Eats columnist for the *San Francisco Bay Guardian,* was a graduate school student who liked reading reviews but couldn't afford to eat at restaurants. He approached the editor of a New Hampshire alternative weekly about doing a Cheap Eats column. She said to write something up and show it to her. "I went immediately to Howard Johnson's, which had a buffet, and pigged out on all-you-can-eat clams. At that time I thought quantity was more important than quality. The editor gave me a regular column. The audience was students and starving artists."

Joan Zoloth, a reviewer for the *Oakland Tribune* for ten years, was a freelance writer when she met the paper's food editor at a social event. After Zoloth bent the editor's ear about food passions and revealed she was a freelance writer, a former waitress, and had taken cooking school classes, the editor suggested she try her hand at a review.

As for **me,** I was the freelance editor of a city magazine, where I wrote a few short reviews, chef profiles, and feature articles about restaurants. Later I wrote reviews on the side for a regional magazine in California. A few years ago I won a contest to write reviews for a weekly paper. For my test, the editor assigned me a review of a top restaurant I had never visited because it was so expensive. I took my husband and blew the entire budget of $160, without even buying a bottle of wine.

I keep the editor's follow-up e-mail to read on days when I'm frustrated about my writing: "I really enjoyed reading your review, because it's obvious you did some research and also obvious that you're at home in good restaurants! To be perfectly honest, so far you're my leading candidate for lead reviewer."

Writing Exercises

1. Using adjectives: Write a 250-word review of the best restaurant meal you've eaten recently, using five descriptive words from the list on pages 122–123.

2. Overcoming your leanings: Recall a food you don't like that was prepared perfectly and served to you at a restaurant. Now write two paragraphs about your experience. The goal is to acknowledge your own prejudices and overcome them for the reader.

3. Do your research: Come up with an ethnic cuisine you've never had and review a restaurant that serves that cuisine. Research the country's dishes and their origins and ingredients before visiting the restaurant, and then write the review.

6

The Cookbook You've Always Wanted to Write

Y ou love to entertain. Friends and co-workers compliment your cooking and ask for recipes. You've spent
years traveling and learning about food and culture. You want
to pass down heirloom recipes to your children. You've collected dozens of recipes and want to share them. Customers
always ask for your recipes. Everyone loves your stories about
people and food.

These are some of the many reasons to write a cookbook.
Notice I didn't say, "You want to get famous and make a lot of
money." If that's your motivation, forget it. Writing a cookbook is too difficult and time consuming to sustain such a
notion. But if you're passionate and obsessed, chances are that
your cookbook will succeed.

Successful cookbook writers begin with an enthusiasm for
food that keeps them going and fuels their ability to come up
with ideas for future books. The hard part is coming up with a
book that excites both you and the outside world. "You're up
against a very competitive market," says Jennifer Josephy, a
cookbook editor at Random House who represents such
authors as Sarah Moulton, Mark Bittman, and Deborah

Madison. "For a sobering experience, go walk around the cookbook section, see if you have anything different from what's on the shelf."

As she implies, it's easy to conjure up a first idea, but the first is not always the best. How to position or shape a book takes lots of pondering and evaluating of pros and cons. You might change your opinion many times. Mulling it over is worthwhile. You can't write a worthwhile cookbook without a good idea. This is true even if you want to self-publish.

This chapter will inspire you to shape your idea, think it through, and visualize the book you've always wanted to write, both in terms of subjects and eye appeal. It will tell you what kind of artwork is reasonable to expect. Since I can't squeeze all the details on how to write a cookbook into one chapter, the following chapter tells you how to write recipes, the bulk of your book. For more on the literary aspects of cookbook writing, see chapter 1.

Once you have the idea for a publishable book, use it to pitch articles to newspaper and magazine editors to float your idea. If they publish the articles, it's a great sign that your cookbook idea has promise. How to get an article published is covered in chapter 4. Once you've overcome that hurdle, you'll need to write a book proposal for an agent or editor, and with any luck, you'll get a contract. How to write a proposal, find an agent, and what to expect from a publisher are covered in chapter 10. But you can't write a proposal without a good idea and an understanding of which cookbooks work and why.

How They Got Started

Everyone has to start somewhere, even successful cookbook authors. Here's how some of them began:

➥ At a class on Chinese cooking, student **Julie Sahni** told fellow students how she used a *balti*—an Indian wok—to cook at home. The students asked her to show them. She began teaching cooking classes, and from the recipes she developed, had the beginnings of her first cookbook, *Classic Indian Cooking*.

�846 **Deborah Madison,** a student of Zen Buddhism, cooked at the San Francisco Zen Center and at Tassajara, a retreat in Big Sur. When the center opened Greens vegetarian restaurant, she became the first chef there. The impetus for her book, *The Greens Cookbook: Extraordinary Vegetarian Cuisine from the Celebrated Restaurant,* was to show customers who had requested recipes how to make the same quality dishes the restaurant served.

�846 **Anne Byrn,** a freelance food writer, became a working mom who wanted to make great cupcakes for her kids but didn't have much time. She wrote a newspaper story about doctoring cake mixes, and based on the response, went on to publish *The Cake Mix Doctor.* The book has sold 1.6 million copies.

�846 **Diana Kennedy** arrived in Mexico in 1957 to join her future husband, a foreign correspondent for the *New York Times.* In 1969, at the suggestion of *New York Times* writer Craig Claiborne, she began teaching classes in Mexican cooking and in 1972 published her first cookbook.

�846 **Martha Stewart** was a caterer in the Hamptons in Long Island, New York, before she became a lifestyle guru.

�846 **Ina Garten,** author of the bestselling *The Barefoot Contessa Cookbook,* also catered in the Hamptons, as did Julee Rosso and Sheila Lukins, authors of the Silver Palate series. (The three books in the Silver Palate series have sold more than 5 million copies combined.)

�846 **Paula Wolfert** went to Morocco because her husband found employment there. Over the years, she became passionate about Mediterranean cooking, watching cooks in their homes, and writing down their recipes. Today she's known as an authority on authentic Mediterranean food.

➥ After taking cooking classes in France, **Julia Child**
opened a cooking school in Paris with two Frenchwomen.
Many of the students were American, and soon Child
decided to write a manual of French cooking for them.
Her radical idea was that all ingredients should be avail-
able in the United States, and that readers should learn
French cooking techniques. Her first book, *Mastering the
Art of French Cooking*, took ten years to produce with her
French co-authors.

What's a Good Cookbook Idea?

Agents and editors often give the same advice to someone who
wants to write a cookbook: You have to have something to say.
That's true, but not very specific. They also say things like
"Everyone reads but not everybody writes. Everyone cooks but
not everyone can write a cookbook. It's harder than most
people think." Agent Doe Coover told me that. Agents and editors are a tough group to impress, but hundreds of people have
done it.

Let's get back to the good idea. Agent Lisa Ekus says she
knows she's found one when she can't stop thinking about it.
Typically, she reads incoming proposals once and puts them
aside. "If I forget about it, it's not a book for me. If it lives with
me and it excites me, I have to believe in the book, have a passion for the topic or writing, or think it's highly marketable."

Author Julie Sahni has more advice on what it takes to have
a new idea: "A cookbook is more than a set of recipes. You
have to have a message, a certain philosophy or technique or
principle to pass on to the audience. It boils down to a simple
concept. You know something more or something different for
the reader. You have to inspire them."

What if you already have a cookbook idea? You've asked

your friends and family if you should write your cookbook and they've said yes. Friends and family are not as hard to please as agents and editors. The very first thing to do, when considering a cookbook, is to make sure you have a workable idea. The second is to scope out the competition. Here are my tests:

You are passionate about the subject: As I've been saying, intense enthusiasm is the most powerful motivator. It's not enough to carry a book idea, but if you communicate excitement, intensity, and knowledge in your writing, it can be contagious. Suzanne Rafer, executive editor at Workman Publishing Company, said in a published interview that a potential author must ignite passion within her and successfully convey a creative spark and vision. Passion may be intangible, but editors and agents know it when they see it.

Martin Yan thrives on it. Now the author of twenty-seven cookbooks, he travels 250 days each year, teaching classes for consumers and chefs, taping television shows shown in fifty countries, and doing research for his cookbooks. "I love to capture some of the essence of individuals around the world and share my experience with people," he says. For one series and book, he targeted Chinatowns worldwide and interviewed chefs at the oldest and newest restaurants. He found families who had lived in each Chinatown for three to five generations, then asked the head of each household to walk with him and buy food for a meal. Yan went back to the family home, watched the cook in action, and shared the meal. "I see the entire picture of their life and heritage," he enthuses. "I am having a good time learning a lot of these things, which I may not experience again."

Laura Werlin was "seized by passion" when she decided to write her first book, *The New American Cheese*. She was a television assignment editor at a station in San Francisco who decided to take classes on food writing. Eventually she narrowed down her food obsessions to artisan cheese from Northern California. When researching her topic, she discovered a national trend of artisan cheese production. "From that moment, I never looked back," says Werlin. She wrote a sixty-page proposal, got an agent and contract, quit her job, and wrote the entire book in three months.

"I had a very steep learning curve, having not written a book or recipe before. I probably did many things the hard way because I knew no other way. I never left my house other than to buy ingredients. I would write until 10:00 PM. On weekends, I sent my husband to a movie, and then I'd meet him at 10:00 PM for a late dinner. I had never been an A-type personality until then." Both this book and her second, *The All American Cheese and Wine Book*, won national awards.

The subject is timely: This is tricky, because few successful cookbook authors actually study trends before writing their books. It's more likely they have good timing because they read widely and talk with other people who love food. Freelance food writer Anne Byrn found an auspicious subject. She made a batch of doctored cake-mix cupcakes for her kids and wrote a story about it for a newspaper. The paper added a sentence asking readers to send in their own cake-mix recipes and received 500 responses in one week.

"The light bulb didn't go on instantly," Byrn admits. She wrote a follow-up story featuring six people who had sent in their favorite recipes. By then, Byrn had a hunch. Just to make sure it wasn't some kind of regional trend (Byrn lives in the South), she called six newspaper food editors across the country and asked whether readers requested cake mix recipes regularly. All said yes, particularly for favorites such as the Better than Sex cake. Byrn wrote her book and then wrote more. *The Cake Mix Doctor, Chocolate from the Cake Mix Doctor,* and *The Dinner Doctor* have sold more than 2.5 million copies combined.

This book was a departure for Byrn, a former newspaper editor who wrote restaurant reviews and traveled to Paris. "I have been such a food snob in my past," she admits. "But I live in a different world now and I have three children. Big deal if I use a Duncan Hines mix." There have been consequences. Certain newspapers will not interview her. Nevertheless, says Byrn,

"I wrote this book for mass Middle America, which I feel very much a part of. I'm not ashamed of that and I do not live in Manhattan."

Alice Medrich capitalized on a trend as well. In her award-winning cookbook *Bittersweet: Recipes and Tales From a Life in Chocolate,* she addresses how to use today's varying grades of high-quality chocolates, which are identified by percentages. Purer chocolate has less sugar and more taste, and recipes need rules of thumb for substitutions and upgrades. An obsessive recipe developer, she writes of her desire to share tools she created for herself, so that readers can "experiment and convert recipes with ease and understanding."

Some authors do keep up with timely topics. "Developing salable ideas is not the same as just coming up with ideas," says author Nancy Baggett in a published interview. "Salability involves meshing what I'm interested in and capable of writing about with what I, and hopefully cookbook editors, think the public might buy." She keeps up by looking at bookstore shelves, reading food magazines and newspaper sections, and following trends and topics surfacing in the national media.

Agents and cookbook editors keep up with trends as well. Says editor Josephy, "Simpler and simpler. That's what people want. Quick and easy. I don't see that changing. It really is a fact of life that people don't have a lot of time."

The idea is about your area of expertise: Werlin and Byrn were not experts when they started their first book, but both became well versed on their subjects in a hurry. Medrich, by contrast, was already a chocolate expert and owner of a Berkeley chocolate store when an agent approached her to write a book. The best authors strive to develop in-depth knowledge of their subject. Even before they write books, they research extensively and write articles about their subject of expertise. They might also speak on the subject and hold cooking classes.

What, exactly, qualifies you as an expert? Let's say you have cooked Sicilian food for years. The recipes were handed down from your mother's side of the family. You might be an expert if, in addition to knowing family recipes, you devour all the information you can find about Sicilian cooking, speak decent Italian, travel to Sicily to watch people cook, write recipes on Sicilian food published in magazines, newspaper articles or Web sites, or give talks about it. A cookbook would be your logical next step.

Steven Raichlen, whose barbecue and grill books have sold more than 2 million copies, said in a newsletter interview that branding himself as a barbecue and grilling expert has helped make a name for himself and build his identity in the food world. "What I've done now that I hadn't done before is focus all my energies on a particular specialty. Of course, the trick is finding a sufficiently broad and deep topic to explore to keep you interested for many years and that has the potential to reach lots of other enthusiasts."

Paula Wolfert has been relentlessly passionate about authentic Mediterranean food since her first cookbook on Moroccan food was published in 1972. It calls for a dessert with hashish seeds. She justified the recipe to her editor by arguing none of the other Moroccan cookbooks had it. Wolfert is one of a handful of successful authors who takes an anthropological approach to further her expertise. She explores villages across the Mediterranean, meets with the women there, and asks them to introduce her to the best cooks. Sometimes she moves in with cooks so she can observe and take notes. "She has knocked on hundreds of back doors in obscure towns, searching for the cook who best executes a particular dish," wrote Peggy Knickerbocker in a profile of Wolfert in *Saveur.*

Wolfert even deals with recipes in languages she doesn't know by developing a network of people who translate recipes from abroad. She brings cookbooks in other languages to the United States and has people translate them for her.

Other cookbook writers who have tirelessly researched other cultures and traditions include:

- ☙ Carol Field, who documents the Italian lifestyle

- Diana Kennedy, who traveled alone through Mexico to find authentic cuisine
- Jeffrey Alford and Naomi Duguid, who travel in Asia for months at a time
- Claudia Roden, who took eighteen years to write *The Book of Jewish Food: An Odyssey from Samarkand to New York*

If you don't have an area of expertise, claim one. Freelance writer David Leite chose Portuguese cooking as his specialty. He decided to write about food to chronicle the Portuguese dishes disappearing from his family's dinner tables as older family members passed on.

How long does it take to become an expert? That's up to you and how much time you spend thinking, researching, traveling, and testing recipes. W. W. Norton vice president and senior editor Maria Guarnaschelli, who edits cookbooks, takes the long-term approach. "Lynne Rossetto Kaspar (*The Splendid Table*) and Rose Levy Beranbaum (*The Bread Bible*) were in their fifties when they wrote their books," she says. "Isn't an important work your life's work? In the end it will pay off."

Your idea is well focused: Lack of focus keeps many potential authors from moving forward. If you imagine a book that has to contain "everything," you might put off doing it forever. Writing about "everything" becomes an overwhelming topic. Because you're in love with it, it's hard to decide what to leave out and what to leave in. As a result, your book idea loses focus.

Examine your idea. Is it too general? Is it "all about" a topic? Think about how you would describe your cookbook to others. When you can form your description into a single sentence, you're much closer. Hone in on the most important subjects for readers, and make a list of points you wish to convey. Then whittle down the subject until it is specific and cohesive. Don't be afraid to discard. Throwing away can be liberating. Keep the ideas you've discarded in a file. You might want them someday for another book. (For example, a book on Mediterranean dishes might be followed by a book on Mediterranean desserts.)

You can be passionate about muffins, explains author Deborah Madison, but ask yourself why they're special to you, why muffins matter. "What is the story? Whom will it delight?" she asks. "Maybe it's stories about family, or maybe you add quick breads, and a book emerges." You could also narrow the idea and make it more specific, such as muffins that are fruit-only, sugar-free, or chocolate.

Madison's enormous reference work, *Vegetarian Cooking for Everyone,* needed lots of forethought on structure and content. The book idea came into Madison's consciousness after teaching a weeklong class on vegetarian cooking at Esalen in Big Sur, California, when she suddenly realized what a shame it was that there was no vegetarian *Joy of Cooking* in which vegetarians could find everything they needed in one place. She decided to write that book.

Even so, it was not "all about" vegetarian cooking. "It took a year just to come up with the table of contents," she recalls. She had to define the scope of the book and make decisions. Should it include breakfast foods, or breads, or recipes already in the culture, such as hummus? She wondered what people would expect, whether to include sandwiches. "I had to become educated," she explains. "I was reading, thinking, and it changed as it went along." This new book was not personal like her prior cookbook, *The Savory Way.* "I wanted to make it a friendly guide for people I didn't know." It took six years to write, contains around 1,000 recipes, and won a national award.

Single-subject books are tightly written books about one ingrediant, piece of equipment, or type of dish. Author James McNair developed a reputation as king of the single-subject cookbook. In 1984, he launched his first book, *Cold Pasta,* and followed it with about thirty more books on subjects such as cheese, chicken, fish, pie, corn, and custards, all with gorgeous full-color photos.

Focus becomes an issue when you research your competition. If you want to write a book on Asian noodles and five books already exist, you'll have to change or narrow your focus to succeed. For more on evaluating competition, see page 253.

You love to tell stories: While publishers once thought of cookbooks as strictly how-to books, today they find it likely that cookbooks will be read rather than used for cooking. Time limitations and changing eating habits mean that the average number of recipes readers try in a cookbook could be as low as two. Think of your own cookbook collection. You may not have made any recipes from many of them, but it doesn't make them any less valuable.

Many people read cookbooks in bed as though they were novels. They provide escape from daily life and a source of guiltless pleasure. With longer stories and full-color photography, cookbooks can take you on a travel adventure, allow you to enter a foreign land, whet your appetite for exotic ingredients, tell the history of a country, and let you imagine a pleasurable dinner party you'll give someday.

The literary aspects of food writing can bring new excitement to a book. Joan Nathan authored *Foods of Israel Today,* an ambitious look at the diverse cultural and culinary lineage of Israel. She said that after senior editor Judith Jones of Knopf edited her book, she asked Nathan to take her and her stepdaughter to the Holy Land. "I introduced her to my Israel," says Nathan. "It was about a week before the Intifada. I had written about a village of vegetarians I'd heard about but had never been to, and Judith was very taken with the idea. We took a cab. We could have been killed! Here we were, three women wandering around a Palestinian village." How's that for a testimony to skilled storytelling and writing? Your own editor is so fascinated by your work she wants to see the place.

You have a new approach: "If I hear there are too many books about Italy, yes, there are, but if you have something new to say about Italy, don't let it stop you," says editor Guarnaschelli. Americans are so in love with Italian cookbooks that they often command their own bookshelf in bookstores. Guarnaschelli worked with Lynne Rossetto Kaspar on *The Splendid Table: Recipes from Emilia-Romagna, the Heartland of Northern Italian Food* in 1992. At that time, "no one thought anyone would be interested in the Emilia-Romagna area of Italy," she recalls. "They couldn't even pronounce it. Even I wasn't sure about using the name in the title." But they went with it. The book won awards and remains in print. Kaspar now has a national radio show of the same name.

A Man, a Can, a Plan: 50 Great Guy Meals Even You Can Make takes an unusual twist on men's cooking. Printed on heavy stiff paper and coated like a children's book so it won't stain, this book gives the not-so-subtle hint that men are like children when it comes to cooking. Recipes have photos of actual cans with plus signs between them. Are the recipes in the book unusual? No. But its unique differentiation, or positioning, succeeds. The book has been particularly successful among college students, says author David Joachim.

Your idea has potential as a series: Agents and publishers like to envision a long stream of revenue from you over the years, and for that matter, so might you. A series sounds like an easy idea, but today's publishers are the ones producing most collections, such as the *Joy of Cooking* series or the *Williams-Sonoma* series. For these series, publishers might hire a different writer to write each book. An example is the *Skinny* series, which includes books on chicken, pasta, soups, grilling, Mexican food, soups, one-pot meals, and Italian cooking. No one author wrote all the books. It made sense as a series because low-calorie cooking was the theme that held together cookbooks on disparate subjects.

A large, well-defined audience will be interested in your book: Publishers want you to define exactly who will buy your book so they can sell to that audience. In the earlier example of a muffin book, you could slice your audience many ways. If the recipes have six ingredients or fewer and can be made in ten minutes, busy moms might snap up the book. If the muffins are gluten-free, vegan, sugar-free, low-fat, or low-cholesterol, you've targeted readers concerned about their health. If your idea is simply "All About Muffins," however, the audience is much harder to define. Who are these people who like muffins? Unless it's a major trend, it's impossible to know.

Your idea is original: I'm talking about being a groundbreaker in the field. Back in 1969, a group of Berkeley, California, college students interested in Eastern religions and meditation gave up meat and created *Laurel's Kitchen,* a classic book on vegetarianism. Little information on meatless cooking and nutrition existed at that time. The group did its own nutrition research, and *Laurel's Kitchen* came out in 1976. "We weren't pushing tahini and weird mushrooms or seaweed, stuff that some of the other cookbooks that came along did a lot of," said co-author Laurel Robertson in an interview. "Mostly we just made normal things without meat." Total combined sales for her first and subsequent four cookbooks are just under two million.

The Whole Beast: Nose to Tail Eating by British chef Fergus Henderson captivated chefs all over the country because it advocates consuming the entire animal. The book includes recipes for pig spleens, duck necks, and whole birds. Eating this way is *de rigueur* for the poor, but Henderson, who serves offal in his renowned London restaurant, St. John, aimed his book at the carnivorous middle and upper classes.

You have exclusive access to information: Let's say you've inherited a box of papers from a well-known person in the food world who has just died. When you search through the box you discover his personal home cooking file for recipes, never before published. There's a good chance a publisher or agent will be all over it, and you. Another way involves doing so much research on a subject you become the expert by default, because no one else has amassed that volume of information, or cares to do so.

Your idea is not esoteric: Sure, your neighbor makes fabulous raw food dishes featuring seaweed, but the audience is too small to attract a publisher. Writing a book on a narrow subject is not the same thing, or entire books on grilled-cheese sandwiches would not exist. Agents and editors often evaluate a book idea by whether the story would be better as a magazine article. "I have to believe there's a large market for the book," says agent Carole Bidnick, who sold Werlin's book on grilled-cheese sandwiches and represents such authors as Peggy Knickerbocker and Fran Gage. "I ask myself how many people would spend twenty-five dollars to read this. If I can't come up with a minimum 10,000 people, I don't believe I can sell the book. If the sales aren't there, publishers are not going to buy the project."

The title rocks: Your ability to convey the meaning of a book in the title is critical. You don't want agents and editor to scratch their heads. Straightforward is fine. One person I worked with came up with *Baking Basics and Beyond.* No confusion there. Strive for brevity, wit, and specificity. Restrain yourself from being cute. Avoid inside jokes or phrases no one but you will understand. If none of your friends gets your title, that's a large clue. Clever puns are acceptable only if truly relevant to your book content. Here are some compelling attributes:

- Titles or subtitles in which the reader benefit is clearly stated, as in *The Meatless Diabetic Cookbook: Over 100 Recipes Combining Great Taste with Great Nutrition.* Other good benefit-oriented words are "fast," "easy," and "foolproof."
- The use of numbers that suggest a wealth of information, such as *1,000 Vegetarian Recipes from Around the World* or *100 Best Hamburger Recipes*
- The use of "greatest" or "best," as in *America's Best RV Cookbook: The Complete Guide to RV Cooking*
- Labeling a book as "new," as in *A New Way to Cook*
- Humor, as in *Help! My Apartment has a Kitchen Cookbook: 100+ Great Recipes with Foolproof Instructions,* which has sold more than 250,000 copies

➥ Secrets, as in *Secrets of a New Orleans Chef:
Recipes from Tom Cowman's Cookbook*
➥ Words that suggest a book is comprehensive or
definitive, such as *The Complete Meat Cookbook* or
The Wine Bible

If you're still stumped, look through your own cookbook collection for inspiration. Ask friends or family to brainstorm with you. No matter what title you choose, don't get too hung up on it, because the publisher has the final say and chances are good it will change.

It's an evergreen: This publishing term means your book will sell for a long time. That excites publishers. It might be a book on diet or self-improvement, for example, neither of which goes out of style. Or it might be a work so distinguished—like *Mediterranean Cooking*—that it's been in print since 1976.

Classic Indian Cooking is approaching its fortieth printing. How can you make your book sell for a long time? Author Julie Sahni says she modeled her ideas after Julia Child, choosing ingredients readily available in supermarkets. And like Child's cookbooks, her's is still in style. "I give the example of crossing a stream with slippery stones," she explains. "You have to make sure your back foot is firm. You have to give the reader simple ways of cooking dishes with supermarket ingredients. Otherwise a lot of people will be put off."

WHEN YOU'D RATHER NOT BE ALONE: COLLABORATING, CO-AUTHORING AND GHOSTWRITING

If you're not ready to write a book by yourself, or feel you don't have the credentials, collaborating can be a great way to become published more quickly. Here are three ways to work with a partner.

Collaborate: Book collaborations work best if a writer works with a more knowledgeable or well-known person, such as a chef who wants to increase the visibility of his or her restaurant. You must have a good enough relationship with a chef to offer to collaborate on a book.

As the writer, you would take the chef's content, recipes, stories, and voice and translate them into a cookbook. You would change the recipes into those appropriate for the home cook, testing to make sure they work: eliminate terms home cooks wouldn't understand such as "flame off"; simplify elaborate or intimidating recipes; and cut down yields to servings of four to eight.

You must have sensitivity, as changing recipes can create a problem if chefs feel the integrity of the recipes will be sacrificed or lost. Many chefs cook without exact measurements, using technique and taste. They also use specialty ingredients not found in supermarkets. It's your job to measure, and to educate the chef on the target audience, usually home cooks.

Discussing the scope and content of the book is a good place to start. It gives you a chance to get to know the food professional, test the waters, and see if you click. You also have to decide whether you are passionate enough about the book's content to devote months to writing it, and whether you can translate the chef's voice and style successfully. Once you've made a good match, the two of you will sign a collaboration agreement, spelling out the responsibilities, deadlines, and compensation.

Collaborators get paid as much as 40 percent of the advance, plus royalties. You must believe the money you receive will be enough to cover your time and effort. A flat fee, called a work-for-hire, is an alternative pay structure where you might receive no money beyond your project fee. Fees range wildly—anywhere from $10,000 to $150,000. Hourly work may cost $25 to $60 for recipe development and testing, or $150 to $180 per recipe as a flat fee. It depends on your skill level and experience.

Once you get a book contract, you'll interview the expert to get his or her thoughts, experience, and knowledge, and spend time in the kitchen observing him. The chef will approve your drafts, recipes, and other writing. If you have made a big contribution to the book, your name may appear on the cover, preceded by "with."

Successful collaborators have agents and can win awards, regardless of whether they co-author or ghostwrite. Mary Goodbody, who has worked with other writers on more than fifty books, received a James Beard Award for co-authoring *Taste Pure and Simple* with Michel Nischan.

Co-author: Co-authors do equal work for equal billing on the cover, where names are linked by "and." An example might be a recipe developer who hooks up with an expert in nutrition because she has less experience in that area. "You need two parties really willing to do their share," explains Nancy Baggett, who had a good experience co-writing some of the books in the *Skinny* series. Each writer divides the work based on time, skill, or whatever criteria seem valid, and signs an agreement. "If one person underestimates and undervalues the time you put in, you're kind of doomed," she cautions.

Some husbands and wives partner on cookbooks. Naomi Duguid and Jeffrey Alford, photographers as well as writers, travel the globe searching for authentic food. Jane and Michael Stern travel around the United States looking for regional treasures.

Ghostwrite: Ghostwriters operate in much the same way as collaborators, but your job is to represent the chef and be invisible. Your name will not appear in the book, unless the author acknowledges you. Usually the more money you receive as the writer, the less credit you get on the book. *Gourmet* magazine contributing editor Barry Estabrook worked with Jacques Pépin on his memoir, *The Apprentice: My Life in the Kitchen*. Estabrook recorded Pépin in long, detailed interviews, "goading him" into talking about and remembering his past. He captured Pépin's voice beautifully and accurately for the chef's dedicated following of fans.

What Kind of Cookbook?

If you're still not sure what kind of cookbook you'd like to write, look through your recipe collection and organize it into groups. See whether you have a surplus of one kind. Do you have more recipes for Greek food? Do most of the recipes fall into a certain category, such as salad, or does your biggest stack focus on a certain ingredient? Or group the recipes by degree of difficulty, or by whether they would appeal to certain groups of people, such as busy working people or singles dining alone.

Here are some of the most popular types of cookbooks:

- Thematic books based on events such as seasons and parties.
- Single-subject books focusing on a specific ingredient or type of dish.
- Appliance books based on tools like slow cookers or pressure cookers.
- Audience-intended books focusing on groups of people, such as diabetics, college students, campers, or the budget-minded. The writing style and recipes would be appropriate to the audience. A cookbook for campers, for example, would have quick, easy portable dishes with few ingredients, and steps that could be made ahead.
- Geographic books, distinguished by country or region. These might be travelogues, full of evocative dishes and photographs.
- Historical books, moving chronologically or covering a period.
- Hybrids. These books are crosses between two themes. Healthy cooking from Provence is two times more focused than a book on French cooking.
- Menu-based cookbooks arranged by meals, such as picnics or holiday dinners.
- General reference books with an encyclopedic,

alphabetical approach. These can also specialize in a single subject, such as vegetables.

➤ Amusing or quirky specialty cookbooks. A romantic dinner cookbook might come with a CD of songs to set a mood, or a book about presidents might detail what they ate.

The most traditional structure, no matter what type of cookbook, is soup-to-nuts: appetizers, soups, salads, main dishes, and dessert. From there you could subtract or add other chapters, such as breads, eggs, side dishes, vegetables, pasta, cheese courses, and fruit. To help determine the order of chapters you'd like to use, look at some other cookbooks you admire.

Once you delineate the appropriate categories or chapters, fill out the book by adding titles of every recipe in your brain. A serious cookbook requires at least 100 recipes. Don't worry about finalizing the list at this point. You don't need finished recipes now either. Putting the names into categories helps you whittle down recipes that should not be included. You might make be famous for your coq au vin, but if you're writing a book on Latin food, it doesn't apply unless you can tweak your recipe to give it a Latin spin. Set aside the recipes that don't fit for your next cookbook.

Which chapters or sections would you include, besides the lists of recipes? You might want to include one of the following:

➤ A shopping resource section to help readers find hard-to-locate ingredients on the Web or in specialty stores in their city.

➤ A glossary or primer, if you are writing an ethnic cookbook that uses unfamiliar foods.

➤ A list or chapter on fundamental techniques, such as how to poach or brine, if you plan to use these methods in many recipes.

➤ A list or chapter on pantry supplies, if your book calls for ready-made ingredients such as canned stocks, roasted peppers, olives, or canned fish.

- A chapter on basics like stocks and sauces. If your book calls for lots of recipes using homemade stocks and sauces like pesto and hollandaise, you might collect these "sub-recipes" in the front and refer to them later within more elaborate recipes. Although I personally don't like sub-recipes much, it makes no sense to keep repeating them over and over.
- A section on premade oils, rubs, and herb mixes. For example, if pre-made pancake mix, rubs for meat, and herb mixes are a focus, you could include all those recipes here.
- A bibliography, if you wish to direct readers to books for additional learning.

Also consider how much narrative you want in your cookbook. If you like to write, you might choose essay-length chapter openers, narrative boxes, or sidebars. Consider whether stories are a central part of your book. They might not be appropriate for beat-the-clock cooking, but if you're writing a book like Grace Young's *Wisdom of the Chinese Kitchen,* which covers her family's recipes, Chinese culture, and the Chinatown where she grew up, you'll want essay-length writing. Young included biographical stories, information about Chinese food and healing, personal memories, and culinary traditions.

How Artwork Fits into Your Idea

Now that you see your book taking shape, you've probably thought about how it will look. Hardly anyone envisions a text-only book. Why bother, when you can have a gorgeous all-color hardcover with photos that illustrate the beauty of each dish, landscapes of rolling hillsides, or gleaming shots of just-picked produce? Not so fast. Color photos are expensive. They require heavier paper stock, glossier paper, and four colors instead of one. Even a text-based cookbook has extra steps for a color insert. Photos are printed on different paper and inserted into the book.

When editors review your book idea, they assess the risk of publishing it. Adding color to your book increases risk because it increases cost. Some cookbooks lend themselves to photography, such as those on the cuisine of other countries or regions. Sometimes the beauty of a chef's presentation makes color photos appropriate. If you are a first-time author, though, there's no guarantee.

Another choice is two-color printing. This works best when it's part of the design, such as illustrations, colored titles or shaded boxes with type over them. If you want illustrations by a certain artist, state as much in your proposal, otherwise the publisher will choose the illustrator for you. Become more familiar with page design and design elements. Thumb through your own cookbook collection or go to a bookstore to discover details you may not have noticed before: the look of sidebars and tip boxes, the length of introductions and headnotes, and the use of pull-out quotes and other elements such as colored titles, boxes, and shading to enliven page design.

Sometimes a book just doesn't warrant color. As Leslie Stoker, president and publisher of Stewart, Tabori & Chang, said in an interview, "A prune cookbook wouldn't have a broad enough book-buying audience to support its production cost. And a meatloaf cookbook just wouldn't have the visual appeal."

Publishers such as Chronicle Books, Ten Speed, Artisan, Clarkson Potter, and Stewart Tabori & Chang routinely print four-color cookbooks. Most of the time the author pays for the photographs one way or another. Three people I worked with got different deals. One received a small advance and the publisher paid for a dozen color photographs. Another got a bigger advance but spent two-thirds of it on the photography. A third author wrote a historical book and had to provide all the photos herself.

A styled color photo costs around $700 to $1,000. If you dream of twenty photos in your cookbook, it will cost between

$14,000 to $20,000. Usually the editor determines how many photos the publisher can afford and hires the photographer, but sometimes the author has a photographer in mind and can negotiate. Photographers like to shoot their food photos in studios so that they don't have to schlep lights and equipment to a location shot. They also shoot in restaurants, home kitchens, and the outdoors. Today most photographers use natural light to bring out the beauty of the food. Some do the food styling, too, but may also use some combination of food stylist, prop stylist, and assistants who move the lights around and other tasks. All these people must be paid, and their cost figures into the advance.

The food stylist prepares all the food for the photos and plays up the natural beauty of a dish. "We make it the way it would look for real," explains photographer Maren Caruso. "Not over-the-top perfect so people are intimidated and will never prepare it." You've probably heard about hairspray on salad greens and shellac on peas. That's more for advertising, explains Caruso, where "the milk splash has to happen in a certain place." I watched a food stylist use mashed potatoes in place of ice cream once. No one could blame her. When a photographer takes half an hour to get the shot exactly right while the ice cream melts under the bright lights, drastic measures become necessary. When I saw the finished photo, it looked like a creamy scoop of ice cream atop a fruit dessert. That's what matters.

A prop stylist provides all the plates, tablecloths, flowers, cutlery, and anything else needed in the shot. I attended a location shoot where the prop stylist drove up in a van and swung open its back doors to reveal a floor-to-ceiling cache. There were plates, platters, vases, flowers, tablecloths, napkins, cutlery, ribbon, and whatever else is necessary for beautiful photos. I couldn't imagine how she kept track of it all.

Do authors style their own food? Rarely. Usually the photo shoot takes place elsewhere, and the author's not part of it. Sometimes, if you have an artistic eye, you're successful, and the photographer trusts you, it can work. Deborah Madison has cooked and styled the food for all her books. "I don't mind when someone else is helping me, but I want the right to say when something is a jumble versus arranged, or to point out when the dish doesn't look like anything I've cooked," she explains. Madison makes some dishes that might be hard to visualize, such as vegetable ragout.

Another example of a book where the author had a hand in the photos is *Dessert University: More than 300 Spectacular Recipes and Essential Lessons from White House Pastry Chef Roland Mesnier.* Because of the complexity of the desserts and because the author had a strong vision of how they should look, he flew into town and stayed near Caruso's studio in Oakland, California. "He came in every day, worked in the studio kitchen in his chef's whites, and helped us create these over-the-top pastries when we needed direction," she says.

So that's a short explanation of how your book might look and what happens behind the curtain. Now, back to your book idea. As you've learned from this chapter, you have lots of thinking ahead. Keep working out the concept and details. Brainstorm with friends. Focus your idea. Look at other cookbooks for reference. Write the table of contents. Get your recipes in order. Next, it's time to start writing your cookbook, right? Yes, to some extent. The next part is to understand how to write most of what's in it: recipes.

Writing Exercises

1. Learn how to focus an idea by drilling down to specifics. Name a country you love and think of the particular region you like best. What are the food specialties of that region? Can you focus on a course? How else might you customize your idea to interest a publisher, based on title concepts I've listed?

2. If you've already chosen the subject of your cookbook, define your expertise. Write a one-paragraph biography.

Doing so helps you feel more confident about the project, and might show you areas where you need more research. Perhaps you have taken cooking classes on the subject, traveled extensively, cooked a special diet, or grew up eating a particular cuisine. Have you written about the subject for a class, newsletter, Web site, or newspaper? If you feel that you need more expertise, make a list of three steps you can take now to enhance your background.

3. When people have trouble describing their book idea to me, I ask them to get the idea down to one sentence. Doing so requires you to focus on the most important points. Ask a friend to help. Keep explaining the idea until you can get it down to one clear concept. Practice this sentence when you tell people you're going to write a cookbook.

7

The Art of Recipe Writing

My immigrant parents never used recipes. When they settled in Canada they had to reinvent the foods they knew—no easy task when neither had ever cooked before. In the 1960s and 1970s it was create or perish: to eat their food, they had to make it. Eventually they recreated most of the dishes, dairy products, pickles, sauces, and sweets they yearned for, tasting from memory and remembering how foods looked and smelled. An exception was the stuffed intestines my father smacked his lips over but my mother wouldn't allow in the house. (My parents were Iraqi Jews, born and raised in China.)

Both parents are gone now, and ironically, they never taught me to cook. I begged for and received a few chicken scratchings on paper that hinted at a recipe form, but when I tried to cook with them, I found instructions I didn't understand, shorthand for techniques I didn't know, or missing ingredients or steps that I didn't discover until it was too late. Nothing turned out right. I kept trying. I cooked a few dishes repeatedly, refining the taste from memory, just as they did. Each time I cooked or baked, I wrote the recipe down, printed it out, and marked it up when I made the dish again. There was always something to improve: more or less of an ingredient, a little more simmering, figuring out how to make a pastry less tough or a step more clear.

Many reasons exist to learn how to write recipes. Perhaps you want to write down family recipes for a son leaving for college. Maybe your neighbor keeps asking you for your recipe for fried chicken. Perhaps you are a chef or cooking school teacher who wants to hand out recipes to students or customers. Or maybe you have a child who needs allergy-free meals, and you want to record the dish so you can make it the same way each time. No matter what your desire, if you want to write a cookbook or feature articles you probably need to write recipes.

A well-written recipe is poetry, like beautiful writing. Agents and editors can see a good one a mile away. Sometimes they test them. Agent Lisa Ekus, who represents both new and established cookbook writers, says if she's found an unknown writer whose recipes look interesting, she will ask the writer or chef to cook for her. "If I can see them in action and taste their food, I can sell the book more passionately. If the book is restaurant based, I try to eat in the restaurant." Agent Doe Coover says she tests recipes from the proposal "all the time," because if an editor tries them and they don't work, "it's going to come back on my head."

A badly written recipe is a disappointment. When I first cooked from published recipes I always blamed myself when the dish didn't turn out. I thought I had not followed a step properly or left something out. Although the author was probably a good cook or baker, it's possible the recipe was not written well, not developed enough, or not tested thoroughly. (I admit that I wasn't channeling Julia Child back then.) Today, when I read a recipe, I can judge whether it will work, or how to adjust it if I think it won't. You don't want readers to second-guess you, though. You want recipes that work the first time. Good recipe writers don't let go until they know their readers can reproduce the recipes faithfully and make dishes that look and taste as good as their own.

The best recipes are not only clearly written but include the personality of the writer. Consider the ending of Quick Cream of Chicken Soup, from my yellowed 1946 edition of *The Joy of Cooking*. After combining chicken bouillon and scalded cream, Irma Rombauer announces, "Add if you want to be luxurious: blanched almonds, ground (about 2 tablespoonfuls to 1 cup soup)." In just a few words, she reveals her playfulness, originality, and need to indulge.

If you are patient, exacting, and detail oriented, you can write a recipe. It's a form of step-by-step technical writing. In this chapter you'll learn how to write each part: the title, headnote, ingredients list, and method. Recipes must be precise, accurate, logical, consistent, clear, complete, doable, and satisfying. The best create visual images in the minds of readers as they imagine making the dish. In the best cases, they are sensuous, immediate, and evocative.

In this chapter you'll find out how to develop, troubleshoot, compose, and test until you have a recipe anyone can follow and get the same results you did. Even if you've written recipes before—for yourself, a community cookbook, a neighbor, or a friend, even for publication—you'll learn tips here that will increase your skill level. You'll also find answers to many common questions, particularly those related to attribution and copyright. I can't go into as much detail as you would find in a whole book on the subject, so I recommend the excellent *The Recipe Writer's Handbook,* by Barbara Gibbs Ostmann and Jane L. Baker.

If you wish to write a cookbook, I can't emphasize enough how critical it is that you learn to write recipes well. That's what readers want most, regardless of whether they are newspaper editors, your children, friends, or purchasers of your cookbook.

Developing a Recipe

You might think recipe writing is linear, where you create a pasta dish, write the recipe, and send it to a friend to see if she can make it accurately. It sounds simple enough. But that's not how it works. Let's say you taste the pasta dish and decide it could use improvement, maybe some parsley and lemon juice. You add "¼ cup parsley" and "1 tablespoon lemon juice" to the ingredients list and make the pasta again. Now it tastes better, but still needs more zing. You revise the ingredients list once more, this time inserting "2 tablespoons lemon juice" and "2 tablespoons capers." You make the pasta again. Now you love it and you're satisfied. That's recipe development.

Three is not the magic number of times to make a dish. What if you realized, upon tasting the third version of the pasta dish, you should have kept the lemon juice to one tablespoon instead of two. Should you make the pasta again, just to be certain? The best recipe writers would say yes. Some have been known to develop a recipe up to twenty times, particularly bakers, where recipe writing is a more exact science because of the chemistry involved. "Those of us who write good recipes tend to be obsessors," admits Alice Medrich. "You have to fight it and go with it at the same time." Sometimes it's all about ingredients. When she's developing a recipe for, say, a layered cake, she might change one of the cake layers to a different type, or change one of the fillings to custard, or take out nuts and substitute coconut.

Other times she will start her development process with an ingredients and measurement grid. Let's say she wants a new chocolate cake recipe. She'll look through other bakers' recipes—those by writers she admires—and then fill in her grid with varying amounts of ingredients they specify. She'll put ingredients down one side and a list of measurements down the other. That way she knows which ingredients are basic and which are changeable. If all the recipes call for similar amounts of flour, Medrich knows the amount is standard, and she probably won't change it. She might test the recipe that calls for the most eggs to see how she likes the results. "It's like doing basic research before a history report," she explains. "It's about finickiness and curiosity, the teeny-weeny little details that make a difference."

Cookbook author Deborah Madison says she often gets inspiration from the garden and farmers' market when she's just "cooking freely in the kitchen. " If she makes a dish she likes, she wants to repeat it. "I cook as intuitively as I can, and make notes like 'needs more tang or sharpness,' and then I start correcting the dish. I go back and forth until I find something I like." She limits herself to making a recipe three or four times.

Recipes may also evolve from dishes she ate in restaurants where she noticed a flavor, unusual food presentation, or the texture of a silky soup. She makes notes on dishes she likes when she's away from the kitchen and refers to them when she's back. Some people have a good taste memory, she says, like her friend Clifford Wright. "He can remember the taste of foods he's eaten abroad. Somehow, he nails the taste." (Wright specializes in Mediterranean cookbooks.)

When you're in the kitchen, tasting your work, take several bites. Savor flavors and textures, considering each separately and as a whole. For a dish with several components, evaluate each part separately before assembling to see how they compliment each other. Take into account appearance, taste, texture, and appropriate serving size. Remember that this is *your* recipe. If your family loves it and you're not satisfied, go with your gut and get rid of it. If you get a negative letter from a reader, replying with the defense of "my kids loved it" isn't very satisfying.

Philosophy of Recipe Writing

You want the right list of recipes to include in your book. How do you think about creating the recipes? "Choose dishes that best reflect your strength," advises Medrich. "You want the best results possible for [the] least time and work spent. Minimize drudgery. Streamline activities, increase convenience." Designing with appearance in mind is particularly important for baking books, which often include color photos.

Many people aren't sure what level of instruction to give. I'm on the side that says not to make assumptions about what readers know and leave nothing to chance. "I've come to the conclusion that we really have to hold people's hands," says Kristine Kidd, *Bon Appétit*'s food editor, in an interview. "Most people today didn't grow up cooking with their mothers. So many of our readers don't have that kind of basic knowledge."

Julia Child took beginning cooks seriously. It's one of the reasons she is one of our most beloved food writers. When she lived in France and studied French cooking, she noticed that most of the cookbooks for serious students were chef's short-hand notes, with not much instruction for such techniques as how to break a sauce or how to poach. Child wanted a "real teaching book" with clear reasoning and every step and technique thoroughly explained. In her first book, *Mastering the Art of French Cooking*, she described how a dish should look at each stage of preparation and told readers what could go wrong with the process, along with corrective measures. Her recipes are long, but they always work. And that is a big reason why readers appreciate her.

Back in the 1950s, Judith Jones was an editor at Knopf (now she's a vice president and still edits cookbooks). She tried some of the recipes when she received Child's manuscript. She found the book revolutionary because it was "like having a teacher right there beside you in the kitchen, and everything really worked," according to an article in the *New Yorker*. Today Jones is still an admirer. "She told us what to expect, how to achieve it, how to taste, how to correct our mistakes, and how to work out our own variations," she says.

Your first task is to accept that readers are probably not exactly like you. They may not prepare ingredients before they start or have the same equipment. They might not understand the meaning of words like "blanch" or read your recipe all the way through first. They also have a life. Madison acknowledges that real life intervenes in the kitchen.

"Cooking is a dynamic and complex process and I'm always trying to look at the whole picture," she explains. "Where in a recipe is there a gap where you can start something for the next day, set the table, or simply sit down and have a glass of wine with your partner? If you think of recipes only in terms of the final dish rather than a process, a meal, or an experience, then it's a rather limited way to see cooking."

Bearing these thoughts in mind, in the next section I detail each part of a recipe, how to think about recipes, and how to write them.

Recipe Titles

Recipe titles should be simple, descriptive, informative, and inviting. You don't want them to read like a menu item in a restaurant. And you don't want them to be vague, so readers can't envision the dish.

Like good writers, good recipe writers have their own styles. I like an accurate, specific title I can understand. Marion Cunningham takes a straightforward approach in *Lost Recipes: Meals to Share with Friends and Family.* Titles are as simple as Southern Green Beans, Stuffed Cabbage Rolls, or Raised Waffles. She wouldn't consider Green Bean Surprise, Organic Cabbage Rolls Stuffed with Long-Grain Rice and Corn-Fed Ground Beef, or Judy's Famous Raised Waffles. Any dish called a "surprise" will be a mystery to your readers because they can't envision the dish. The second title belongs on a menu. The third won't mean anything to readers, since they don't know Judy. It's best to credit Judy and explain her significance in the headnote.

It's easy to write a confusing title. You might think Stone Fruit Ice Cream is perfectly fine. But now you've asked readers to work. "Which fruits have stones in them?" they might wonder. "Does she mean plums? That doesn't sound good." And then they turn the page. If peaches make the best and most appealing ice cream, call it Peach Ice Cream, and list other types as variations.

Readers want to be enticed. Even something as simple as James Villas's Creamed Leeks with Italian Sausage sounds good, because he added "creamed" and "Italian" as descriptors. Leeks with Sausage wouldn't do it for me. "Easy" or "quick" are always inviting if they fit the style of book. You could use adjectives like "the best" or "sublime" but in a way, it's cheating. You probably think almost all of your recipes are the best or sublime. Let the title speak for itself.

For recipes from world cuisines, most authors go for the recipe title in its original language first, followed by an explanation in English. In *The Book of Jewish Food,* Claudia Roden names Chicken Soup with Rice in Arabic first: *Shorba bi Djaj.* Julia Child titles a recipe *Choux Brocoli Blancis,* followed by (Blanched Broccoli—Plain Boiled Broccoli). Grace Young, in *The Wisdom of the Chinese Kitchen,* calls my favorite dim sum dessert Sesame Balls, then *Zeen Doy* in smaller type, perhaps placing the original phrase afterward because people are unfamiliar with Mandarin and Cantonese.

If you are writing a cookbook, compile a list of titles for each chapter. Study them to ensure variety and liveliness. Alternate style, wording, and length.

The Headnote or Introduction

Here's your second chance to draw readers into the recipe. Headnotes set a mood, give the recipe a personality, or tell a story. You need headnotes for several reasons. One is because without them, the first thing readers will see after the title is "2 pounds pork butt, well trimmed."

These days, headnotes contain more narrative and read like novels. They tell stories or entertain. They're written in a conversational style. You might have a funny story about a kitchen disaster, or a particular memory or occasion you'd like to share. If you have no story, don't feel you have to fill a void or make one up.

Instead, write about the connection of food to history, dining rituals, and celebrations. Or encourage readers to make the dish. Inventive sales pitches are fine, such as "This is one soup I make all winter long which has the double virtue of being scrumptious and effortless" (Laurie Colwin); or, "My favorite chicken dish was the ring mold with wild-mushroom sauce served on a beautiful Sunday afternoon in late spring when the doors could be left open and the warm rays of the sun streaked across the dining table, saluting my mother for her efforts in presenting a beautiful meal gathered from field, forest, garden and barnyard." (Edna Lewis)

When you read a good headnote, you appreciate it. Your readers will want to do the same. Give them context for the larger issues. Janet Theophano, author of *Eat My Words: Reading Women's Lives Through the Cookbooks They Wrote*, explains: "As cooks, we must first taste a dish in our imaginations, see it on the table, share it with guests—sometimes more fanciful than real—and then actually reproduce it from a text. A longing for the pleasures of the table reflects a concern for balance and harmony and an integration of the physical and spiritual nature of our existence. In this way, cookbooks are a meditation. Preparing a dish or a meal is not merely an effort to satisfy physical hunger but often a quest for the good life."

John T. Edge, author of *Southern Belly: The Ultimate Food Lover's Guide to the South*, says there are five kinds of headnotes. Here are his examples:

- *Cultural:* In this neck of the woods, we eat hominy when . . .
- *Historical:* The Hot Brown sandwich was first concocted by Chef . . .
- *Personal:* I remember the night Aunt Minnie slipped on that banana peel . . .
- *Instructional:* Only soft winter wheat will do for this . . .
- *Sensual:* This cake rises so high that it looks like an Eisenhower-era bouffant.

Most of all, headnotes are practical. They tell readers what to expect. They state benefits such as saving time, releasing creativity, or using up leftovers. Sometimes headnotes are no more than a set of brief, descriptive instructions. Simplicity can be beautiful. Here's an example from *Feasts for All Seasons,* by Roy Andries de Groot, a book on seasonal cooking that came out ahead of its time in 1966: "We like to serve asparagus as a separate course, before the main dish. The problem of cooking asparagus is simple. The tips are tender and should never be in contact with boiling water. The stems, on the other hand, must be boiled."

At a minimum, your job is to consider readers' needs, explain the recipe, and establish trust. For example:

- If the recipe looks long and complicated, or is made in stages, reassure readers that it's worth their trouble, that they can make parts in advance, or that the dish comes together quickly.

- If the recipe calls for advance preparation, let them know.

- If the method uses a new technique critical to the recipe's success, say so here so readers can prepare for and focus on the task.

- If the recipe includes an unfamiliar ingredient, explain where to procure it and why it's worthwhile. If the recipe calls for several unfamiliar ingredients, you're on thin ice, unless you're writing a book on a relatively unexplored ethnic cuisine and want to be accurate. A cookbook with lots of recipes calling for obscure ingredients makes agents and editors very nervous. Reassure readers that if they can't find the exact ingredient, a substitute will work. For example, in her recipe for Zinfandel of Beef, Julia Child declares, "If you are out of zinfandel, use another good young red wine and call it simply Beef Stew in Red Wine."

- If the dish can be made with variations, explain how adding or changing an ingredient works as an alternative.

- If the dish is hard to imagine, describe it with specific words—not by saying delicious, wonderful, or great, but instead something like, "this sharp, refreshing sauce."

➡ If the dish is traditionally served during certain holidays, or goes well with other recipes in the book, let readers know.

➡ If you think it would taste best with certain wines or beers, make suggestions.

➡ If the recipe needs a hint, help readers out. In *The Way to Cook,* Julia Child suggests soaking one cup of beans in ten cups of water to get rid of "the rooti-ti-toots" they bring on.

I would be remiss if I did not include my pet peeves here. Please do not state in the headnote, "Add a green salad and a crusty loaf of country bread for a complete meal." You could say this about any Western or European entrée. Or that a dish is the best thing you've ever tasted. You'll make readers suspicious. Instead, show the reader how good it is with description.

At the end of the headnote, state the number of servings. Sometimes servings are based on precise measurements, such as "makes four half-cup servings," and sometimes you might have different sizes based on whether the item is an appetizer or main course. List cookies by the dozen.

Now we get to attribution, an issue usually discussed in the headnote. How do you address using a recipe with an unknown origin—such as a handwritten recipe from an aunt who got it from a friend? It might be an heirloom, from a restaurant, or taken from a cookbook. It's best to find the origin, even if you changed the recipe in at least three major ways. When in doubt, give credit, and you'll create fewer problems. Even if you have no idea, you can still say your best friend's mother gave it to you in the 1950s on a handwritten card. Or that it was adapted from or based on another recipe, or your recipe was suggested by it. Even if you've completely reworded the recipe, to be safe, say where it came from.

As to the question of copyright, most publishers register cookbook copyrights in the author's name. The common belief, however, is that only the headnote and method can be protected, not the ingredients list (you can't copyright "1 cup flour," for example, because it's too generic). If you are self-publishing, you may register with the United States Copyright Office at the Library of Congress, (202) 707-9100 or http://www.copyright.gov, if you wish. For freelanced articles, usually recipes become the property of the publication, and they own the copyright.

RECIPE WRITING FOR CHEFS AND CATERERS

If you're a food professional who wants to write recipes for home cooks, you will have challenges other cookbook writers do not. Most chefs and caterers create recipes to feed crowds. It's different to make a dish for four. You might also make assumptions about reader knowledge and experience. My favorite example of a chef trying to write a recipe for home cooks is an opening sentence a friend read to me: "Roast a duck as you would for any occasion." If you don't understand why this is funny, you won't be successful writing for a home cook.

My friend had that recipe because she was rewriting a chef's recipes for home cooks. For best results, take your best shot at a recipe and hire a recipe developer or experienced cookbook writer to rework it for you. Have someone who represents your reader test it. For more details, see "When You'd Rather Not Be Alone: Collaborating, Co-authoring and Ghost-writing," on page 155.

Ingredients List

Think of the ingredients list and the directions that follow as a formula. The most important rule of this formula is to list ingredients in the order they will be used in the directions or method. That way, if some ingredients require preparation, as in toasted nuts or thawed berries, readers see it right away. Or if they lose their place in the method, it's easy to scan the list to see which ingredient comes next.

The other rule about listing ingredients is that there's no such thing as being too specific. Instead of oil, say olive oil. State the type of milk, and whether the butter is salted or unsalted. Specify onions and potatoes by size, such as "1 large onion, chopped." Sizes of cut vegetables range from smallest to largest: minced, diced, or chopped.

Measurements can be tricky. Some recipe writers like to say "2 carrots, peeled and chopped." Since carrot sizes vary, I prefer "½ cup chopped carrots (about 2)." Readers know the exact amount for the recipe and the number of carrots, in case they have to shop. Some writers prefer to state the weight, as in "½ pound carrots." Since most cooks don't have a scale at home, I don't like that idea. If a food is sold by weight, however, give reader both measurements, such as "1 cup strawberries (about 8 ounces)."

When using canned foods, state the size, as in "1 (14-ounce) can whole tomatoes, drained." If possible, use the whole can of broth or orange juice to make life easier for readers. In the "making life easier" department, canned stock is acceptable in most cookbooks, and beans don't have to be soaked overnight. State your preference for dried beans, but also acknowledge that canned beans will work. If you only tell readers the amount required for a soak, they won't know how many cans of cooked beans to buy instead. (By the way, one pound dried beans equals five-and-a-half to six cups cooked.)

In baking, know the difference between liquid and dry measure. Do not use a scale to measure ingredients, even if you think it's more accurate. American home cooks do not use scales, even in baking. They do not use metrics either, so keep measurements in cups, tablespoons, and teaspoons. If you are converting a foreign recipe, make these conversions. Use large eggs, the standard size. If it matters whether water is ice cold, rather than cold, say so.

Consider whether a food should be measured before or after use. Distinguish between "1 cup almonds, chopped," or "1 cup chopped almonds." Similarly, "1 cup sifted flour" is different from "1 cup flour, sifted." Make sure you figure this out, as imprecise measurements drive recipe editors crazy.

Many people get stuck on how to refer to ingredients used twice in a recipe. Avoid double listing. Write "¼ cup plus 1 tablespoon olive oil," for example. In the oil's first mention in the method, tell readers to add the "1 tablespoon olive oil," not "the oil." Later tell them to add "the remaining ¼ cup olive oil." Some writers use the term "divided" to follow a single amount, but often readers can't figure out what it means until they read the method. If you call for flour in two parts of a recipe that has different components, such as a pie, separate the ingredients with subheadings and groups, such as "For the piecrust" and "For the berry filling." Keep the method for each sub-recipe within, not after, the overall method (you can set apart the sub-recipes by breaking them into separate steps), unless the sub-recipe can stand alone and will be referred to elsewhere in the book, such as for piecrust.

Recipes with parts need subgroups with subheadings. Irene Kuo's Beef in Black-bean Sauce [sic] has a recipe for the "slippery coating," followed by a general recipe for the dish, and a third recipe for the sauce. I like this method because it's clear immediately to marinate the beef, stir fry it, and add sauce. Breaking up the recipe is particularly important with a lengthy recipe. If your recipe calls for a sub-recipe on another page—such as stock or a sauce—cross-reference the dish. Too many sub-recipes will make readers turn the page. Most don't like flipping from one page to another, or seeing that they have to prepare three parts first before assembling them all in the final fourth.

When it comes to type of ingredient, call for the most

commonly available whenever possible. This is particularly important for recipe writers who present food from other countries or particular regions of the United States. "We like to do things in authentic ways, but authentic ways are not necessarily the way to make things accessible," said Mark Bittman, *New York Times* columnist and author of *How to Cook Everything,* in an interview. If you really want readers to use the hard-to-find ingredient because it's essential to the dish, or because the dish won't taste as good with a substitute, say so in the headnote. Give readers an incentive and enough information to search for it. The same is true with brand names. Avoid them unless you think a dish will be diminished by not using a particular brand. Name it in the headnote, not in the ingredients list. If you list an optional ingredient, a substitution, or a variation, test each recipe that way to evaluate whether the change worked.

Method or Directions

The method is where you tell readers how to make the dish. At its most basic, it is systematic technical writing, written in a lively voice. At its best, method writing has personality. Editor Jones advocates writing directions that sound like you're standing next to a friend in the kitchen, helping that person cook. "You want to give the impression you have done it many times and can cook with confidence," she explains.

When Jones reviews recipes, she looks at the quality of the writing and use of language. "It's not that the recipe per se is striking and new," she explains. "It's what the writer does with it." One of her authors, Lydia Bastianich, wrote "a whole meditation on what you're doing while stirring risotto," she explains, "what you listen for, see, and smell. Writing like this comes from something within."

Put each step in a separate paragraph. Sometime they are numbered, but most often not. I like recipes that start with a verb, such as rinse, chop, or beat.

Often the first direction is to heat the oven, but this is not necessarily correct. Make sure readers do so at the right time. If you ask them to "marinate meat for 20 minutes," or "put cookie dough in the fridge for 1 hour," you'll want them to turn on the oven later.

Specify the size of commonly available pots and pans by small, medium, and large. Don't make readers guess what size they need and pick the wrong one. Baking, particularly, requires specific pan sizes.

I'm not a fan of the term "set aside." As Jones is likely to say, "What else are you going to do with it? Throw it away?" Instead, give specific instructions only when necessary, such as "cover and refrigerate for at least 1 hour."

Jones, as you may have guessed, has strong opinions on recipe writing. She tries to undo formulaic writing. The word she likes least is mixture. "You mix milk with bit of salt, now it's called the milk mixture," she says incredulously. She suggests specific language instead, such as batter, dough, custard, dry ingredients, and liquid ingredients. Jones also likes Child's mastery of visceral action words, such as toss, dump, pour, plop, and scrape. The term she dislikes most is "in a bowl combine." "Recipe writing has become very sterile," she says. "People think you take the bowl out first. You don't always do it in a bowl, and why do you have to use six bowls?"

As you write your method, watch the length. There is such a thing as too much explanation. If the method becomes too long, simplify instructions or put preparation into the ingredients list, such as "1 cup cooked rice, "or "2 red peppers, roasted and cut into thin strips."

When you state a time on how long to cook, stir, or bake, use a timer to ensure the times are accurate. Give a second visual description for doneness, such as "bake until the custard is set, or until the top becomes golden brown." Or "sauté butter until it turns to a nutty brown." Watch food as you cook and come up with accurate language, such as "stir until sauce thickens, hardens, or reduces."

Try not to use expensive or specialized tools readers might not have in their kitchens. Not everyone has a standing mixer or a food processor. Don't refer to appliances by brand names, such as the Cuisinart.

If you're writing a diet book or a book about nutrition, you'll want nutritional information at the bottom of your recipes. These statistics require nutritional analysis software. For a list of programs, contact the Food and Nutrition Information Center of the U.S. Department of Agriculture, (301) 504-6409.

ACTIONS WORTH EXPLAINING

People cook less and less. You don't want to intimidate them by using a term they don't understand. Doing so makes people feel stupid, then mad at themselves because they don't know the word.

The following words are some you should either avoid or, if using, explain exactly:

- Blanch
- Blend
- Braise
- Combine
- Cream
- Cube
- Deglaze
- Dice
- Dredge
- Flame off
- Fold
- Julienne
- Pan-broil
- Poach
- Reduce
- Sweat

I'm holding out on sauté, although many writers now explain that too.

Some terms require complex explanation and may bog down your method. Greg Patent, author of *Baking in America*, suggests that, because describing how to fold can take several sentences, you include a technique section where you can describe it once.

Sidebars or Notes

Sidebars come into play when you want to give miscellaneous information in more detail. They are often presented as part of the design, and might have a shaded background, lines around the text to create a box, or colored text. Subjects include:

- tips for preparation or technique (e.g., how to roast a pepper)
- serving suggestions or variations if you have a long list
- how to choose a particular ingredient (e.g., look for clams that are tightly closed)
- additional details about ingredients
- history or customs related to a dish

Notes often serve the same purpose but go at the end of the recipe.

As you develop, number, and date each recipe version. When you finish making the dish and have marked up and dated your recipe draft, print a revised version. Keep all drafts. When you think you have a winner, review your recipe with a critical eye.

- Ask yourself whether your readers would make this dish. Does it meet their needs? Is it too complicated? Have you written a headnote that would draw them in?
- Make sure ingredients are listed specifically.
- Look for opportunities to explain a step more clearly.
- Look for missed steps, or steps in the wrong order.
- Check the ingredients list against the method.
- Check temperature times, yields, and pan sizes.
- Check that you have specified low, medium, or high heat and pan size when cooking on the stove.
- Check whether you handled all foods according to food-safety techniques.

➥ Look for wordiness or illogical reasoning.
➥ Examine earlier drafts to ensure you purposely changed the amounts.
➥ Check for typos.

Joan Nathan says that even when she thinks she is done, she will spot test a few recipes at random to ensure there are no mistakes.

Once you start writing recipes you'll notice a certain amount of duplication in phrases and directions. Create a style sheet to ensure your recipe language is consistent. Use it to record unusual spellings and as a check on whether to use articles (a, an, the) in the method. Some styles have become standard: figures always come first in an ingredients list; and tablespoon, teaspoon, pound, and cup are always spelled out. When you get a book contract, publishers usually give you their own recipe style guide to follow. Magazines and newspapers have certain styles as well. If you're uncertain, read the publication's published recipes to see what style they prefer.

If you're planning to self-publish, it's fine to use a software program such as Master Cook. I don't recommend it if you want to be traditionally published. The recipes don't export well into Microsoft Word files, as publishers prefer.

Testing, the Final Frontier

I know this book is about writing, but you are not done with recipes until you or someone else tests them and successfully reproduces the dishes. I'm a fan of having mere mortals—or whomever best represents your potential readers—test your recipes. Otherwise you run the risk of making assumptions about what readers know or of leaving errors they might find.

On the other hand, I've interviewed experienced recipe writers who rely on their own judgment, since they are ultimately responsible for their own recipes. Mark Bittman says emphatically, "I develop and test. I don't hire testers. I don't really trust anyone else anyway." He adds, "My *Times* column is read by one million people per week. I probably get two or three mistakes a year, such as calling something Turkish when it should be Greek." Deborah Madison has written thousands of recipes and feels confident about the process. Sometimes she sends recipes to family, friends, and readers to try, but most often, she relies on herself. Paula Wolfert had not used testers until recently, when she met food enthusiasts from all over the world on e-mail through Egullet.com and used them to test her recipes. "It was incredibly eye-opening," she says.

Nathan says she likes to test everything in her book and still finds things she takes for granted. "I gave my daughter a recipe that asked for one pound of carrots. She gets everything from farmers' markets. She said she doesn't know what a pound is. So I decided it was about seven carrots." Nathan likes to keep in touch with readers. She finds that their result is not always the same as hers, even when they tell her they have made the recipe exactly. Readers also give her ideas. Someone who was allergic to coconut milk suggested using soy milk with coconut flavoring as a substitute. Nathan says she would never have thought of that.

She spends a day making six or seven recipes, hosts a dinner party for twelve, and then asks guests for their honest opinions. "My social life surrounds my cookbooks," she explains. Many other writers I've interviewed use this technique instead of recipe testers. Some feel recipe testers are not always trustworthy, as they might make unauthorized substitutions that will influence whether the dish succeeds, such as canned chilies instead of fresh ones, or kidney beans instead of pinto beans.

Some authors have testers come to their homes and cook. They watch the tester make a recipe. "Sometimes people get so excited about the process that they forget a step or ingredient," says Nathan. Like many authors, Nathan uses an assistant to help her cook. She uses college interns three days per week, with one day set aside for cooking. Other writers might have assistants shop for them or prepare ingredients.

When testing your recipes, it's best not to give them to family members and friends. Chances are they will not be entirely honest in response, even if you give them a test sheet (see Test Sheet Sample Questions below) and tell them to be brutal. They may decide not to bring up something they don't like because they think their opinion isn't as valid as yours, or because they don't want to hurt your feelings. I also wouldn't give a recipe to a culinary school student or a professional recipe developer, unless they are your target readers. You want people you know slightly, who like to cook.

Many recipe writers don't pay testers. Others have found drawbacks to that system. Unpaid testers take forever and are less likely to provide thorough feedback, said David Lebovitz, author of *The Great Book of Chocolate,* in an interview. "When money is involved, people take it more seriously." He has paid home testers fifty dollars to test three recipes. Others reimburse testers for ingredients. Regardless of how or whether you pay, acknowledge testers in your book.

Nancy Baggett, author of *The All-American Cookie Book,* saved her developing and testing notes so she could show documentation if anyone asked. "Just for curiosity's sake," she adds, "I totaled up the testing and found I had made 38,000 cookies."

By the end of this system of developing, writing, and testing, you should have a batch of well-written, accurate, consistent recipes. Look at all the benefits: If you've always wanted to create a lasting chronicle of your cooking, you will have succeeded. Great recipes means editors will take you seriously. Readers who need explicit instructions will be grateful. And those who fantasized about making a dish like yours will get it right the first time.

TEST SHEET SAMPLE QUESTIONS

If you can, state the questions in such a way that you do not get a simple yes or no answer. Here are examples.

- Are ingredients listed in correct order? Were the measurements clear or did certain words seem to be misplaced (for example, "1 cup peanuts, chopped" versus "1 cup chopped peanuts")?
- What kind of questions did you have about the directions?
- Did the ingredient quantities seem to work, or would you have added or subtracted anything? Were any ingredients difficult to find? What was your substitution, if any, and how do you think it may have affected the dish?
- How would you evaluate the time it took to prepare the dish?
- Was there anything confusing about the recipe steps?
- How did you choose which utensils, cookware, or equipment to use? Would you prefer that be specified?
- How were your results? What did you like or dislike about the flavors, textures, and tastes of the dish?
- What was visually appealing about the dish?
- How would you evaluate portion sizes, preparation times, and level of difficulty, on a scale of one to ten for each? Please elaborate on your answer. Say if anything was too hard or too time consuming.
- How does this dish taste to you, on a scale of one to ten?
- How likely would you be to make this dish again? Why or why not?
- How did this recipe compare with similar ones you have tried before?
- Overall comments?

REFERENCE BOOKS

You don't have to reinvent the wheel. Books exist to help you with recipe questions you might have as you go along, even your own cookbook collection. The first two books, plus my own collection, have been invaluable to me.

- *The Recipe Writer's Handbook,* by Barbara Gibbs Ostmann and Jane Baker. The bible on how to write recipes, with much more detail than I could ever include here.
- *Recipes Into Type: A Handbook for Cookbook Writers and Editors,* by Joan Whitman and Dolores Simon.
- *Food Lover's Companion,* by Sharon Herbst. Definitions of culinary terms, origins of foods, and explanations of techniques.
- *On Food and Cooking: The Science and Lore of the Kitchen,* by Harold McGee. Scientific explanation, culinary lore, and food history in a fascinating compendium.
- *Cookwise: The Hows and Whys of Successful Cooking,* by Shirley Corriher. Explanations of how certain outcomes of cooking occur and will help you understand how to make changes.
- Your own cookbook collection. When words fail me on how to explain a technique, write a headnote, or describe an ingredient, I often turn to trusted authors to see how they do it. Aside from the ones mentioned in this chapter, other outstanding recipe writers are Richard Olney, Craig Claiborne, Rose Levy Beranbaum, Madeleine Kamman, and Flo Braker.
- For historic recipes, consider the work of Escoffier, Caréme, and Pomaine.
- Other styles: Edouard de Pomaine, an early twentieth-century food writer, often wrote the method in the second person, telling you what you see and smell. Elizabeth David writes recipes in narrative style rather than listing the ingredients first. Instead she specified them within the method, and the method is all that appears. James Beard used this style as well in *Delights and Prejudices.*

Writing Exercises

1. Write a recipe for your favorite sandwich. Include a head-note at least three sentences long. Now check your ability to be specific. Did you ask for a certain type of bread, or for slices of a certain thickness? Did you specify the type of mustard (not the brand name)? If you called for an exotic mayonnaise like aioli, did you include the recipe? Did you specify special equipment, such as a panini maker? If so, describe how readers can make the sandwich without it.

2. Find origins. In your files, find a half-dozen handwritten recipes given to you by others, with no credit listed. Contact each person to find out where the recipe originated. If they can't remember, consider how you would alter each recipe to make it your own, or what you would write in the headnote to explain the situation.

3. Determine the sophistication level of your readers. Look in your cupboards and refrigerator, and list all foods and spices you think your target reader probably will not have. Determine how to approach these ingredients in your cookbook if you plan to include them, particularly in terms of substitutions. If you can't answer this question, you probably haven't done enough research on your target reader.

8

Memoir and Nonfiction Food Writing

I n the last decade or so, hundreds of books on every possible subject related to food have flooded the shelves. Fueled by the success of Ruth Reichl's best-seller memoir *Tender at the Bone: Growing Up at the Table,* they picked up steam. Food history books, once thought obscure and esoteric, entered the mainstream with books like *Cod: A Biography of the Fish that Changed the World* and *Salt: A World History.* Single-subject books on topics such as chocolate, oranges, and vanilla abound. Guidebooks on food and travel, biographies, and exposés such as *Fast Food Nation: The Dark Side of the American Meal* have crossed over into other categories of the bookstore. Reference books demystifying foods, their origins, and uses are plentiful.

The growth of the noncookbook food-writing world excites me so much that I wonder if the cookbook section of bookstores will have to be renamed. So if you prefer not to write a cookbook, or if you've already written a cookbook and want to try another form, consider food-based books. To succeed at narrative food writing, you have to be a great detective and researcher rather than an expert. After all, what is the appropriate background of someone who wants to write a book on, say, the history of barbecue?

Take Andrew Smith, author of several books including the *Oxford Encyclopedia of Food and Drink in America,* who had no expertise in food when he started writing for publication. In fact, his field is international relations. Smith entered the food-writing world after using a candy bar to explain complicated international topics to fourth graders. He pointed to a map of the world to show where chocolate comes from, where it's manufactured, and where the money from candy bar sales goes. He realized that talking about food is a great way to get people interested in "all the things they wouldn't normally care about," such as history, culture, and science.

Memoir is the largest category of noncookbooks and the closest to a traditional cookbook, since it usually includes recipes. From there you'll find lots of other possibilities that will help you with your own ideas of what to write. The message in this chapter is exhilarating: the door's wide open for food-based books.

Food-based Memoir

Many of my students want to write memoirs. Why are we attracted to this genre? We use our love of food to access family, culture, and emotions. First-person books based on food memory are usually joyous, even when the memories evoked are bittersweet. Some are filled with intimate memories of life, love, and food, particularly the memoir-like *The Gastronomical Me* by M. F. K. Fisher.

One of Fisher's disciples, Ruth Reichl, editor of *Gourmet* and a former food critic, came out with her own memoir in 1986. She single-handedly fired up a new generation of food memoirists with the best-selling *Tender at the Bone,* a sensuous coming-of-age tale of a career spent following her appetite. Her sequel, *Comfort Me with Apples: More Adventures at the Table,* gave further credibility to food-based memoir as a category. One year later year, Frances Mayes caused a sensation with *Under the Tuscan Sun,* a memoir about fixing up a rural Italian villa, living with her husband, and cooking. It also included recipes.

These memoirs aren't just about food, and that is why they succeed. Adept storytellers write about people and relationships, where conflict between characters is as important as stellar meals. The most successful food-based memoirs combine extraordinary stories with beautiful writing. "It seems to me that any good memoir is about relationships and telling events so it doesn't matter if it's about food or not," says Amanda Hesser, *New York Times* columnist and author of *Cooking for Mr. Latte.* "Food can provide an organizing principle to the book or can serve as a sensual element or symbolism, but if the core narrative isn't there, it's not going to be a very interesting memoir."

Food-based memoir has its own characteristics. It may sound obvious, but the stories must center on food. "This is both limiting and liberating," explains Shoba Narayan, author of *Monsoon Diary: A Memoir with Recipes.* "Limiting because you don't include aspects of your life story that are not food related. Liberating because this gives it a tight structure and therefore one less thing the writer has to obsess about."

While many excellent books can guide you through the general topic of memoir writing (see Great Books on Memoir Writing, page 194), they do not cover the specifics of this particular genre. Here are the most important characteristics:

Food memories: Reconstruct meals and dialogue around the table, cooking events, and how you learned about food and food traditions. Describe the sights, tastes, sounds, and smells of the kitchen and who was there. Tell people about what they couldn't possibly have tasted or known by themselves.

Focus on the senses: Most of your scenes will take place in locations where food and eating are at the forefront, whether it's in the kitchen, dining room, garden, restaurant, market, cooking school, cafeteria, picnic area, or the woods. Put the reader there with you, experiencing all the sensations. Here's an example from *Comfort Me with Apples,* where Reichl watches a chef at work in the kitchen: "Mr. Chen told me to taste it and then asked if I could guess the secret ingredient. I felt as if it was a test, so I tried really hard. There was an indefinable richness to the dish, and I thought of that golden liquid, and guessed chicken fat. Mr. Chen was delighted with me."

Sophisticated storyteller Isabelle Allende's *Aphrodite: A Memoir of the Senses,* her lusty celebration of sex and food, takes a different approach by combining more than 100 recipes with poems, stories, photos and drawings, and discussions on the sensual art of food, attracting your mate, and the effect of smell on libido.

Recipes: Just about every food memoir I've read includes recipes, except for those by restaurant critics and the memoirs of farmer Mas Masumoto such as *Epitaph of a Peach: Four Seasons on My Family Farm.*

The number of recipes to include seems to be up to you. Some books contain just one or two at the end of each chapter. Some have dozens. Reichl said on a panel that in her first book the story drove the recipes, while in her second the recipes drove the story. Hesser's book contained more than 100 recipes, on the other hand. Says Hesser, "I included recipes because I'm a cook and I wanted readers to be able to taste what I was talking about —if they were motivated, that is."

Decide whether recipes are fundamental to your book's story, whether they deepen it and add texture and context. In Hesser's book about her relationship with Mr. Latte, a man who later became her husband, she detailed the meal her future mother-in-law made, the first meal Hesser made for Mr. Latte, and the first meal he made for her. These events are critical to the book's story line.

Memoir has characteristics particular to its genre as well. The first is that it covers a certain period of time, perhaps a single aspect of your life. It's not your life story, or you would call it an autobiography. Memoir tells of an emotional, physical, or psychological journey you experienced. The best memoirs read like novels. This style is called literary nonfiction, or narrative non-fiction, in which the quality of writing is as important as the story. Here are the elements of memoir:

- Insights are critical. The story is not just about what you did, but how what you did changed or affected you. Without these insights, the book will be a recounting, with little liveliness and depth. Here's an example: "Growing, buying, preparing, serving, eating food—the whole tasty subject— captured and framed so many of my memories that in a curious way it has not only sustained me but given me life," writes restaurateur Alexander Smalls in *Grace the Table: Stories & Recipes from My Southern Revival.* While recording his life, he includes internal thoughts.
- The story evokes emotion from the reader.
- Strong characters come alive on the page. Even more minor characters need vitality. Describe the person's appearance in specific detail to create a picture for the reader. One writer who excels at character study is Ludwig Bemelmans. His hilarious memoir *Hotel Bemelmans,* a behind-the-scenes tell-all about a New York hotel in the 1920s, has recently been reissued.
- The dialogue of your characters rings true. In writing *Kitchen Confidential: Adventures in the Culinary Underbelly,* author Anthony Bourdain said in a published interview that he "did not want real working cooks and restaurant people to read the thing and say, 'What the hell is this? I don't know any chefs who talk like this! This is not my life!'"
- You tell the truth. "If you're not honest, it's boring," says Hesser. "It's the texture of relationships that's interesting, and if you smooth it all out, it's going to be insipid."
- You use plot devices from fiction, such as conflict, suspense, and tension, by creating desire. "All storytelling from the beginning of recorded time is based on somebody

wanting something, facing obstacles, not getting it, trying to get it, trying to overcome obstacles, and finally getting or not getting what he wanted," writes Sol Stein in *Stein on Writing*.

� Your book has a story arc. This is the critical point in a novel, where tension is at its highest, and you have used suspense to build up to this moment.

➥ Your conclusion shows how your life and impressions have changed, and the consequences of that change upon you.

You might start by figuring out the reason you want to write a memoir in the first place. Does it fill a powerful need? Do you have an unusual story or a life-changing experience? Was it the first time you did something? Did you overcome adversity in a way that will inspire others? Do you want to record an event from the past, your accomplishments, family history, meals you ate, or recipes?

If you're worried your life might be too boring, you're not alone. Hesser said as much when talking to an interviewer about *Cooking for Mr. Latte*. Even though she was already a full-time *New York Times* writer, she said she was afraid she wouldn't be able to find or gather stories. "I didn't want it to be just self-involved blather about my life," she admitted. Even though it's hard, keep your inner critic at bay. Hesser knew she had a good story. She probably felt vulnerable by publishing such personal aspects of her life. You must believe you have a good story, too, particularly if you have told it and people respond positively.

GREAT BOOKS ON MEMOIR WRITING

➥ *Writing Life Stories,* by Bill Roorbach
➥ *Inventing the Truth: The Art and Craft of Memoir,* by William Zinsser
➥ *Writing About Your Life: A Journey Into the Past,* by William Zinsser

➥ *Old Friend from Far Away: How to Write a Memoir,* by
Natalie Goldberg
➥ *Unreliable Truth,* by Maureen Murdock

When thinking about your topic, consider how your experiences relate to readers and their lives. Sometimes things that fascinate you will not translate well to your readers. If you deal with universal themes of accomplishment, such as graduating from culinary school, taking a fantasy trip abroad, or serving a series of meals to family and friends, you are more likely to succeed. Make readers feel as though they are experiencing your story, help them learn, or give them inspiration to duplicate your experience for themselves. Show them how the world works. To do so, you'll have to get out of the way. Otherwise readers will be passive, reading about you and what you did, and not experiencing your story directly. Be part of the scene without dominating it.

Here's an example from A. J. Liebling, who pays for his feasts in Paris with money wired from his parents. He writes in *Between Meals,* "At the Credit, I would be received with scornful solemnity, like a suitor for the hand of a miser's daughter. I was made to sit on a bare wooden bench with the other wretches come to claim money from the bank, all feeling more like culprits by the minute. A French bank, by the somber intensity of its addiction to money, establishes an emotional claim on funds in transit. The client feels in the moral position of a wayward mother who has left her babe on a doorstep and later comes back to claim it from the foster parents, who now consider it their own."

Can't you imagine Liebling at the bank, seething? You share his disgust and discomfort, right down to how it feels to sit on a hard surface. You agree that the bank is unreasonable to treat him this way, because things like this have happened to you. And you're having fun reading his diatribe because it's witty. On the other hand, he could have written, "I really hate going to the bank. I don't like the way they treat me. I feel like I've done something wrong. They have no right to keep me from my money." Now, it's all about him, not about the scene. You don't know where he is, you feel no compassion or outrage, and there's no humor to provide levity. You watch him have a tantrum, from a distance. That's boring.

Your story must seem real to readers, and you must have enough distance to make realistic assessments of where you were emotionally at the time you're talking about. If readers are not convinced, it doesn't really matter what happened or how it unfolded. Many people use memoirs as a form of therapy. It's fine to do so, but your story may not be publishable if you are the only one who understands the course of events, or if there is no action or dialogue. You must be capable of objectivity about that period in your life. If not, turn it into fiction.

In memoir as in fiction writing, your character and tone are essential to the book. As Amanda Hesser said earlier in this book, she had to make herself into a character as well, even one that wasn't exactly true to life. I like memoirs that show a writer's excitement about that fascinating part of his or her life and the wonder of it. Victoria Riccardi, author of *Untangling My Chopsticks: A Culinary Sojourn in Kyoto*, said in an interview that her approach was, "What a gift to be here." Another way to show character is to use humor and self-denigration in your writing.

Be an expert on you. If you want to write a memoir about summers you spent on tourist farms in Umbria, you're the expert about your experience. You don't have to be an expert on farming or food. Those subjects are secondary to the story. Simply do enough research on these subjects to put your tale in perspective and provide enough context.

In food-based memoirs, nostalgia can be boring. I saw this firsthand when I judged an annual book award that included many food-based memoirs. Their focus was so familiar: perfect pasts of discovering food during childhood, where a loving mother and grandmother were ingenious cooks who made complicated meals by hand. Avoid sentimentality as your main theme. Be willing to write about something mundane. Write about how the person across from you at the restaurant ate lunch. It will train you not to be so emotionally attached, and your writing will change for the better.

Memoir writing includes extensive research so that you can choose which details to include. If your memoir captures your family's past, look for documents other than recipes that give clues about that time, such as marriage and death certificates, letters, maps, family trees, photos, and magazines from that era to give you a sense of the times. If you are planning to write about a certain time while you are living it, such as that spent cooking on a houseboat in France, collect and save the things around you to unlock memories later. Take photos. Write in a daily journal. Save menus, tickets, and relevant newspaper stories. If certain people are critical characters in your story, interview them now. You think they'll always be around and there's time, but you can't be certain. I conducted oral histories with my aunt and mother before they died. Now I have a transcript of their memories. I can listen to the tapes to add texture and credibility to my characters. On the tape, I hear how my auntie paused to take long drags on her cigarette, for example, and the raspy quality of her voice.

Know how the story ends. A big part of defining your memoir is to determine where it stops. You have to be over the experience to put it into perspective. When you write your story, you will lead up to the end, foreshadowing it throughout the book, and you must know what to conclude. Your book must have a definable beginning, middle, and end.

The structure of a memoir can be a series of anecdotes, vignettes, or essays strung together. It can be chronological or written as diary entries. A memoir is not about every event, or even the most important ones during that time, unless they are relevant to the central story of your book. Organizing a long project like this requires vigilance. You will continuously distill and discard, and it may take you some time to get to the exact theme to pursue. You may write a list of points you wish to make, or a skeleton or outline, and change it several times. That means you're making progress because you're thinking it through.

If you feel apprehensive about exposing certain thoughts or incidents, there are ways to create boundaries between yourself and readers. Just as you want to be careful not to overdo the emotional aspects of your past, you must be prepared to live with whatever you disclose about yourself. Reichl, when talking on a panel about her memoir, said she "didn't talk about the really bad stuff in the first book. I didn't want to hurt people's memories." At the same time, your duty is to tell the essential emotional truth, and not get lost in what you think you should be feeling. You don't have to reveal everything about yourself. Choose what's essential to the story, and reveal these secrets throughout the book.

To play it safe, some writers employ false names for individuals they want to protect, those who might be hurt or upset by the way they are portrayed. Because I was trained as a reporter, I'm not fond of this technique, where emphasis is on telling the literal truth. Since no two people remember an event or individual exactly the same way, however, I suppose writers can take license, as long as the point is to bring out the inherent truthfulness of the story. Some authors also merge characters or alter the setting or timing. That sounds like fiction to me, but you have to decide what you can live with. If you're afraid you can't accurately reconstruct a conversation, put a disclaimer in the front of the book saying you did your best to get the essence of what people said.

Typically, you shouldn't let people read your manuscript before it's published, because they will find things they don't like. Find ways to reassure your mother or spouse without getting specific about their role in the book. If you're afraid you'll hurt or embarrass a loved one, make that person look less identifiable in the book. If you write something potentially damaging, a publisher might ask for a written consent form from that person.

Reichl got permission from Colman Andrews, former editor of *Saveur*, to write about their affair. She didn't send him the manuscript. Andrews told me the story: "She took me to lunch at Fleur de Sel in Manhattan and told me she had written about me and our relationship in the book, then asked my permission to use my real name and the actual circumstances. If I was uncomfortable with that, she said, she would be willing to give me a pseudonym and change some identifying details. She added that she didn't think I'd mind anything she had written.

"On the principal that one probably shouldn't do anything in life that one wouldn't be willing to read about later, I told her to go ahead and use the 'real' me. And as I told her later, it turned out I did mind some of what she had written, not because it made me seem like a cad (which I probably was), but because it made me sound so humorless about food and wine, which I'd like to think I wasn't. But ultimately, I can't complain. She did a good job of capturing the spirit of the times (and of our relationship), even if she played a bit fast and loose—as she readily admits—with the facts."

For more on memoir writing, I recommend you read some of the books I listed or take classes to jumpstart your writing. Now, let's go on to all the other kinds of books that are neither cookbooks nor memoirs. Below are genres of food-based books for you to choose from. Many of these categories cross over each other, so there's no need to feel limited.

Food History

Do you wonder about the history of foods, cooking, food preparation, and food etiquette? Consider writing about food from the past and providing new insights. Many forms of food-based books include history. For memoir, you'll want to find your own culinary history and family information about who cooked where and what they made. For a book about travels in Mexico, you might want to investigate the origin of tortillas, if that's part of the adventure. Researching origins and significance of foods in history make the material come alive.

If you are passionate about a subject that requires delving

into history, your book can bring fresh perspectives to old stories, says Sandy Oliver, publisher and editor of the *Food History News* newsletter. So many questions need answers. Here are some of the ones she poses on her Web site, Food History News (http://www.foodhistorynews.com): "What did the pilgrims eat for the first Thanksgiving? Was the Italian Catherine de Médici responsible for French haute cuisine? Is it true that people spiced meat highly in past times to hide the bad taste of spoilage?"

While many food history books languish in obscurity, some make their way into the mainstream, as demonstrated by Mark Kurlansky's *Cod* and Mort Rosenblum's *Olives: The Life and Lore of a Noble Fruit*. Most historians wouldn't think of food as an appropriate category, says author Andy Smith. The field was wide open when he entered it twenty years ago. He believes it still is. "Anybody can pick a topic," he says. "The secret is to talk to people about things they know but have never thought about before, and are shocked and surprised when you start giving them context." Smith is now at work on an encyclopedia of fast food and junk food.

What all good food history books have in common is the hundreds of hours of careful research authors put into them. Accuracy is paramount. "If you're working from your own memory [as in a memoir], no big deal, but in a historical context, you have to be right," says Oliver. To research historical cooking, you must go past theorizing and recreate the food as accurately as possible, she says. If you're interested in fireplace cooking, for example, "Go find a fireplace and cook something in it. Or take a vacation. Or visit house museums. Living History museums sponsor all kinds of weekends," Oliver advises.

To get started, she suggests you "go to the library and read everything you can lay your hands on for a week or more. Or do library research on the Internet. Use Google. Find out what the standards are." Rather than work in isolation, get to know other food historians who can advise you on how to write food history well. She lists food history groups across the country on her Web site.

For general information on writing food history, and for a lively discussion as food history is being made, two resources are particularly useful. Rachel Laudan, author of *The Food of Paradise: Exploring Hawaii's Culinary Heritage,* wrote an excellent pamphlet on food history writing and how to do it on her Web site, http://www.rachellaudean.com which is downloadable. You can also join the Association of the Study of Food and Society's Listserv, where academics and historians exchange information about everything from cannibalism to vegan diets. A listserve allows you to broadcast a message to a group without knowing the addresses of each member. Go to http://food-culture.org to sign up.

How long does it take to write a history book? Oliver estimates that writing a one-subject book can be covered in a year or two. "Grab something out of your life experience that interests you terribly," she advises. That's good advice for any kind of book.

Cultural Anthropology and Philosophy

These books study the social, symbolic, political, and economic roles of food and cultures. Often written by academics, they may require peer review and are often published by university presses. Some emerge from masters' theses or doctoral dissertations.

These books have a hard time getting into the mainstream, partly because they are written in a scholarly tone for a specialized audience. Many cite previous works and are heavily footnoted, perhaps intimidating the casual reader. Plus, they are not as accessible as books in the cookbook section of bookstores. Instead you'll have to search for them in the history, philosophy, or anthropology sections. For example, my paperback edition of *No Foreign Food: The American Diet in Time and Place,* by geography professor Richard Pillsbury, suggests on its back cover that it be placed in "American/cultural studies."

Some books in this category cross over. *Much Depends on Dinner: The Extraordinary History and Mythology, Allure and Obsessions, Perils and Taboo of an Ordinary Meal,* by Margaret Visser, tells the story behind ordinary items found on the American dinner table, such as butter, salt, and roast chicken. *We Are What We Eat: Ethnic Food and the Making of Americans,* by Donna R. Gabaccia, was reviewed in *USA Today,* which said, "Today's multiethnic American diet offers intriguing insight into the character of the nation. . . . Gabaccia explores the journey of these ethnic foods from pushcarts to the national marketplace and how . . . ethnic cuisines have retained their essential and often ritualized role in American life."

Another well-known book is the anthology *Food and Culture: A Reader,* edited by anthropology professors Carole Counihan and Penny Van Esterik. It examines the social, symbolic, and political-economic roles of what—and how—we eat. While M. F. K. Fisher and Frances Moore Lappé (*Diet for a Small Planet*) penned two of the essays, others are written by academics, historians, cultural anthropologists, and researchers. Topics in this kind of food writing can be challenging to the general reader. Take this opening sentence from the essay "Food as a Cultural Construction," by Anna Meigs, an associate professor of anthropology: "Eating for the Hua people of the Eastern Highlands of Papua New Guinea is one of several ways in which physical properties and 'vital essence' are transferred between objects and organisms." I'm sure she wrote a distinguished work, having made it into this anthology, but the subject matter caters to a narrow audience.

Reference

These books are structured as a series of listings, like dictionaries, where you look up something to do with food. Sharon Tyler Herbst has spent years refining and updating the *Food Lover's Companion.* Her latest is the *New Food Lover's Companion: Comprehensive Definitions of Nearly 6,000 Food,*

Drink, and Culinary Terms. Altogether, her book has sold more than one million copies.

Smaller reference works on the subject of your passion might be a bit less ambitious and more doable. Former *New York Times* restaurant critic William Grimes wrote *Eating Your Words: 2,000 Words to Tease Your Taste Buds,* as the kind of book he could have used on the job. It includes a long list of types of mushrooms from agaric to yellowfoot, a definition of court bouillon, and short essays on such topics as defining a hoagie. If general topics seem too enormous, tackle a more narrow subject that serves as more of a guide, such as *Atomic Kitchen: Gadgets and Inventions for Yesterday's Cook; Kitchen Garden A to Z: Growing, Harvest, Buying, Storing;* and *A Lady at the Table: A Concise, Contemporary Guide to Table Manners.* Some of these books do quite well. Ben Schott's quirky *Schott's Food & Drink Miscellany* contains an addictive blend of oddities, such as how to cook a swan, how Hemingway liked his martinis, and why asparagus makes your urine smell. *Newsweek* called it "as hilarious as it is addictive," and *Vanity Fair* reviewed it as "utterly indispensable."

Gary Allen wrote *The Resource Guide for Food Writers* after collecting information for a book on herbs and spices. He couldn't find the data he wanted past the usual twenty spices covered in most books, and decided to go back to school to refine his research skills. His instructor suggested he put together a list of resources for food writing. His three fifty-page lists became the basis of his book. *The Resource Guide* took a year and a half to write and came out before Allen graduated from Empire State College in New York, where he now teaches food writing. Here's his philosophy on how he approached it: "I make a set of cubbyholes and throw things into them until a book emerges. I trust the material enough to generate the book."

Even the big reference books don't take forever. Editor Andy Smith told me his *Oxford Encyclopedia of Food and Drink in America* was published three years after he got the contract. He hired Allen as one of dozens of freelance writers who wrote entries and indexes. Like other big reference books on food, the *Encyclopedia* is an invaluable research tool. If you don't want to buy these huge books, go to a library large enough to keep them. The best-known are

- *The Cambridge World History of Food*
- *The Oxford Companion to Food*
- *The Encyclopedia of Food and Culture* (part of Schribner Library of Daily Life)
- *The Oxford Encyclopedia of Food and Drink in America*

Literary lists are another form of food reference. If you enjoy searching publications for pithy quotes, you could collect your findings in a book like *Since Eve Ate Apples: Quotations on Feasting, Fasting and Food from the Beginning,* a compendium of witty one-liners and quotes about food. *Dunces, Gourmands and Petticoats: 1,300 Words Whose Meanings Have Changed Throughout the Ages* traces the history of words and explains their usage. *Great Books for Cooks* lists hundreds of cookbooks by categories. Lists of historical cookbooks or food-based poems, bibliographies by people who collect cookbooks, and books with meal suggestions for reading groups are just a few of the categories that might inspire you.

If you like essays, anthologies are a good way to get your first book or essay published. Get permission to collect essays, book excerpts, or other writing forms and write an introduction. Holly Hughes created an instant annual work when she compiled the first *Best Food Writing* in 2000. She guaranteed her success with a foreword by Alice Waters, and the series is still going strong.

Guidebooks, Both Local and Abroad

If you like to travel—even locally—and you've devoted yourself to finding insider information, you could write a guidebook. Packed with useful, practical information, these books are written by those who pick an area and become experts on it, guiding the reader with careful research. A few examples are *Patricia Unterman's Food Lover's Guide to San Francisco, Food Festival: The Ultimate Guidebook to America's Best Regional Food Celebrations,* and *Pennsylvania Snacks: A Guide to Food Factory Tours.*

Laura Taxel spent two years writing *Cleveland Ethnic Eats,* a guidebook she updates every year. If you're considering writing one of your own, here is her advice:

- Look for an unmet need, a lack of organized, easy-to-use, easy-to-access information on a topic people want to discover.
- Define a specific geographic area to cover.
- The yellow pages already exists, so don't think all you have to do is gather names, addresses, and phone numbers. A guidebook's value is in the personalized, value-added information a knowledgeable author provides.
- Invest time and legwork in gathering a significant sample of your listings and put together a meaningful representation of the book's content before you take your idea to a publisher.
- A guidebook requires a big investment of time and out-of-pocket expense up front. You'll have to pay for your own transportation costs, food bills, and telephone calls.
- View your guidebook as an ongoing project. Regular updates require a steady infusion of new and corrected information.

If you've written a book that sells, you'll have to keep it up-to-date. Taxel revises hers annually. "You won't make big bucks fast, but it can become a steady source of revenue and make you a recognized expert in a particular market, which leads to many other writing and speaking opportunities," says Taxel. "That's what *Cleveland Ethnic Eats* has done for me."

Take the same kind of guidelines and go abroad to your most beloved tourist destination. Two examples are *Food Lover's Guide to Paris,* by Patricia Wells (actually, she lives in France) and *The Food and Wine Lover's Companion to Tuscany,* by Carla Capalbo. You might write a book for the *Eat Smart* series from Gingko Press, such as *Eat Smart in Poland: How to Decipher the Menu, Know the Market Foods & Embark on a Tasting Adventure.* What you decide to write depends on your area of interest, your ability to find information meaningful to other visitors, and whether you have the means to travel and pay your own bills.

Biographies

Fascinated by a certain figure in the food world? Write a biography. Laura Shapiro, an accomplished author of two historical books, *Perfection Salad: Women and Cooking at the Turn of the Century* and *Something from the Oven: Reinventing Dinner in 1950s America,* turned to a biography of Julia Child for her latest work. After Child's death, says Shapiro, she realized there was room for a second biography of her life. Her book will be "an extended essay about Child and her impact on the culture, who she was and what she meant. I could only do it after her death. It will be more of an appreciative analysis," she explains.

How do you come up with the right person to profile? It can be anyone who strikes a chord. "You have to want to lose yourself in that person. That person has to be big and interesting enough, or small and interesting enough, with depth you can throw yourself into," says Shapiro.

Here's a sample of the variety of subjects publishers have found worthwhile. *Stand Facing the Stove: The Story of the Women Who Gave America the* Joy of Cooking chronicles the lives of *Joy of Cooking* author Irma Rombauer and her daughter. *Cooking for Kings: The Life of Antonin Careme, the First Celebrity Chef,* examines the life of Europe's most famous chef. Heads of companies make good profiles, too. In *I'd Like to Buy the World a Coke,* David Greising's biography of Roberto Goizueta, he examines the life of a chemical engineer who first worked for Coca-Cola in Cuba and went on to become the youngest vice president ever at the company.

Shapiro says the biographies she used as guides are two about James Beard: *Epicurean Delight: The Life and Times of James Beard,* by Evan Jones, and *James Beard: A Biography,* by Robert Clark.

Food and Health

Health writing uses food as a vehicle to help readers feel better. Most are advice-based cookbooks, written by doctors, nutritionists, and dietitians. If you're interested in writing about a diet of eating and cooking, you'll probably end up writing a cookbook, with a few chapters of advice in the front.

Some reference books on health issues have succeeded, such as Jean Anderson and Barbara Deskins's *The Nutrition Bible: The Comprehensive No-Nonsense Guide to Foods, Nutrients, Additives, Preservatives, Pollutants, and Everything Else We Eat and Drink,* which covers more than 1,500 foods and beverages. In *The Green Pharmacy: The Ultimate Compendium of Natural Remedies from the World's Foremost Authority on Healing Herbs,* Dr. James Duke mixes folklore and medicine, discussing how ginger can alleviate morning sickness and how anise can help asthma. Employing a similar idea in *Food: Your Miracle Medicine: How Food Can Prevent and Cure Over 100 Symptoms and Problems,* author Jean Carper shows how scientific studies illustrate the healing power of food.

Again, your decision about what to write will be fueled by your enthusiasm, interest, experience, and ability to find credible information. If you feel you need expertise, team up with an expert and co-write the book. Ask experts for access to their information and credit them in the book. Or interview experts and quote them to give more credibility to your project.

Kitchen Science

The best-known book on kitchen science is *On Food and Cooking: The Science and Lore of the Kitchen,* by Harold McGee, a reference book that explains everything from lactose intolerance to the composition of a corn kernel. He wrote it as a companion guide to cookbooks in which readers could discover more in-depth information about cooking, particularly the chemistry, history, and uses of foods.

McGee taught English and writing at Yale University, and trained as a physicist and astronomer. Recently he updated and expanded the book into a more general food reference book. His biggest problem was knowing where to stop. "Writing half a page about coffee isn't going to cut it anymore," he admits. He thought ten pages would be better, but "each subject is fascinating and could be a book." When I asked him how he could verify the accuracy of hundreds of entries, he said, "You do the best you can, then the world decides whether you did a good job. It has to do with personal standards. If you skim the subject, you are most likely to make mistakes. I try to burrow down a few stages and then I feel confident about the material." This is excellent advice for researching any kind of book, but then again, it took him ten years to write the second edition.

If you want to write about how to become a better cook by understanding science, this category might be for you. To see what's required, research a few books that have done well. These books include lots of recipes, while McGee's book does not. They cover similar topics but have their own personalities. Here are some examples:

- *What Einstein Told His Cook: Kitchen Science Explained* answers more than 100 questions on such topics as why water boils and freezers burn, and which frying pan is best. Author Robert Wolke is a retired chemistry professor who writes a column for the *Washington Post.*
- Biochemist Shirley Corriher wrote *Cookwise: The*

Hows and Whys of Successful Cooking, about the way food works in a recipe, to enable cooks to get the results they want. Her book explains such things as why cookies made with butter turn out flat and crisp, while cookies made with some shortening are soft and puffy.

➺ *I'm Just Here for the Food: Food + Heat = Cooking,* by the Food Network's Alton Brown, explains cooking principles to people in their twenties and thirties.

➺ Russ Parsons's *How to Read a French Fry: And Other Stories of Intriguing Kitchen Science* focuses on scientific principles as well.

Adventures, Journalism, and Essays

Many of the categories in this chapter overlap, particularly here, where adventure-based, journalistic books are likely to include memoir and food history.

If you're interested in chronicling a hands-on experience, such as attending cooking school or working in a restaurant, you've come upon a topic publishers like. Bill Buford, editor of *Granta* magazine, wrote *Heat: An Amateur Cook's Adventures as a Kitchen Slave, Pasta Maker, and Apprentice to a Dante-Quoting Butcher on a Hilltop in Tuscany.* That's the longest subtitle I've ever read. In *The Making of a Chef: Mastering Heat at the Culinary Institute,* Michael Ruhlman explains how the most prominent cooking school in the country trains chefs, and included his own thoughts as he went through the process. Both books are also memoirs.

Speaking of culinary adventures, *A Cook's Tour,* chef Anthony Bourdain's politically incorrect world tour, chews up and spits out the usual food/travel journalism where a writer might typically discuss more rarified meals such as a long, luxurious dinner at three-star Taillevent in Paris. (Not that there's anything wrong with it. *A Meal Observed,* by

Andrew Todhunter, does just that.) Bourdain, a first-rate chef, takes a high-testosterone gonzo approach that involves extreme eating and inebriation. Here's his first sentence, a letter to his wife, Nancy: "I'm about as far away from you as I've ever been— a hotel (*the* hotel, actually) in Pailin, a miserable one-horse dunghole in northwest Cambodia, home to those not-so-adorable scamps, the Khmer Rouge."

If you have a reporting background and don't mind causing trouble, you might investigate a part of the food industry. *The Jungle,* a novel by Upton Sinclair, set the standard in 1905 when Lewis exposed the inhumane conditions of Chicago's stockyards. Most investigative reporting is nonfiction, however. Eric Schlosser's *Fast Food Nation: The Dark Side of the All-American Meal* enjoyed a deservingly long ride on the best-seller lists because of his prescient timing, excellent journalism, and passionate writing. *Food Politics: How the Food Industry Influences Nutrition and Health,* by Marion Nestle, takes an insider's perspective. It's an eye-opening read as well.

Company profiles are popular ways to write about food and who controls the food industry. You might wonder how many books we need on candy companies. Each of these takes a different focus. *The Emperors of Chocolate: Inside the Secret World of Hershey and Mars* looks at the chocolate wars between the two industry giants. There's also *Crisis in Candyland: Melting the Chocolate Shell of the Mars Family Empire.* These are tales of secretive and tightfisted organizations by writers from the outside looking at their impact. A background as a reporter would be particularly useful here, as these are not vanity books, where the company approves the book before it can be published and often controls its content. A related book, *Candyfreak: A Journey Through the Chocolate Underbelly of America,* takes more of a travel memoir approach from the perspective of the candy-obsessed author, Steve Almond.

Another type of nonfiction book combines self-contained stories written in essay form. Most often, these books comprise stories previously published in a magazine. The writing can be literary, entertaining, or educational—or all three—and often combines reporting and adventure. My favorite witty, hilarious essayists are Jeffrey Steingarten of *Vogue* magazine; Calvin Trillin, a freelancer for the *New Yorker;* and Alan Richman, a freelance food critic, whose book *Fork it Over: The Intrepid Adventures of a Professional Eater,* says it all. You might get essay ideas from James Villas, the former *Town and Country* food and wine editor, who has written *Stalking the Green Fairy: And Other Fantastic Adventures in Food and Drink,* and Robb Walsh's *Are You Really Going to Eat That?*

Fran Gage's first book, *Bread and Chocolate: My Food Life In and Around San Francisco,* began as a book about nuts. Her book proposal included a fervent, long essay on chestnuts. When her agent showed her proposal to an editor, he liked the chestnut piece so much he asked Gage to write more for a book about the Bay Area food scene, with recipes. At that point, the sum of Gage's published writing experience was a newsletter about her defunct bakery. "I just started writing and it sort of worked out somehow," she says modestly.

To come up with topics for her essays, she made a list of foods divided by those she felt passionate about, those she knew could become a story, or those for which she could visit the people who made or grew the foods. When she found crayfish in a farmers' market, for example, she figured she could write about the crayfish itself and going fishing with her children when they were little. Gage asked the crayfish vendor to accompany her on her fishing boat, and "There I had an essay in three parts." Gage thought up an essay based on a trip to the market, a memory, a conclusion that research would be doable, and a fishing trip with a vendor. Sometimes great ideas can be serendipitous in the way they come together.

I hope this chapter made you as excited as I am by this expanding category. The variety shows how mainstream the subject of food has become and how it can be translated into many of styles of nonfiction writing. If several book ideas popped into your head as you read, capture that list. Book ideas have to come from somewhere, and one of my goals in writing this book is to help you generate yours.

Writing Exercises

1. Generate food-based memories for your memoir. Map out the street where you lived as a child and write about the food you tasted from other homes. Draw the street where you grew up on a sheet of paper. Add a drawing or X marking the spot of each house. Add the names of families you knew or kids you played with. Now draw upon your memory of eating foods for the first time. Write about three or four times when playmates or their parents presented you with a food you had never eaten before. Create the scene. Remember your apprehension or excitement. Recall the taste on your tongue.

   Once you have documented a few strong images, weave them together in a story. Write about how you felt eating those new foods, how they changed you, and whether you eat any of them today.

2. Flex your research skills with an essay on food history. Name your favorite spice. Now write 500 words about it. Discover the country of origin and how the spice is harvested, processed, and sold. Find out whether it was used in a famous historical dish or prized by certain people. See whether traders took it on trade routes to another country, and how that country used the spice. Say how it's used today and how you cook or bake with it. If you like, conclude by developing a recipe using the spice.

9

Writing about Food in Fiction

So far this book has been about nonfiction, the biggest category of food writing by far. But writing fiction, it turns out, is not that different from nonfiction. In both cases, your job is to convey passion, put the reader in the scene, let the food play the leading role, and write a story with a beginning, middle, and end. Both fiction and nonfiction include suspense and tension to drive the narrative. Both use food to establish the place, time, culture, and mood. If you've read the other chapters, you've spent your time well preparing for fiction.

Fiction writing is fun. You get to make up characters, plot, and dialogue. Your story can take place anywhere in the world, during any time period. You get to merge people you know into a single person and take revenge on people you don't like—as long as they won't know it. If some events haven't turned out well in your life, they can turn out well in your fiction piece. If you've always hated your mother's cooking, a character can have a mother who's a celebrated chef.

In fiction, food is a device that helps you develop characters based on how they cook, which foods they like, and how they eat. It also creates a mood or sets a scene, and establishes the time. "Food is everything," says Phyllis Richman, former restaurant critic of the *Washington Post* and author of *The Butter Did It: A Gastronomic Tale of Love and Murder, Murder on the Gravy Train,* and *Who's Afraid of Virginia Ham?* "It's part of the relationship between Chas [Richman's main character] and her lover, Chas and her daughter, and it's the murder weapon. While they're having an argument, the daughter cooks and Chas sets the table. Food is what occupies them. It facilitates working out problems among characters, explains characters to one another, and identifies people."

In that vein, here's how a skilled writer shapes a character's personality based on how the character handles food and how and when he eats. In *The Garden of Eden,* Ernest Hemingway writes: "He went out to the empty kitchen and found a tin of Maquereau Vin Blanc Capitaine Cook and opened it and took it, perilous with edge-level juice, with a cold bottle of the Tuborg beer out to the bar. He opened the beer, took the bottle top between his right thumb and the first joint of his right forefinger and bent it in until it was flattened together, put it in his pocket since he saw no container to toss it into, raised the bottle that was still cold to his hand and now beaded wet in his fingers and, smelling the aroma from the opened tin of spiced and marinated mackerel, he took a long drink of the cold beer."

Wow. I've read that paragraph at least two dozen times and it still slays me with its muscular sensuousness. Hemingway is not the kind of guy who would just write, "The man went to the kitchen, found some fish and drank some beer." Look at the specific language, how he slowed down the moment. Now, what do you know about this character? He's strong, masculine, sexual, and deliberate. He takes great pleasure in food. He doesn't litter.

In some fiction, food itself becomes a character. In *Five Quarters of the Orange,* by Joanne Harris, an orange becomes the villain by taking on evil powers. The smell of oranges brings on a woman's crippling headaches. She will not permit them in her house. Her daughter steals an orange and uses it to control her by placing it on her mother's pillow, triggering migraines. Other negative roles food can play include dismay, disgust, detachment, disillusion, destruction, danger, or even death—the all-important D-words.

The assent to eat—sitting down to dinner, taking a cup of tea—can become the catalyst for action. In *Anna Karenina* by Leo Tolstoy, Levin, the main character, drinks an awful lot of tea, often at the start of a paragraph as a way to begin a scene. He might order tea sent to his study, signaling the beginning of work. Or he might sit with others and have tea, as in "Levin was sitting beside his hostess at the teatable and had to keep up a conversation with her and her sister, who was sitting opposite him."

By default, much of the dialogue in novels with food themes takes place over food at parties, cafés, and particularly at dinner tables. Edith Wharton's *The Age of Innocence* uses food to advance the plot, eventually: "After a velvety oyster soup came shad and cucumbers, then a young broiled turkey with corn fritters, followed by a canvas-back with currant jelly and a celery mayonnaise. Mr. Letterblair, who lunched on a sandwich and tea, dined deliberately and deeply, and insisted on his guests doing the same. Finally, when the closing rites had been accomplished, the cloth was removed, cigars were lit, and Mr. Letterblair, leaning back in his chair and pushing the port westward, said, spreading his back agreeably to the coal fire behind him, 'The whole family is against a divorce. And I think rightly.'"

Sometimes the plot relies on the elaborate meals the main character makes and the dialogue that results. In *Serving Crazy with Curry* by Amulya Malladi, a woman gets fired from her job and suffers a miscarriage. Feeling shame for abandoning her traditional Indian family, she attempts suicide. Her mother saves her life. She moves in with her parents but refuses to speak, taking up cooking instead, and prompting her family to engage in conversations over meals that draw them closer.

There are all types of culinary fiction, from murder mysteries to novels based on food to joint themes of food and sex. While many classic writers are never thought of as food writers, they write beautifully on the topic, as illustrated above by Hemingway, Tolstoy, and Wharton. Even children's books with food themes present a satisfying challenge. This chapter explores all types of food writing in book-length fiction. Its goal is not to teach you how to write fiction, but to generate story ideas by giving you examples of successful titles and plot lines, and to help you shape your individual voice, style, and view of the world.

Culinary Crime Capers

Great dining has often been a part of mystery novels. In the 1960s, Nero Wolfe, Rex Stout's sleuth, had a rule that no one could interrupt a meal, including those prepared by his personal chef, Fritz. Meals were an integral part of the plot in Agatha Christie books, from arsenic in the food to the way the murderer stalked his victim at a dinner party to exposing the murderer at tea. More modern examples of culinary crime are Nan Lyons's *Someone is Killing the Great Chefs of Europe,* and Chef Anthony Bourdain's thrillers set in the restaurant industry and seasoned with culinary detail: *Gone Bamboo* and *Bone in the Throat.*

Some writers create food-based murder mysteries based on ordinary characters. They have moved the genre away from stories about hard-boiled detectives who never eat, to cozies, books that focus more on character and relationships. Joyce and Jim Levine, who have written more than forty books together, teach a six-week online course on writing cozies at Writerscollege.com. Since they are the experts, I'll let them describe the genre:

> Cozies are light mysteries depicting real-life people solving mysteries in unusual ways. The genre is steadily broadening as their popularity increases. Traditionally, the cozy was a British novel featuring sweet elderly women and other harmless protagonists. Probably the best known is Agatha Christie with her *Miss Marple* series.

Today's cozies occur in every place and time with men and women as sleuths. They have an amateur detective, although there is often a police officer in a supporting role. The amateur sleuth gathers clues by listening to gossip and by paying attention to surroundings. The cozy sleuth attracts murder. Murders happen everywhere around him or her. The sleuth has access to a large number of people, usually through a career.

The cozy is heavy on dialogue, light on gritty depictions of death and the murder itself. They are full of suspense and dark corners of intrigue. But cozy murder mysteries are tamer than their thriller counterparts. Descriptions of the crime scene are toned down. Sex is never graphic. The stories are thoughtful rather than thriller. The books generally have strong, quirky characters and are set in interesting places. Cozy sleuths come from many different walks of life and from any time or place.

That means the main character could be a food journalist, baker, caterer, innkeeper, chocolate maker, or coffeehouse owner, as they are in the books I've discovered. Here, the plot ideas are often campy and the titles full of puns and double entendres. Recipes are always part of the form, although the amount varies.

Phyllis Richman, the formidable top reviewer of the *Washington Post* until her retirement in 2000, wrote her three cozies while working full time. "I had been doing my job for so long I needed some freshening," she explains. "I had been thinking for decades about doing mysteries. I also thought if I wanted to get published, it would be easier to do so from the *Post* than from retirement." She stayed home one day a week to write, and after fifty-two weeks, her first book was ready.

Richman used her insider knowledge of the restaurant business as a theme for three books, as cozies are usually written as a series. In *Murder on the Gravy Train*, Chas Wheatley, restaurant critic for the fictional *Washington Examiner*, flies to Paris with her chef lover for a benefit gala. When her lover dies of an apparent heart attack from soaring cholesterol, Wheatley knows better. She continues writing her reviews and recipes while investigating his death. In *The Butter Did It,* Wheatley finds something rotten with the food at one of Washington's most popular new restaurants. The head chef is missing. Wheatley tracks down the dead chef, eating her way from one restaurant to the next and giving readers an inside look at the restaurant business. In *Who's Afraid of Virginia Ham?* a new reporter, angling for Wheatley's job as food editor, dies by eating lethal Virginia ham at a work function.

At first Richman had to get used to new tools of plot, character development, point of view, and dialogue. But there's nothing that different about fiction, she decided. "It's just another form of restaurant reviews and travel writing."

Probably the most famous of the food-themed cozy writers is Diane Mott Davidson. She has written twelve culinary mysteries, some appearing on the *New York Times* and *USA Today* best-seller lists. When starting out, Davidson wrote two mysteries before selling her third, *Catering to Nobody,* to St. Martin's Press. An avid cook and fan of Julia Child, she convinced the publisher to include four recipes.

Davidson's writing group suggested she focus her murder mystery on Goldy Korman, a caterer, who was then a minor character. "For Goldy, cooking heals," said Davidson in an interview. "If she can cook, she can get a feeling of control over the world. Cooking is more than just comfort food, it's about nurturing oneself while nurturing others." Davidson's recipes come from food ideas suggested by friends, colleagues, restaurant dishes, or sometimes right out of her head, featuring ingredients she thinks would taste good together.

Like Richman, she has a good time while writing her books. Some of Davidson's culinary capers are:

➡ *Dying for Chocolate.* Korman, a divorced culinary artist, starts Goldilocks Catering in Aspen Meadows, Colorado, to support herself and her teenage son.

- *Killer Pancake.* While Korman caters a cosmetics firm's low-fat luncheon, a sales associate dies in a hit-and-run while animal-rights people demonstrate in front of her store.
- *The Last Suppers.* On Korman's wedding day, her husband gets arrested for a homicide. She includes a recipe: Dark Chocolate Wedding Cake with White Peppermint Frosting.

While Davidson started out as a mystery writer, Joanne Fluke wrote psychological thrillers before moving to culinary capers. Now all of her murders have to do with baked goods. In some of her books, the pastries provide a clue. In *Lemon Meringue Pie Murder,* the protagonist, Hannah Swensen, discovers one of her pies at a crime scene and finds out how it got there. Baked goodies win friends and get people to talk, says Fluke, particularly at Swensen's own bakery and coffee shop in Lake Eden, Minnesota. There she hears local gossip and private conversations as she refills coffee cups. Food is also a facilitator, says Fluke, where Swensen uses her cookies and desserts to soothe pain and calm nervous people, thus disarming them and prompting them to talk.

Fluke catered in college to make extra money, but the author traces her passion for baking back to childhood. Her grandmother was an assistant pastry girl for a wealthy family. "Gammie used to bake every winter morning to warm up the kitchen, and all it took was a whiff of vanilla, chocolate, or cinnamon to get me out of bed in plenty of time for school," recalls Fluke. "When I was old enough to reach the table, Gammie and Mom taught me how to bake. It was something we all did together and I'm sure that's why the kitchen is still my favorite room in the house."

Fluke wrote her first culinary mystery, the *Chocolate Chip Cookie Murder,* in 2001. Swensen returns home upon the death of her father and opens the Cookie Jar bakery. She becomes an amateur sleuth when she finds a dead delivery truck driver still holding a chocolate chip crunch cookie in his hand. A few of Fluke's other books are:

- *Strawberry Shortcake Murder.* Swensen judges a dessert bake-off. Someone finds one of the judges face down in Swensen's own strawberry shortcake.
- *Blueberry Muffin Murder.* The baker finds the dead body of a cookbook author and tracks down the killer.
- *Sugar Cookie Murder.* The baker compiles a cookbook of the locals' favorite recipes for the Christmas party at the community center. Swensen finds her mother's silver cake knife stuck in the chest of one of the guests, who is lying dead in the parking lot.

A CULINARY MYSTERY WRITER TELLS YOU HOW

I asked Joanne Fluke to pass on some simple ways to get ideas and writing going for your upcoming food-themed book. Her three-notebook idea, which follows, is particularly good. I've learned from experience that when I go back to notes I've taken at the scene or soon thereafter they're so much more detailed than if I wait. I always carry a little notebook around to jot down ideas as they come up.

Her advice about honing your skills is something you've read before in this book, but it can't be said enough. Here are her suggestions:

- Buy three notebooks. Use one to jot down all your favorite dishes, especially if you're going out to dinner and trying something new. Write down the name and your impressions. You may think you'll remember the great meal you had at that little French bistro, but you won't. Use the second notebook to take notes while you read everything you can get your hands on in the genre you've chosen. Write down what the authors do that you like. Use the third notebook to note what the authors do that you *don't* like.
- Start writing. Try the techniques from the second notebook

to see if they work for you. Avoid the things in the third notebook like the plague.

�406 Hone your skills. Take a writing class or join a critique
group if you think it'll help you. Get a copy of the *Writer's
Market* and study it for practical advice and information.

�406 When thinking about your story, jot down little notes
about the characters. When the story and characters are
clear in your mind, outline it so that you won't forget.

�406 Begin writing your book. If that first paragraph eludes
you, try writing the last chapter first. Then, when you
write the first chapter, you'll know where you're going.

�406 Write every day. Work hard. Be optimistic, but don't give
up your day job.

Two other writers who write culinary capers are Mary Daheim
and Joanna Carl. Daheim crossed over from a career as a historical romance writer. Her Bed and Breakfast series includes *Just
Desserts,* where an innkeeper solves the mystery of a murdered
visitor. Other titles I love are *Nutty as a Fruitcake* and *Legs Benedict.* In *The Chocolate Frog Frame-Up,* part of the Chocolate
Chocoholic mystery series by Carl, small-town chocolatiers debut
their chocolate frog at a Fourth of July party. The first customer to
buy it dies and a chocolate clue leads to solving the murder.

Certainly, you can read these books for fun. While you do
so, notice how authors advance the plot, throw in plot twists,
and create suspense and tension. Without suspense, there's not
much of a mystery at the end, when you reveal the culprit. You
need narrative drive, or the promise that something's going to
happen. These authors know how to build events and suspi-
cions to a crescendo. If you're interested in learning how to
write mysteries, see Useful Reference Books for Fiction Writers
on page 222.

I love how these writers don't take themselves so seriously. I
can't resist telling you about a few more ways writers create
funny titles and plots:

- In *On What Grounds,* by Cleo Coyle, the manager of a historic coffeehouse arrives to find her assistant manager dead. In *Through the Grinder,* business is booming but customers seem to be dying after drinking her house coffee blend.
- In *Too Many Crooks Spoil the Broth,* by Tamar Myers, a mean-spirited innkeeper solves the murder of a dead guest. *Eat, Drink and Be Wary: A Pennsylvania Dutch Mystery with Recipes,* and *Parsley, Sage, Rosemary and Crime* are two more titles I love.
- *Death by the Glass: A Sunny McCoskey Napa Valley Mystery,* by Nadia Gordon, investigates the seamy side of the restaurant and wine world. Wine professionals, cooks, and gourmet friends help a chef-owner of a Napa Valley restaurant solve a crime.
- In *A Catered Murder,* the best-selling author of vampire fiction drops dead at an affair the main character caters. Isis Crawford, a caterer and travel writer, wrote the book.

When your characters are caterers, bakers, innkeepers, restaurant critics, chefs, and candy makers, you can live vicariously by fictionalizing their lives. Take a moment to imagine one of these characters, the hero of your book, coming upon a dead body. In your mind you've already constructed the scene, imagined your hero physically, and identified the body. These details could be the start of your own mystery book. Write down the scene while it's still fresh.

USEFUL REFERENCE BOOKS FOR FICTION WRITERS

This chapter offers just a taste of fiction writing. For more, try these books:

- *Stein on Writing: A Master Editor of Some of the Most*

Successful Writers of Our Century Shares His Craft Techniques and Strategies, by Sol Stein. Immediate, useful advice on how to fix flawed writing, improve good writing, and create excellent writing.

- *How to Write a Damn Good Novel: A Step-by-Step No Nonsense Guide to Dramatic Storytelling,* by James Frey. Detailed descriptions of common pitfalls and how to avoid them.
- *Write Away: One Novelist's Approach to Fiction and the Writing Life,* by Elizabeth George. A personal approach to mastering the tools and techniques necessary to writing the novel.
- *Description,* by Monica Wood. Includes advice on how to use description to awaken readers' senses. Part of the Elements of Fiction series.

If you're interested in mysteries, you'll find around a dozen books on how to write them, many written by successful mystery writers. A few I recommend are:

- *How to Write a Mystery,* by Larry Beinhart. Advice on narrative drive, the promise that something will happen. Not step-by-step, but useful advice on how to approach plot, character development, and other writing techniques.
- *How to Write Killer Fiction: The Funhouse of Mystery & the Roller Coaster of Success,* by Carolyn Wheat. Lots of useful tips and insights on such things as the difference between mystery and suspense and how to plant clues.

Main Characters in the Food Business

Lots of novels have main characters in the food business as well. If you are not a food professional, why not write about the business?

Cookbook author and novelist Bharti Kirchner was traveling in Japan and stayed in a hotel that had a bakery nearby. When she visited the bakery she was surprised to find it full of beautiful French pastries. She kept turning the scene over in her mind, she says, picturing a Japanese man with a passion for French baking. Kirchner wrote *Pastries: A Novel of Desserts and Discoveries,* about a bakery owner who struggles when a competitor opens a bakery down the street. For research, she read industry trade magazines to learn about running a business, interviewed several bakers, and hung out in their kitchens. Over time, she understood the life, character, challenges, and work of a baker, and the atmosphere of a bakery.

Good Grief, by Lolly Winston, has a different baking theme. A woman quits her job and discovers her talent as a baker. She opens her own bakery, and the town paper describes her porcini and Brie cheesecake as "sure to be a hit." Winston's book is also a laugh-out-loud funny and poignant story about surviving the loss of a spouse.

Here are more sample characters and plots based on the food business, to give you ideas for your own story:

Food writer: The best-selling *Heartburn,* by Nora Ephron, tells the story of a food writer whose husband cheats on her. Ephron makes a convincing case of how her heroine got into food writing, starting out as a journalist (how Ephron got started in real life), then writing a food column for a newspaper. Recipes are included.

In *Cooking for Love,* by Sharon Boorstin, a Beverly Hills cookbook author dreams about food and the man who got away. She finds him on Google twenty-five years later, leading to a culinary adventure halfway around the world with her girlfriend.

Restaurant owner, chef, waiter, or reviewer: If you've ever worked in a restaurant, owned one, or have been a reviewer, you must have lots of material for a good yarn. If you haven't and would love to imagine this lifestyle, consider these plotlines:

- *Crawfish Dreams: A Novel,* by Nancy Rawles. A Creole who moved her family from Louisiana to South Central Los Angeles opens Camille's Creole Kitchen and recruits her family to help her get the restaurant on its feet.
- *Eating Crow,* by Jay Rayner. A London restaurant critic attempts to redeem himself after a chef commits suicide because of a bad review.
- *Liquor: A Novel,* by Poppy Z. Brite. A New Orleans alcohol-themed restaurant's bumbling owners close the place down. The author's husband was a chef at Commander's Palace.
- *Love and Meatballs.* A daughter works in a family restaurant and becomes torn between two men. Author Susan Volland is a classically trained chef who had written freelance articles and recipes for magazines and cookbooks.
- *How I Gave My Heart to the Restaurant Business: A Novel,* by Karen Hubert Allison. A woman and her boyfriend open a successful restaurant in Manhattan and give up their outside lives.
- *The Food of Love,* by Anthony Capella. Based on Edmond Rostand's *Cyrano de Bergerac,* but set in Rome, an Italian Casanova falls in love with an American art student and tells her he's a chef. He can't cook, but his less attractive friend can, so he uses his friend's skills for a culinary seduction.
- *High Bonnet: A Novel of Epicurean Adventures,* by Idwal Jones. Written in 1945, this book reveals a restaurant world in Paris entirely devoted to food. Anthony Bourdain called it "porn for cooks."

Chocolate shop or sweetshop owner: In *Chocolat,* by Joanne Harris, a woman opens a chocolate shop in a rustic French village and angers the church by appealing to pleasure-starved parishioners. You can taste the chocolates in your mouth as you read.

Cheesemaker: In *The Mammoth Cheese,* by Sheri Holman, an artisan cheese maker and his daughter go on a historic journey to re-create a huge Cheshire cheese once given to Jefferson, presenting it to the president.

Television producer: My Year of Meats, by Ruth L. Ozeki, features a Japanese-American documentary filmmaker invited to work on a Japanese television show meant to encourage beef consumption. She becomes increasingly aware of the beef industry's practice of using synthetic estrogens on cattle and plans to sabotage the program.

Food and sex: Some novels focus on the dual pleasures of food and sex, filling the senses to near overflowing. Why do food and sex go together so well? "Food is our most public sensual pleasure," explains Richmond. "It's second only to sex in terms of sensuality, and since you can't really do sex in public, reading about it fulfills a basic need."

Perhaps the best-known book in this category is *Like Water for Chocolate: A Novel in Monthly Installments with Recipes, Romances, and Home Remedies,* by Laura Esquivel. The daughter of a rancher falls in love and uses magical realism to pour her emotions into her cooking. Each chapter opens with a recipe. Another example is *In La Cucina: A Novel of Rapture,* by Lily Prior, which tells the story of a girl growing up on a Sicilian farm who spends most of her time in the kitchen. She meets an Englishman in Palermo, and together, they explore their culinary and sexual passions.

What about Recipes?

Some culinary fiction authors swear by including recipes in their works. Others put them in grudgingly, and some don't do it at all.

"If I didn't include recipes, my house would get egged, people would call to yell at me on the phone, and I'd receive a slew of angry e-mails and letters," says Fluke. Twice now, she's written in passing about a cookie and a cake without including their recipes. She mentioned Lisa's White Chocolate Supreme Cookies in the *Chocolate Chip Cookie Murder*. "I got so many letters and e-mail messages I had to create a recipe and put it in *Blueberry Muffin Murder*," says Fluke. "I also got in trouble when I wrote about Rose's Famous Coconut Cake in *Lemon Meringue Pie Murder*. I didn't have a recipe for that either, but hundreds of people asked for it in e-mails so I had to come up with one and put it in *Sugar Cookie Murder*."

Other fiction writers dislike the switch from writing narrative to writing the instructions that recipes require. "Recipes destroy the flow of the story," says Kirchner. "They take away from the literary quality of the novel." She prefers to write about cooking in more general terms, such as how someone baked a cake. Richman's restaurant-based mysteries include a recipe at the back of each book. In the narrative, she makes a point of writing about dishes in enough detail that they're workable; some chef-readers have tried them out and told her about their efforts. Ephron uses a similar technique in *Heartburn,* but with more specific measurements and instruction, so it reads more like a recipe. Twenty recipes appear in the book, inserted conversationally as part of the story. It's an effective way to keep the narration going, but the style makes these recipes harder to read than those in a more traditional structure.

As you can see, there's no one right way to add recipes. I prefer to see them at the end of each chapter, in traditional recipe format, with an index by title in the back of the book so readers can look them up alphabetically.

Food in Classic Literature

I'm not the type who thinks you shouldn't read while writing or you might write in the style of the author you're reading. I don't know how you can become a good writer without reading great writing. Earlier I provided examples to show how classic writers inserted descriptions of food or meals to move a story along or to depict emotion. Once you start looking at classic literature, you'll find useful examples everywhere.

Marcel Proust's wistful passage about a madeleine in *Swann's Way* introduces the relationship between food and memory: "But when from a long-distant past nothing subsists, after the people are dead, after the things are broken and scattered, taste and smell alone, more fragile but more enduring, more unsubstantial, more persistent, more faithful, remain poised a long time, like souls, remembering, waiting, hoping, amid the ruins of all the rest; and bear unflinchingly, in the tiny and almost impalpable drop of their essence, the vast structure of recollection."

Henry Fielding's witty eighteenth-century *The History of Tom Jones, A Foundling* has a narrator who says literature is like a meal, in which the paying customer expects to be entertained and satisfied.

F. Scott Fitzgerald's *The Great Gatsby* details summer parties out on the famous lawn: "On buffet tables, garnished with glistening hors-d'oeuvre, spiced baked hams crowded against salads of harlequin designs and pastry pigs and turkeys bewitched to a dark gold."

In Edith Wharton's *The Age of Innocence,* a man engaged to a society girl longs for a life of passion with someone else, set against a New York backdrop of grand dinners and parties. And *Down and Out in Paris and London,* by George Orwell, includes his experiences in the unpleasant hotel and restaurant world in which he worked in the 1930s. Even *Moby Dick,* by Herman Melville, describes foods of the times as a way to show authenticity and detail. Here's a picture of seafood chowder: "It was made of small juicy clams, scarcely bigger than hazelnuts, mixed with pounded ship biscuits, and salted port cut up into little flakes; the whole enriched with butter, and plentifully seasoned with pepper and salt."

For a taste of many writers and their love of food, read *Feast of Words: For Lovers of Food and Fiction,* by Anna Shapiro. She pairs inventive menus and recipes with passages of fiction by authors such as Dickens, Lessing, and Hardy. Her book is instructive because it is organized by themes found in classic novels, such as "Starved Love," "Penitential Meals," and "Eating the Social Index."

Children's Books

If you've always wanted to write children's books, why not combine your passions and write about food? Food in children's literature can serve several purposes, no matter what your intention. Primarily, of course, it tells a good story, just like adult fiction. *Stone Soup* (there are various versions by multiple authors) tells an old French tale of three hungry soldiers who convince inhabitants of a village to make them a soup that starts with boiled rocks. In *Blueberries for Sal,* by Robert McCloskey, two sets of mother and child, one a momma bear and cub, go on a hunt for blueberries and end up intermixed. In Maurice Sendak's *In the Night Kitchen,* a boy stumbles into a night kitchen where bakers prepare cakes for the morning.

Food is not only a source of entertainment for kids, but it's also an educational and experiential tool. Here are some other ways it can be employed in children's fiction:

It can make eating look enticing: *Eating the Alphabet,* by Lois Ehlert, shows fruits and vegetables so enticing that even finicky kids will want to eat them. *The Seven Silly Eaters,* by Mary Ann Hoberman, comprises rhymes about how a mother accommodates picky children who will only eat certain foods such as applesauce or eggs.

Aids you can't use in adult novels can help younger readers indulge their senses. *The Wiggles: Yummy, Yummy Fruit Salad,* published by Grossett and Dunlap, has fourteen scratch-and-sniff stickers in flavors like apple, banana, watermelon, and grape.

It can introduce foreign foods: Some authors build songlike lyrics around food. Amy Wilson Sanger's *World Snacks* series explains sushi, dim sum, Mexican food, Jewish "nosh," and soul food. Here's a line from *Soul Food:* "When I wake up I smell biscuits/and gravy for our grits./ I say thanks for smoky ham/cut into little itty bits."

It helps children understand other cultures. In *Henner's Lydia,* by Marguerite De Angeli, readers see how a Pennsylvania Dutch community makes cider in the backyard and what kinds of food the community members eat, such as apple butter and half-moon pies. Artist and poet Grace Lin's *Dim Sum for Everyone* describes the pleasures of a Chinese dining tradition.

Food can be a learning tool: In *Chicken Soup with Rice: A Book of Months,* by Maurice Sendak, children learn activities they can do during different months and seasons while sipping this soup. In January they eat it while slipping and sliding on the ice, while in July they find a turtle selling it at the bottom of the ocean.

Whether you write a mystery about a cook, a novel with food-based theme, or a children's book, all the fiction writers I've interviewed share similar advice. They suggest joining a critique group with regular meetings and producing work to share with the other members. They recommend reading books on how to write novels, and reading novels to understand how authors use food to craft scenes, plot, and character. They suggest you take classes. And most of all, if you want to be a writer: Writers write. Do it every day.

Writing Exercises

1. People in your book or short story must seem believable to your readers. Build up characteristics by writing a sketch. Go to a restaurant with a pad of paper and take notes about your waiter. Describe the person visually, then get inside his head and imagine his life in the workplace and at home. Does he work fourteen-hour days,

ending with drinks at bars at three in the morning? Does he spend tips on heavy-metal music? Describe his home, how he cooks, what he likes to eat, and whether he is a food snob.

2. Write a dramatic dialogue between you and the waiter, based on the food. This is a next step in developing the waiter's character, where you imagine a conversation based on your personality and what you know about him. Write several lines of dialogue suggesting the beginning of a relationship that may continue later in your story. You can choose to create conflict and tension (you hated the food; he was snippy), but not all drama is negative. In the previous example, perhaps he stalks you later for revenge. If it's positive, maybe he's a flirt and you build suspense that the two of you will meet elsewhere.

3. Choose a food, then write a story that is set in a particular historical period. If you chose baked beans, for example, you could write about cowboys hunched over a fire, camped out at night while driving a herd of cattle. Next, write a dialogue between two people who are consuming your chosen food. Incorporate action related to the food in the scene, such as how one cowboy slurps the beans from a tin cup, or how another tears bread and leaves crumbs in his mustache. Try writing three paragraphs.

10

How to Get Your Book Published

Writing a nonfiction book will make you better known, but there's a problem: publishers prefer authors who are already known, since it's less risky for them. Lots of people rush to get their book proposals out the door before they have the credentials to interest a publisher. When I suggest they write a few articles, teach a class, or speak on the subject, they resist. "I just want to write the book proposal," they say.

Yes, but without the necessary credentials, a finished book proposal won't do you any good. An agent or publisher will want to see your "platform," industry-speak for your ability to bring in a base of readers before the book is even out there. A newspaper or magazine columnist, a cooking teacher who does fifty classes per year, a television show host, a well-known restaurateur, chef, or caterer, or a consultant who speaks all over the country are examples of people with platforms. Potential purchasers of their books know them, and they can get in front of their readers with regularity.

Working on your reputation before you write your book will dramatically increase your chances of success. And here's a great side effect: once you establish your credentials, your self-confidence goes way up, and you'll write a stronger and more convincing book proposal.

The best and easiest way to beef up your credibility is to get published. Stories with your byline show that someone else thought your writing was good enough to publish and make you more desirable. If you don't believe me, consider this quote from Rux Martin, executive editor of Houghton Mifflin, who has edited cookbooks by *Gourmet* magazine and Jacques Pépin. "It would be virtually impossible for someone to have a proposal that would excite me and be worthy of consideration who had never written for publication."

Write on the subject of your book as a way to test the idea and confirm its value. It also shows publishers that readers are interested in the subject. A restaurant review and a recipe for grilled salmon are better than nothing but won't get you very far if you want to write a cookbook on birthday party cupcakes. If you have not begun writing for publication, read chapters 2 and 4 on increasing your credentials through freelance writing.

Do you need prior publication if you are writing a novel or are planning to self-publish your book? As a novelist, you will be more attractive if you get short stories published first, but this may not be essential. To approach agents and publishers with fiction, you don't need a proposal. You write the whole book first and send agents or editors a cover letter with a few sample chapters. If you plan to self-publish and sell your book, readers may be more likely to buy your book if you are published first, although it's not essential. The exception is if your book is only for yourself or family members, or you are compiling a community book or recipes to raise money. If so, you might want to skip ahead to the self-publishing section on page 257.

But if you are hoping to have a nonfiction book traditionally published and you've already written the whole thing, I'm sure you're not happy that I'm telling you to do more work. You'd rather submit your book to a publisher; maybe not even bother with an agent. Unfortunately, that's not much of a strategy, and it rarely works. Editors hardly ever accept manuscripts as a first step to working with an author. Many big publishing companies don't accept unsolicited manuscripts at all, let alone read them. In fact, the rejection rate just for book proposals from both agents and publishers is the same, around 90 to 95 percent. Why not get into the 5 to 10 percent that succeeds?

On first contact, agents and editors will want to know who you are, how you came up with your idea, how you will promote your book, who you know in the media, whether you have a built-in audience, and if you've ever been published. If you send your finished book with a cover letter that says, "Please publish this," you're not answering any of these questions. You're not selling yourself. Selling is a big part of the game, as is understanding where your book fits into the landscape and having something new and fresh to say.

The document that answers editors' and agents' questions is called a book proposal. Not only does it discuss your book, it sells you as the author. This chapter shows you how to write a killer proposal. You'll also learn whether you need an agent, how to find one, and how to query prospective agents. The section on contracts explains what happens when a publisher wants to buy your book. Finally, you'll find a section on self-publishing, which is of increasing interest to more and more of my students and clients.

The Landscape

Around the world, more than 24,000 food and wine titles are published each year, according to Edoard Cointreau, founder of the Gourmand World Cookbook Awards. In the U.S., according to Ipsos-NPD, a market research firm that tracks cookbooks, the biggest-selling cookbook to date has been *In the Kitchen with Rosie: Oprah's Favorite Recipes,* by her personal chef, Rosie Daley. It has sold 5.4 million.

While publishers keep churning out cookbooks, the market

is getting tougher, says agent Jane Dystel, head of Dystel and Goderich Literary Management. There are too many cookbooks, and some publishers have cut back or cut out publishing them, she says. But on the other hand, "There are always going to be new cooks and new consumers who want to do fresh things." And perhaps the rise of non-cookbook-based food books shows there are lots of opportunities outside the cookbook world.

The competition will be intense. "We get around 500 proposals a year and publish twenty books, and we're a big cookbook publisher. Probably five are our idea to begin with, so only fifteen cookbooks come from outside," explains Bill LeBlond, editorial Director of Cookbooks for Chronicle Books. By "our idea" he means that an editor suggested a book idea to a previously published author, perhaps as her next book. Or the editor has invited someone, such as a chef, to write a book.

Even though it's a tough market, you can succeed. You have to know what agents and editors want, which can be elusive. "It really boils down from personal taste," explains agent Doe Coover, who represents such authors as Jacques Pépin, *Gourmet* magazine, and Marion Cunningham. "Some decisions stem from what I think is salable. I have to feel passionate about it. I have to know I'm not going to be daunted if the first two publishers turn it down, or the first six. I have to know I'm in it for the long haul." Coover has represented first-time authors as well as the stars, but obviously she's picky. If you follow the advice in this chapter, you'll have a much better shot at getting an agent at her level or a good editor and publisher.

The Proposal: Once you have a solid book idea, it's time to write the book proposal. A book proposal is a document you send to agents and editors. It introduces you and tells them why they should be interested in both you and your book. It includes your bio, a table of contents for the book, sample recipes if you're writing a cookbook, and samples of your writing. It explains the target market, the potential competition, and how your book differs from it, and how you will promote the book. Regardless of whether you want an agent or plan to submit directly to a publisher, you need a proposal. It's normal to spend at least six months writing it.

You might have heard that you can send a one-page query letter instead of a proposal. That's true, and it's a lot less work. But if agents or editors like it, they will say, "Yes, this sounds interesting. Please send the book proposal." Now what? You haven't written it. Six months or a year from now, when you finish the proposal, your cover letter will say, "Remember when I sent you that query and you liked the idea. . . ." Write the query letter after writing the proposal, so the proposal's ready to go if you get a green light.

Think of a book proposal as a sales pitch that provides vital details about your idea and shows your voice and writing style. It might be as long as fifty pages double-spaced. Remember that you're writing it to agents and editors, not readers, so keep your audience in mind. Think about what an editor and agent want to know. The only sections you write directly to readers are the writing samples and recipes, because they are samples of what will appear in your book. A book proposal must answer these questions: Why you, why now, and who cares? Here are the main elements:

Title page: Create a cover page with the title of book, subtitle, and all of your contact information.

Table of contents for the proposal: If your proposal is long, it needs a table of contents listing sections by page number.

Summary or concept: Agents and editors are busy. Lorena Jones, publisher of Ten Speed Press, says she spends about 25 percent of her time acquiring manuscripts, 35 percent editing, and the rest managing her staff. She's responsible for about 120 books per year, including those by Charlie Trotter and Molly Katzen. A summary gives someone like Jones an immediate understanding of the book. Write two dynamite paragraphs that sum up the book, the market, and you. Here's the summary I wrote for my proposal for *Will Write for Food:*

No current book focuses solely on food writing as a career. How can this be? The food industry is booming, with 21 million Americans in 2003 who consider themselves food enthusiasts, according to Mediamark, a multimedia audience research company. Many of these enthusiasts dream of turning their passion into a writing career. Where do they go to learn? *Will Write for Food* targets food lovers who want to express themselves, guiding them from their earliest creative impulses to building up a portfolio to dealing with their taxes (answering everyone's favorite question, "Can I write off all my meals out now?").

Interviews with successful writers like Jeffrey Steingarten, Colman Andrews, Mimi Sheraton, and William Grimes, and well-known food editors and agents, fill out a portrait of the life of a food writer, giving readers the background they need to get started and follow through. The book covers the subject in comprehensive yet accessible chapters ranging from restaurant reviewing to cookbooks to memoir. Focused exercises at the end of chapters stimulate creativity and help organize thought, building practical skills. *Will Write for Food* will be the first and conclusive guidebook to the incredibly popular world of food writing, written by a veteran editor and writer.

You probably do not know enough to write the consummate summary right now. Write a draft summary and leave it as a placeholder. Go back when you've finished the proposal and punch it up. By then you'll have a stronger and more focused notion of what it should say.

Overview: This is the proposal's introduction. It tells the agent or editor what kind of book you plan to write and why. The overview is like a mini-proposal that sums up all the points you will make. Even though it comes first, write it at the end, because it's hard to sum up the proposal and the book idea at first. Writing the proposal forces you to think about the book in more detail than you have before. Often you're still fleshing out and refining the book as you write. The overview:

- must engage the agent or editor immediately, in the first few sentences. They may stop by the bottom of the page if you have not dazzled them or made them curious or excited
- establishes your idea as solid and salable
- describes the book's main points, scope and breadth, material to be covered, your writing style, and the book's special features
- tells how readers will benefit from reading your book
- makes a case for why the market needs a book on this subject now
- explains how your book is different or unique
- explains why you are qualified to write this book
- tells the reader the size of the manuscript or how many recipes it contains, and how long it will take you to complete it.

To begin your overview, pull readers in. Former cookbook agent Martha Casselman has said she likes an overview that reads like a novel or news story, pulling readers along, involving and exciting them, creating sensual images in their heads. An anecdote might work at the beginning—even statistics, if they grab attention.

Once you hook your readers, summarize the elements listed above in a few compelling paragraphs. Help them visualize your project by outlining the material you will cover, the main points, the philosophy behind the book, its unique conception, and its organization. Explain what you will include, such as the number and types of recipes, special sections, or sidebars. Be as specific as possible without resorting to a list of chapters (that comes later). If appropriate, use anecdotes or name a few dishes and describe them, using all the senses. Think of this section as the book jacket copy. If you're not sure how to word it, read a dozen or so jackets of books you have at home.

Describe your voice. Will it be friendly, knowledgeable, or witty? Will you attempt to break down complex concepts? If you've described your book as humorous, do you know how to use humor? It's not enough to say, "The book will be funny." Demonstrate humor within the proposal. Tell how the book benefits your readers, what's in it for them. Close the overview with a strong statement that reinforces your most important point.

Do not insist that the book must look a certain way. The publisher determines the design. If you think photos or illustrations are critical to your book's success, explain why. A guidebook on identifying oysters, for example, would be harder to use without visual images. If you plan to provide your own artwork, such as illustrations, historical photographs, or old letters, say so here. For more on the visual aspects, see page 160 in chapter 6.

Target audience and market: Agents and publishers want to know if a definable market exists for your book. This is part of what constitutes your platform. The target audience identifies who will buy the book and why.

Even though you'd like it to be so, your book is not for everyone. Saying so implies you have not thought through who will buy it. Look for definable populations. Quantify the groups by finding statistics or other identifying information. Identify your readers in as many ways as possible, such as income level, gender, or frequency of visits to fine restaurants.

It's okay to identify more than one kind of reader, as long as you build a solid case for each. When Andrew F. Smith began compiling the audience for his book *The Tomato in America: Early History, Culture, and Cookery,* he found tomato-lover societies, huge tomato festivals with 25,000 attendees, and tomato-growing contests attended by tomato lovers. When he wrote *Pure Ketchup: A History of America's National Condiment, With Recipes,* Heinz bought 5,000 copies. For *Peanuts: The Illustrious History of the Goober Pea,* he found a peanut-lovers' association with 41,000 members.

Say whether you have a built-in strategy to reach potential readers, such as targeting customers at your restaurant or students in your cooking classes, or creating a newsletter or Web site dedicated to potential readers. Describe any strong contacts or connections in the culinary field or the media who might help promote your book.

Establish that your topic interests the media. Perhaps magazines or television shows have covered the subject recently. Knowing your reader base will help you choose which publications, Web sites, televisions shows, and other media might have articles or content that applies.

Identifying your target audience will make your book more focused. The more you know about your readers, the more you know what they desire, what they need to know, or what will benefit them. When you write your sample chapters or recipes, you will be able to visualize your target readers sitting across the desk from you. When you write directly to them, you make a connection that comes through in your book.

Promotion plan: Unfortunately, you can't count on publishers to promote your book very much. Often they have paid large advances to authors whose books are coming out the same time as yours, and those books get the bulk of the marketing money budget. Publishers want to know how *you* will help them sell the book. That means getting in front of your target audience and promoting it. While this section of your proposal will be based on a theoretical plan, it must be realistic. If you say you plan to appear on *Oprah* and get your own television show, unless you can state how you plan to do it or demonstrate that you have made inroads, agents and editors probably won't believe you.

The best ways to promote your book may be on a television show, in a cooking class, in a restaurant, or at a speaking event. If you have a cooking class coming up, or a cooking school plans to feature you, mention it here. If none of these other ways apply to you, figure out how to hold a class on the topic of your book and where to speak on it. Do you have a Web site where you can promote the book? Can you write articles for publications on the subject of the book? If so, which ones? Will you do demonstrations at department stores? Will you try to get interviewed on radio stations, and if so, for which shows? Make contacts and state them in your proposal.

You might benefit if a significant figure in the food world or media writes an endorsement—called a blurb—on the back cover or a foreword to the book. If so, it's best to ask that person to commit now, so you can say so in this section. You may be nervous about sending a letter asking for a commitment, but often people are honored.

Describe outlets other than bookstores, mega-stores, and culinary stores that might sell your book, such as wineries, home-design stores, or specialty stores for products such as cheeses and chocolate. If there are events where you could promote your book, list them, and contact organizers in advance to get actual commitments.

About the author: Here's where the agent or editor gets to know you. Don't write your life story or how you've always wanted to write this book. Create a bio highlighting the experiences most related to your book. Many people I've worked with say they had no idea their bio could be so long until they thought it through. When you've never compiled your accomplishments in one place, it can be very satisfying to do so.

Look deeply into your past. Publicity, experience, jobs, volunteer work, research, awards, travel, and special skills might qualify. Maybe you've had a life experience that provided a valuable lesson and material for your book. Brainstorm lots of ideas, but pare them down to the ones that apply most. Even if you are proud of all the quilts you've made and belong to a quilting group, leave this information out unless it somehow relates to your topic.

Join organizations and take classes to punch up your bio. If you become an officer of one of these associations, your bio will look even stronger. See if you can speak or do a demonstration on the topic of your book.

If you already have a press kit that includes your biography, skip this section and include the press kit with the proposal.

Analysis of the competition: Choose three to five books that either you or your target readers would find competitive because of the subject or approach. A book with a similar title and completely different content may still be a competitor if it would appear next to yours on the bookshelf. List all information about each book, including title, author, price, whether it's a hardcover or paperback, and publication date. In a paragraph or two, describe each book's contents briefly and compare it to yours. End by stating how your book will be better and different. Do not be disrespectful. You never know whether the recipient of your proposal sold that book, published it, or is best friends with the author.

Table of contents: There are two. The first is a short list of chapter titles that fits on one page so agents and editors can grasp the book's concept, content, and structure. On the next page, start a chapter-by-chapter outline that describes the book in more detail, from introduction to index. Write up to a one-page description of each chapter, describing what it will cover, its purpose, and how it benefits the reader. Follow with a list of all recipes. Include sidebar names, if known. Other parts of the book to list might include a glossary, pantry list, resources list and buying guide, and bibliography.

Ten to twelve chapters are common. The structure usually starts with the simplest elements and flows to the more advanced aspects. Make sure the chapters flow in some logical way. For more details on cookbook organization see page 158.

Sample recipes and/or sample chapter: This section shows that you not only have a well-thought-out understanding of your book, but you can deliver. It must be substantial, and it must be your best writing. If your book is primarily recipe-based, submit up to one dozen recipes, each on a separate page. Recipes must be foolproof and flawless, showcasing the range of your skills and knowledge. You must have tested every recipe before submitting it, because agents and editors can tell whether recipes work just by reading them, and they might even test them. Each recipe should be complete. If it includes tip boxes or a sidebar, include them with the recipe. If your book is recipe based but contains lots of narrative writing, submit a few chapter openings or other text as examples.

If your book is not a cookbook, submit at least one complete chapter. Do not submit the introduction, because much of its content is already covered in your overview. Review your table of contents and choose a meaty chapter in the middle somewhere, one that is also not too long, perhaps 6,000 words at most.

Supporting materials: At the back of the proposal, include any freestanding information that is likely to promote your book idea. Most important are recent articles you've written on the subject. If you don't have any, include copies of your published work. Choose pieces that appeared in prestigious publications, show the variety of your work (if appropriate), and are samples of your best writing. If you have not been published in print, perhaps you have Web copy to include. Include any stories written about you, and a video clip if you appeared on television. Photos are optional. Start the section with a list of the supporting materials in the order readers will see them.

Format: Double-space your proposal with 1- to 1.5-inch margins all around. Include page numbers, beginning with the table of contents, with either the title of the book or your name. Do not make the proposal hard to read by using all caps, which looks like shouting. Do not use colors or other gimmicks that detract from the substance of your text. Bold-face and italics are acceptable for headings. This is not a design project. Clean text in one font and size lets readers see the quality of your writing. Bulleted lists are easy on the eyes. Do not print on both sides of a page. Do not bind the proposal in any way. You may staple a set of supporting materials together if you have many.

Cover letter: Whether you're writing fiction or nonfiction, introduce your proposal or sample fiction chapters with a short cover letter written specifically to your target editor or agent. Spell the person's name correctly. Get the title right. These sound like small details, but agents and editors always complain about them when they're not done right.

Overall: No typos, punctuation, or grammatical errors. I cannot overstate the importance of proofing, proofing, and proofing again. You are selling yourself. Copy with errors reduces your credibility, even if there are just a few typos. Print out your proposal and read it several times. Have other people read it for mistakes you did not catch. You may have to do this a half-dozen times. It's worth it.

HELPFUL BOOKS ON GETTING PUBLISHED

While there's only so much I can say in one chapter, these books are devoted entirely to getting published. I recommend them highly and bring most of them to classes when I teach food writing.

- *How to Write a Book Proposal,* by Michael Larsen. A clear, thorough, nuts-and-bolts guide from an agent dedicated to helping writers succeed.
- *The Fast Track Course on How to Write a Non-Fiction*

Book Proposal, by Stephen Blake Mettee. A short but well-focused book from a seasoned editor. It includes a sample proposal, sample contract, and glossary.

➤ *Nonfiction Book Proposals Anyone Can Write: How to Get a Contract and Advance Before Writing Your Book,* by Elizabeth Lyon. A solid, detailed book with a proposal template and models for success.

➤ *Thinking Like Your Editor: How to Write Great Serious Non-fiction and Get it Published,* by Susan Rabiner and Alfred Fortunato. An agent and her husband, a freelance editor and writer, offer useful advice on how books succeed and why.

➤ *The Shortest Distance Between You and a Published Book: 20 Steps to Success,* by Susan Page. Advice and strategies all the way from goals for the book to getting a contract to writing it to dealing with doubt and procrastination.

➤ *Literary Agents: What They Do, How They Do It, and How to Find and Work with the Right One for You,* by Michael Larsen. How to launch your career as a writer, with an unexpected plus: it helps deal with rejection.

➤ *Be Your Own Literary Agent: The Ultimate Insider's Guide to Getting Published,* by Martin P. Levin. If you want to do it on your own, try this book.

Do You Need an Agent?

If you want to be published, rather than self-published, you probably need an agent. The exception is if you plan to pursue small publishers, such as university presses and regional presses. Your chances of being published are exponentially better with a good agent. If you don't believe me, look at the *Writer's Market,* which lists information on book publishers every year. Each listing gives the percentage of books a publisher accepts from agents versus authors. You'll notice that:

- the number of books publishers accept from agents (versus unrepresented authors) is usually higher, frequently much higher.
- typically, the larger the publisher, the more books it publishes from agents. At HarperCollins, only 5 percent of its books come directly from writers.
- the smaller the advance ($10,000 and under), the more writers the publisher accepts directly. Rutgers University Press accepts 70 percent of its books from authors without agents and offers a $1,000–$10,000 advance.

If you're thinking you just want to get published and you don't care about the advance or quality of the publisher, snap out of it. You will "live, sleep, and breathe that subject, 24/7, for two or more years, and it will take money away from your other jobs," says agent Carole Bidnick, who represents such authors as Peggy Knickerbocker and Fran Gage. For such hard work, you deserve a good deal.

Aim high with a good agent who will be your advocate and guide. Author Mark Bittman once wrote in a newsletter, "An agent will change your career. If your idea is a good one and you're capable of delivering on it, an agent can recognize that and convince an editor you're worth a gamble. Yes, you might be able to do it yourself, but the process will work better, faster, and more profitably with an agent. Most experienced authors agree that doing it yourself is a complete waste of time and money."

Harriet Bell, vice president and editorial director of William Morrow Cookbooks, says she'd hire an agent if she wanted to get published. "If I ever wrote a book—and I have no intention of doing so—I'd hire an agent even with twenty-five years in the business," she says. "An agent allows the author/editor relationship to be about the work, not the business or money, and an agent is there for contingency purposes. If anything goes wrong, authors need someone on their side to navigate the waters." She's talking about after you get the contract. Contrary to what people believe, agents do lots more than just get you in the door.

The agent's job: Agents understand the industry and can evaluate your book's chances. If they take you on as a client, they should review your proposal and give suggestions on how to improve it. You will sign a contract in which you agree that the agent receives a 15 to 20 percent commission of all money due you. You may also be charged for office expenses relevant to your proposal, such as phone calls and shipping. Agents will target the most appropriate publishers for your book and send out your proposal with a cover letter. Right there, you've got a huge advantage. Editors drown in proposals and query letters. Most take boxes of mail home at night to keep up. They pay attention to cover letters from agents. Rux Martin, executive editor at Houghton Mifflin, says 95 percent of the proposals she sees come from agents.

Lorena Jones, publisher of Ten Speed Press, describes a typical Ten Speed sorting process. An assistant sorts proposals into piles of A, B, and C. The A's are top priority and could come from "someone previously published, someone with name recognition or someone recommended by a friend of the house, such as an author, agent, or employee. Or anything that matches up with trend spotting, appears to be well written, or ideally, is original," she explains. "B might be modest in scope but has commercial appeal. It could be well written but not referred from an agent we know. C is interesting to look at but doesn't fit with what we need right now." Many publishers put unsolicited, unagented proposals into what's called the "slush pile." It's a derisive moniker for low-priority reading. That shows you how much editors rely on referrals, authors they've already published, and agents.

If you've managed to work with an agent who specializes in cookbooks and food-based books, you'll be in the A pile. Agent Coover explains, "We have a more intimate relationship with editors because editors, like agents, specialize. It's our job to know the editors' tastes, what they're looking for, and what's on their lists [which books they publish]."

Agents decide whether to send the proposal to just one editor or make multiple submissions. Sometimes they think a certain editor would love your book and call that one editor first. Or they might ship out the proposal to ten or twelve editors and wait for replies.

Some agents spend up to three years trying to sell a book, but it usually takes less time. If every appropriate editor turns it down, that's the end. If editors say they would buy your book if it were different, you and the agent will decide whether to change it. If an editor makes an offer, the agent evaluates it and negotiates it on your behalf. This is another advantage, as contracts are often ponderous documents with small type and obscure language. Agents know the terminology and which items to pursue. "An agent is your buffer, but also your advocate, always looking for more: more advance money, more public relations and marketing, more design input, more photographs, and so on. Your agent is also your reality check as to what's reasonable and possible," says agent Lisa Ekus.

What If You Still Don't Want an Agent?

Some publishers will read your query letter or proposal, regardless of whether you have an agent. "Editors read unsolicited material because some good stuff comes in that way. You may be surprised by a proposal with an unusual take on something. You can't take anything for granted," says Bill LeBlond, editorial director of cookbooks at Chronicle. San Francisco caterers and twins Sara Whiteford Corpening and Mary Corpening Barber came to him without an agent, with an idea for a smoothies book that sold 250,000 copies, he says.

Jones says 70 percent of Ten Speed Press's authors have no agent. Of those, about half have been published and may have had an agent in the past. "These people are more entrepreneurial, more DIY [do it yourself]," she explains. "On the East Coast, books come through agents, that's the normal protocol. We don't need that level of insulation. It's easier to negotiate the contract with an agent, that's the only holdup."

If you want to be published by a small publisher, a regional publisher, or a university press, you don't necessarily need an agent. Agents may not be interested in you anyway because the advances are much lower than from traditional publishers. Andrew F. Smith, a prolific author of food history books, says he's been successful by networking and getting to know editors at small publishers without the help of an agent. Another way in the door is to get a referral. Editors look harder at references from friends, writing instructors, and colleagues than at unsolicited submissions. Seek them out.

Before you send off your proposal, do your homework. Find out which publishers would be most likely to publish a book like yours by looking for similar books in the library or bookstore. Don't send a proposal on regional foods of Kentucky to Random House, for example. Find out how each editor likes to be approached by calling a junior person in the editorial department of that publishing house. Some want e-mail, some only want proposals, and some want mailed query letters. If an editor makes an offer on your book, hire an attorney who specializes in publishing to review the contract.

Most publishers have Web sites with submissions guidelines. Read them before submitting your query or proposal, and send your letter or query directly to the editor who receives cookbooks and food-related projects. Do not send a generic letter that says "Dear Editor."

Finding and Getting an Agent

Agents are elusive. Since they reject 95 percent of all book ideas, many limit their visibility. At the same time, they sincerely want to discover fresh talent. To contact them, avoid a phone call, unless you've been referred and know they want to have a conversation. If they don't know you, go through traditional channels by sending them queries and proposals.

You'll have lots of competition. Like editors, agents also drown in queries and proposals. Coover says she gets 100 to 125 proposals per month. Jane Dystel, who represents Lydia Bastianich and Bobby Flay, says she sees around 40 per month, with food-based books representing only 10 percent of the books she represents. Like editors, agents want to be contacted a certain way. Some like e-mail, some want regular mail; some want just the query, some want the whole proposal. Call the office or look at their Web sites to find out how and what to submit before doing so.

All agents say they want new writers and new voices, but most don't take on writers who will attract low advances. Lisa Ekus is different. When she started her agenting business, Ekus dedicated half of her list to first-time writers. "I felt it was critical to give new voices a platform," she says. "Publishers are more resistant to an unknown first-time writer. I've sold about 80 percent. Almost all are working on a second and sometimes a third book. I want to nurture new writers along through many book projects." Ekus also has businesses that teach media training and offer public relations services to writers.

To find agents, try these tactics:

Look in the acknowledgments section of a book: When authors thank their agents, they do so in the acknowledgments section.

Join the International Association of Culinary Professionals: If you are a member of the food industry, a cooking teacher, restaurateur, or a published food writer, membership entitles you to go to the annual conference that agents attend and to receive the directory, which contains contact listings for agents who specialize in food-based books.

Join other food-based associations: Agents might be members or attend events. Members might know agents and be willing to help you. Associations include:

- Slow Food: http://www.slowfood.com
- Women Chefs and Restaurateurs:
  http://www.womenchefs.org
- The American Institute of Wine & Food:
  http://www.aiwf.org
- COPIA, The American Center for Wine, Food & the
  Arts: http://www.copia.org
- The Research Chefs Association:
  http://www.researchchefs.org/
- The American Culinary Federation:
  http://www.acfchefs.org/
- Les Dames d'Escoffier: http://www.ldei.org

Go to writing conferences: Agents often speak at conferences, teach classes, lurk in the audience and sign up for short meetings that are a little like speed dating. Sometimes you can pay extra and have an agent evaluate a few pages of your proposal.

Take a writing class or join a writing group: The instructor might know an agent and refer you, or someone in the group might know an agent.

Someone you know, or a friend of a friend, must have written a book: That person might have an agent—ask.

Go to book signings: Agents might attend to support their clients.

Research online databases: At Publishers Marketplace, http://publishersmarketplace.com, look under agents who specialize in cookbooks. Literary Marketplace, http://www. literarymarketplace.com, lists agents in alphabetical order by name, with limited contact information. My search on the word "cookbooks" turned up five agents. This number is off by a long shot, but might be based on which keywords agents put in their listings.

When you find an agent who wants to represent you, make sure you have good chemistry and that you trust the agent. You want an agent who returns your calls and keeps you up to date, someone who is truly excited about your book.

Reasons for Rejection

When you've compiled your list of agents or editors, send out your proposals or queries all at once. Unless you have a connection, waiting for a response takes forever because agents and editors take weeks, often months, to answer. Be prepared for rejection. Agents and editors reject projects for several reasons, not necessarily because they don't like you or your book idea, such as when:

- ✦ An agent has already sold a similar book, or it conflicts with a current project in the pipeline at a publishing house.
- ✦ They find the material well written and well presented, but are not interested in the subject.
- ✦ They think the idea's too narrow and will attract too few readers.
- ✦ The subject's been done to death.
- ✦ The trend has already passed. (Most books at big houses take almost three years from first contact to publication, so trend-based books can be dangerous there. Smaller publishers often can turn around a book more quickly.)
- ✦ Your idea is too trendy or not substantive or interesting enough for a whole book. It might be best for a magazine article instead.
- ✦ They don't like your writing.

Most often, however, agents reject queries and proposals because the author has not done a professional job. "It's amazing how many people can't be bothered to do the simplest things when they submit proposals," says LeBlond. "If you're going to the trouble of submitting it, why not get it right? We get badly copied proposals that were tossed into one envelope, rejected, and then stuck into another envelope with a photocopied letter that says 'Dear editor.' They look shabby and worn." Ekus has had similar experiences. "Often I receive proposals that are incomplete, poorly researched, about a subject that's been done to death, or even illiterate."

Sometimes publishers think your book has the germ of an idea and may suggest how they'd like to see it. Lori Longbotham wanted to write an unillustrated cookbook of lemon recipes, both savory and sweet, says LeBlond. Chronicle recast it as a book on lemon desserts, with only sixty recipes and beautiful photography. *Luscious Lemon Desserts* is now in its tenth printing.

The Contract

Regardless of whether you go it alone or use an agent, you'll receive a contract once you and your editor agree on the sale. Contracts vary in size and complexity, but all cover the main issues you will negotiate:

The advance: An advance is a loan against royalties. You will not earn any further income until after book sales reach the amount of the advance. Typically, advances for first-time authors range from $5,000 to $25,000. If you have worked on and developed your platform, the amount could be higher. You do not have to repay the advance to the publisher if the book fails to sell.

The royalties: Let's say you are offered a $10,000 advance, with the cover price of the book estimated at $20.00. Typically, royalties are 10 to 15 percent of the price of a hardcover, and 7.5 percent of the price of a paperback. If the book has color photographs throughout, the advance will be lower. At 7.5 percent, your take is $1.50 per book. Once the publisher has sold

6,667 books, equal to $10,000, you will begin receiving royalties if more books sell. Some publishers, particularly very small houses, pay royalties on a percentage of net sales rather than on retail price.

Agents try for the biggest advance they can get because most books do not earn past their advance. Regardless of whether you use an agent, you may have to use the funds from your advance to pay for photography, illustrations, recipe ingredients, researchers, testers, and an index.

Timing: The time publishers give you to write your book varies. It could be nine months or three years. Usually they publish twice a year, in spring and fall, though some publishers have a winter season as well. The season they choose determines the deadline. (Publishers determine which books to produce in a particular season based on when they think the book will do best. For example, it makes more sense to publish a cookbook of soups and stews in the fall—when readers are looking for hearty comfort foods—than it does in the spring. And most gift books come out in the fall, in time for the holidays.)

The fine print: The publishing industry has its own private language of bonus clauses, subsidiary rights (the rights to use the material in abridged, adapted and condensed versions), options, and discounts you get for buying books. (To fully explain the various options and legalese would take pages, but since my expertise is in writing and not contracts, I suggest you refer to Helpful Books on Getting Published, on page 245, to learn more.) If you have an agent you still have the final say on whether to accept the offer. Once you agree, it takes two to three months to get a signed contract and the first advance check.

If you've been doing the math as you've been reading, you'll see that writing a book is not much of a moneymaking proposition. If you spend one year writing a book for a $15,000 advance, it's not exactly a living wage. Now that you know you're not going to make much money, what's another 15 percent of not much money anyway? Agents are worth it. They want you to succeed, they'll work hard to get the best deal, and they'll help you move forward with your next book.

Agents want you as a long-term investment, not a one-shot deal. "Advice, recommendations, inspiration and consolation are also necessary components of a strong author-agent relationship," says Ekus. "I think of myself as a combination pitch woman, negotiator, and mother—which includes nurturing and nagging."

The Publishing Experience

Congratulations. You have a contract and you've started writing your book. The editor who purchased your book may be your editor, but not necessarily. You may work with someone new. The new editor could leave and you'll get another editor. Agent Coover says one of her authors was assigned to a new editor who had rejected her book idea earlier at another publishing house!

It's your job to establish a relationship with your editor and to meet your deadlines. The editor is supposed to review your manuscript, edit it, and send it back for revision. Here, your editor looks at the big picture in what's called a developmental edit—whether material in one chapter would be better in another, whether a section lacks focus or you've left things out, or whether you've written too much. He or she may query you on anything that seems confusing, tangential, incorrect, or poorly phrased. Once you make the corrections and adjustments, your work goes to a copy editor, who will edit it to fit the style of the publishing house and for punctuation and grammar. The copy editor will also question whatever appears to be unclear. Meanwhile, the art department works on a book jacket. Page proofs will appear for further checking, and from there it's on to production and printing.

A print run of 5,000 to 10,000 books is considered typical, unless you're a big name. The number is based on pre-orders for the book. Publishers would rather print fewer books and reprint than keep thousands of books in their warehouse and pay storage charges. Most publishers depend on backlist books that continue selling long after publication. Some books stay in print decades after they were written, particularly if they don't include photos, which date the book.

Pros and Cons of Self-Publishing

Whether you choose self-publishing depends on your goal. If you're writing a cookbook or memoir for yourself or your family, and you have no intention of selling it, self-publishing is a great idea. It also depends what you mean by self-published. In the broadest sense, self-publishers are authors who pay the full cost of publishing their books. If you print your file out on 8½ x 11-inch paper, make twenty copies, and put each in a binder, that's self-published. If you want to produce a bound book, you have a few choices:

Print it yourself: You've got a big research project ahead. You will:

- ➡ hire a copy editor
- ➡ find a graphic designer to design the book and create the cover
- ➡ choose the size and paper stock
- ➡ decide on whether to include color, photographs, or illustrations
- ➡ evaluate bids from printers
- ➡ take receipt of your published books and store them

In short, writing the book is just the first step. You make decisions on all aspects of design and production.

If you're writing a cookbook, hire a custom publisher that specializes in them: If you don't want to print it yourself, these publishers print customized high-quality cookbooks for food companies and non-profits such as Junior Leagues. Services include editing, marketing, and distributing your book. (See Selected Resources for Self-Publishing on page 264)

Use Print on Demand (POD): Your book is stored in an electronic database. The company manufactures one book at a time when a sale comes in over the Internet. A POD book is a trade paperback (5.5 x 5.8 inches) with a colored cover. POD cannot handle color photography or glossy paper. Most cannot produce a hardcover book.

POD has advantages. The company mails the book and processes the funds. You don't store the books. You can make revisions by submitting new copy and printing a new edition. POD companies give you royalties when copies are sold. On the other hand, usually bookstores will not stock POD books. Some PODs will help you publish e-books, which are downloadable books sold through the Web.

Several good reasons exist to self-publish. See if any of these are right for you:

- Profits go directly to you. You pay all the expenses up front, and if your book sells enough copies to move past breaking even, all the money is yours.
- Get into print faster than traditional publishing. Traditional publishing typically takes between eighteen months and two years from the time you submit your manuscript to the time you hold a finished book in your hands. Self-publishing is often a few months away.
- Keep the copyrights and subsidiary rights to your work. It is possible to keep the copyright with a traditional publisher, but difficult to keep the subsidiary rights, which include foreign rights and first and second serial, audio, and theatrical rights.
- Establish a track record to sell to a traditional publisher,

if you are a first-time author. "If someone came to me with high sales, such as 10,000 copies in a year, and had a track record of public speaking and demonstrations, I would consider them," says agent Carole Bidnick. Ten Speed Press's Jones agrees. "Whenever someone's committed enough to typeset, design, and print, to us, that is symbolic of the personal investment and drive behind a book that's going to enhance our investment," she says. "There's something quite charming about a person who has made an effort to sell the book one copy at a time."

➻ Control every aspect of the entire process, from editorial to design to marketing. If you are the type who doesn't want anyone telling you what to do, self-publishing is a better fit for you. You don't have to hire an editor to judge your sentences, content, or structure. You design the cover. You decide on the book's size, paper quality, and typeface. You control every aspect of the book's production, no matter how small. Some people relish this new learning experience.

➻ Print a small number of copies. If you don't have much money, don't want stacks of books in your garage, and don't want to process and ship each order, POD makes sense.

JUDY KANCIGOR'S FAMILY COOKBOOK

"It all started because a favorite aunt was dying at the same time my daughter-in-law was expecting her first grandchild," says Judy Kancigor, author of *Melting Pot Memories: The Rabinowitz Family Cookbook and Nostalgic History*. "I wanted to preserve history of the family. I told everyone, 'If you're related by blood or marriage, you can be in the book.'"

She wrote a letter to all her relatives, suggesting the kinds of recipes she wanted. Some responded right away while others had to be nagged. "My cousin's husband copied my aunt's entire handwritten recipe book, because she was the primary cook in the family," she recalls. "She was close to ninety, she remembered everything. We went through her book page by page and she told me which recipes to put in."

At first, Kancigor became overwhelmed by the task, but eventually she worked on it full time. "If you can get people to help you, delegate," she advises. Three years later, she had a cookbook with 850 recipes about her family's Jewish heritage and foods. Working with a custom publisher of cookbooks, she sent in handwritten recipes on separate pages. A typist typed them into Microsoft Word files. Kancigor made "this huge leap" and ordered 500 copies, with 300 earmarked for friends and family. The other 200 sold. She made revisions and ordered more. "Another 500 were gone in six weeks," she says.

"My cookbook was very expensive," admits Kancigor. "I wanted the photos a certain way, and I wanted heavier stock and dividers." In total, she published 10,000 copies and has sold almost all. She did so by speaking to Jewish women's groups, putting a coupon in the back of the book for ordering, and getting the book into Judaica shops, cookbook stores, and temple gift shops. She put it on Amazon. Even so, her book was not much of a moneymaker. She jokes that her dad used to say, "You lose money on every sale but make it up in volume."

Kancigor writes terrific, funny recipes. Here's a sample: "If doubling the recipe, don't put it all in the food processor at the same time, because it overflows from the bottom. This I learned from personal experience. In my daughter-in-law's kitchen yet." "The writing is what I enjoy more than the cooking. I crack myself up. I sit there, enjoying me," she says.

"My kids are still scratching their heads and saying, 'How come people are reading about our family?'" she says. "People buy the book because they have photos like that, or they see their own family. The immigrant story is universal. People will buy the book for a daughter-in-law who's not Jewish and coming into their family, or for bridal showers."

Kancigor has never slowed down. She still promotes the

book all over the country. At a book signing at the International Association of Culinary Professionals annual conference, editors approached her. Later that year, she signed a contract. Workman Publishing will publish her book of the same title in 2005.

Reasons to Hesitate

Before you get all excited and rush to self-publish, there are just as many reasons not to do it. If you plan to sell the book, you will have to promote it. Your chances of success are higher if you have a built-in marketing system or platform. You might already:

- teach cooking classes
- own a restaurant
- own a retail store
- have a television show
- have heavily-trafficked Web site
- distribute a newsletter seen by hundreds of people.

In each case, your book will appear in front of readers who could buy it. Carol Fenster self-published a book on dietary restrictions and sold it through the lecture circuit. "She had the numbers, database, touring, and platform within her area of expertise," says her agent, Lisa Ekus, who sold Fenster's self-published book to Putnam/Penguin in a two-book deal.

One of the writers I've worked with, Melissa Guerra, had a PBS television show called *The Texas Provincial Kitchen*. She self-published 5,000 professionally designed color paperback cookbooks and sold them at the end of each show for $19.95, then reprinted another 8,000 when those were gone. Her book sold around 12,000 copies before the show went off the air. She's still selling it on her Web site, http://www.melissaguerra.com, at the rate of five per week.

While her cost per book was around $5, she says she broke even, and wouldn't have done so if she did not have free storage. (Do the math: 13,000 books at $5 each equals a $65,000 initial cash investment.) "The worst thing a novice writer can do is not listen when people tell you how the book industry functions," says Guerra. "Writing for a publishing house is definitely the way to go." Her query letter attracted the interest of eight agents, and her second book will be published this year, from Wiley.

Here's my problem with self-publishing. When you publish traditionally, you receive a check. The publisher produces and distributes the book. With self-publishing, *you* write the check, you figure out how to publish the book, and most often, you sell it yourself. It's almost impossible to get into bookstores and other retail stores with a self-published book.

Here's my list of reasons to hesitate:

- You believe your book will sell a million copies and you're going to get rich. This is not a good reason to publish anything, no matter how it's produced. It's too hard to write a book if money is your only motive.
- Your book will have less credibility than a traditionally published book. The stamp of a traditional publisher means that someone in the business thought your work was worthwhile. Otherwise, anyone can publish anything they want, regardless of quality. Granted, people start their own publishing companies to publish one book, and it's getting harder to tell whether a book is self-published.
- You have to store several thousand books. "I didn't realize it," says Judy Kancigor, author of *Melting Pot Memories* (see page 259). "They come to your house. In your garage, you have to get them up on top of something in case your washing machine overflows." She stored her books in clear plastic cartons, raised off the floor.

➻ If you sell one at a time, it will take forever. Most stores buy from distributors, and most distributors don't take self-published books. Some self-publishing companies offer more distribution than others, but it's still limited compared to traditional publishers.

➻ If you don't like the idea of promoting yourself, it's going to be awfully hard to sell all those books.

➻ You have to become an expert on every aspect of publishing, including editing, design, paper stock, production, and printing. If you just want to write, these responsibilities can be overwhelming.

➻ Unless you choose POD, fulfillment is your responsibility. That's a fancy word for processing the order: cashing checks and taking credit cards, boxing up books and mailing them out, one by one.

➻ You want a full-color, hardcover coffee-table book. Forget it, unless you are very wealthy.

➻ Self-publishing can be astonishingly expensive. You pay all up-front costs, and you get stuck with the leftover inventory.

SELECTED RESOURCES FOR SELF-PUBLISHING

These Web and print sources provide lots more information, should you wish to pursue this type of publishing. The ultimate authority on self-publishing is Dan Poynter, at http://www.para publishing.com, author of *The Self-Publishing Manual: How to Write, Print and Sell Your Own Book*.

Print-on-Demand publishers to explore:
➻ Trafford On-Demand Publishing Services: http://www.trafford.com
➻ Booklocker: http://www.booklocker.com
➻ Authorhouse: http://www.authorhouse.com

Custom publishers specializing in cookbooks:

- ♦ Favorite Recipes Press: http://www.frpbooks.com. Custom cookbooks require a 5,000 minimum press run. Community (fund-raising) cookbooks require a 3,000-book order.

- ♦ Wimmer Cookbook Distribution: http://www.wimmerco.com, requires a minimum 1,000-book order for its standard cookbook template, and a 3,000-minimum order for its custom cookbooks.

- ♦ Cookbook Publishers: http://www.cookbookpublishers.com, has a download-able price sheet that calculates cost based on how many recipes you plan to print and how many books you want to publish.

- ♦ Morris Press Cookbooks, (800) 445-6621. Type your recipes into the company's own software program to save on costs. Minimum order is 200 books.

- ♦ Fundcraft: http://www.fundcraft.com, specializes in personal fund-raising books for charities.

General self-publishing options:

- ♦ iUniverse: http://www.iuniverse.com
- ♦ Xlibris: http://www.xlibris.com
- ♦ Vantage Press: http://www.vantagepress.com

Publishers who offers self-publishing and POD:

- ♦ Infinity Publishing: http://www.infinitypublishing.com
- ♦ iUniverse: http://www.iuniverse.com.

If you're not planning to sell your book to a traditional publisher, MasterCook and Cookbook Maker are two types of software programs that let you store and organize recipes, then print them ready for binding. Traditional publishers want all your recipes in Microsoft Word files, so if you land a publishing deal, you'll end up doing lots of retyping and reformatting if you start with a software program for recipes. Search the Web for more details, as neither product has a Web site.

In the End

You've made it to the end of this book. From *Will Write for Food*'s first chapter, my goal has been to help you write about food, whether for yourself or for publication. I hope you have the tools to express your ideas, thoughts, and opinions in words. Now it's up to you to believe you have something to say and a compelling way to say it. Believe in yourself and your ideas, and believe that you can move forward. Keep writing, even if it's only for twenty minutes per day.

At least half of the path to publication is about not giving up. Just remember that even Julia Child was rejected the first time an editor saw her manuscript. Imagine how much we would have lost if she gave up right then. As editor Harriett Bell told me, "Every successful cookbook author was once someone who just had an idea." Discovering a promising new writer is one of the things editors and agents love most about their jobs. Give them the opportunity to find you.

Appendix

Interview Subjects

- Allegra, Antonia, creator and director of the Symposium for Professional Food Writers at the Greenbrier
- Allen, Gary, author of *The Resource Guide for Food Writers*
- Anderson, J. P., restaurant editor, Chicago Citysearch.com
- Andrews, Colman, former *Saveur* editor in chief
- Baggett, Nancy, cookbook author
- Bauer, Michael, executive food and wine editor and restaurant critic for the *San Francisco Chronicle*
- Bell, Harriet, vice president and editorial director of William Morrow Cookbooks
- Bidnick, Carole, literary agent, Bidnick & Company
- Bittman, Mark, *New York Times* columnist and cookbook author
- Boorstin, Sharon, book author
- Bourdain, Anthony, TV chef and author of memoirs, novels, and cookbooks
- Byrn, Anne, cookbook author
- Carpenter, Maile, editor, *Time Out New York*
- Caruso, Maren, food photographer
- Coover, Doe, literary agent, The Doe Coover Agency
- Doyle, Amanda, associate editor, *Where* magazine, St. Louis
- Dystel, Jane, literary agent, Dystel and Goderich Literary Management

- Ekus, Lisa, literary agent, Lisa Ekus Public Relations Company
- Estabrook, Barry, contributing editor, *Gourmet* magazine
- Fletcher, Janet, cookbook author, food writer for the *San Francisco Chronicle*
- Fluke, Joanne, author, culinary mysteries
- Furiya, Linda, freelance food writer
- Gage, Fran, book author and essayist
- Geary, Tom, tax accountant, San Jose, CA
- Goldstein, Darra, editor, *Gastronomica: The Journal of Food and Culture*
- Grimes, William, former restaurant reviewer, the *New York Times*
- Guarnaschelli, Maria, vice president, W. W. Norton & Company
- Guerra, Melissa, cookbook author
- Hesser, Amanda, *New York Times* editor and former restaurant reviewer
- Holmberg, Martha, former editor in chief and publisher, *Fine Cooking*
- Jay, Sarah, managing editor, *Fine Cooking*
- Jones, Judith, senior editor and vice president, Alfred A. Knopf
- Jones, Lorena, publisher, Ten Speed Press
- Kancigor, Judy, cookbook author and columnist
- Kidd, Kristine, food editor, *Bon Appétit* magazine
- Kirchner, Bharti, cookbook author and novelist
- Knickerbocker, Peggy, freelance writer and cookbook author
- Laudan, Rachel, author and food historian
- LeBlond, Bill, editorial director of cookbooks, Chronicle Books
- Leite, David, freelancer as well as editor and publisher of Leite's Culinaria (Web site)
- Leone, Dan, "Cheap Eats" columnist for the *San Francisco Bay Guardian*
- Londre, Patti, principal, the Londre Company, Inc. (marketing and public relations firm)

- Madison, Deborah, cookbook author
- Martin, Rux, executive editor, Houghton Mifflin Company
- McGee, Harold, author of *On Food and Cooking*
- McManus, Jeanne, former food editor, the *Washington Post*
- McPherson, Heather, food editor, the *Orlando Sentinel;* past president, Association of Food Journalists
- Medrich, Alice, cookbook author
- Moskowitz, Dara, freelance food writer and restaurant critic for *City Pages*, Minneapolis, MN
- Narayan, Shoba, author of *Monsoon Diary: A Memoir with Recipes*
- Nathan, Joan, cookbook author
- O'Neill, Molly, essayist, author, and former *New York Times* food columnist
- Oliver, Sandy, editor and publisher, *Food History News* newsletter
- Pack, Mary Margaret, food writer and restaurant reviewer, the *Austin Chronicle*
- Parsons, Russ, food editor and columnist, the *Los Angeles Times*
- Patent, Greg, freelance writer and cookbook author
- Reigler, Susan, restaurant critic, the *Courier-Journal,* Louisville, KY
- Richman, Alan, *Bon Appétit* editor-at-large
- Richman, Phyllis, author of culinary mysteries and former restaurant reviewer for the *Washington Post*
- Sahni, Julie, cookbook author
- Severson, Kim, food reporter, the *New York Times*
- Shapiro, Laura, author and food historian
- Sheraton, Mimi, former *New York Times* restaurant reviewer
- Sietsema, Tom, food critic, the *Washington Post*
- Smith, Andrew F., author of food history and reference books; teaches culinary history at New School University
- Steingarten, Jeffrey, book author and *Vogue* magazine columnist
- Taxel, Laura, freelance writer and guidebook author

- Trillin, Calvin, freelance writer, book author, and columnist for many publications, including the *New Yorker*
- Unterman, Patricia, restaurant reviewer and guidebook author
- Werlin, Laura, cookbook author
- Wood, Virginia, food editor, the *Austin Chronicle*
- Yan, Martin, cookbook author
- Zoloth, Joan, former restaurant reviewer, the *Oakland Tribune*.

Bibliography

Ackerman, Diane. *A Natural History of the Senses*. New York, NY: Random House, 1990.

Alexander, Brian. *Atomic Kitchen: Gadgets and Inventions for Yesterday's Cook*. Portland, OR: Collector's Press, 2004.

Allen, Gary. *The Resource Guide for Food Writers*. Oxford, UK: Routledge, 1999.

Allen, Moira Anderson. *Starting Your Career as a Freelance Writer*. New York, NY: Allworth Press, 2003.

Allende, Isabel. *Aphrodite: A Memoir of the Senses*. New York, NY: Perennial, 1999.

Allison, Karen Hubert. *How I Gave My Heart to the Restaurant Business: A Novel*. New York, NY: Ecco, 1997.

Almond, Steve. *Candyfreak: A Journey Through the Chocolate Underbelly of America*. Chapel Hill, NC: Algonquin Books of Chapel Hill, 2004.

Anderson, Jean and Barbara Deskins, *The Nutrition Bible: the Comprehensive, No-Nonsense Guide to Food, Nutrients, Additives, Preservatives, Pollutants, and Everything Else We Eat and Drink*. New York, NY: William Morrow & Co., 1995.

Avakian, Arlene Voski, editor. *Through the Kitchen Window: Women Writers Explore the Intimate Meanings of Food and Cooking*. Boston, MA: Beacon Press, 1997.

Baggett, Nancy. *The All-American Cookie Book*. Boston, MA: Houghton Mifflin, 2001.

Beard, James. *James Beard Delights and Prejudices*. Philadelphia, PA: Running Press, 2002.

Bemelmans, Ludwig. *Hotel Bemelmans*. New York, NY: Overlook Press, 2004.

Beranbaum, Rose Levy. *The Bread Bible*. New York, NY: W. W. Norton & Company, 2003.

Bittman, Mark. *How to Cook Everything: Simple Recipes for Great Food*. New York, NY: Wiley, 1998.

Bly, Robert W. *Secrets of a Freelance Writer: How to Make $85,000 a Year*. Second edition. New York, NY: Owl Books, 1997.

Boorstin, Sharon. *Cooking for Love: A Novel with Recipes*. Lincoln, NE: iUniverse, Inc., 2004.

Bourdain, Anthony. *A Cook's Tour: In Search of the Perfect Meal*. Waterville, ME: Thorndike Press, 2002.

———. *Gone Bamboo*. New York, NY: Bloomsbury USA, 2000.

———. *Bone in the Throat*. New York, NY: Bloomsbury USA, 2000.

———. *Kitchen Confidential: Adventures in the Culinary Underbelly*. New York, NY: Ecco, 2001.

Brenner, Joel Glenn. *The Emperors of Chocolate: Inside the Secret World of Hershey and Mars*. New York, NY: Broadway, 2000.

Brillat-Savarin, Jean-Anthelme and M. F. K. Fisher (trans.) *The Physiology of Taste: Or Meditations on Transcendental Gastronomy*. New York, NY: North Point Press, 1986. Originally published in 1825.

Brite, Poppy Z. *Liquor: A Novel*. Three Rivers, MI: Three Rivers Press, 2004.

Brogan, Kathryn S., 2005 *Writer's Market*. Cincinnati, OH: Writers Digest, 2004.

Brown, Alton. *I'm Just Here for the Food: Food + Heat = Cooking*. New York, NY: Stewart, Tabori & Chang, 2002.

Brown, Marcia. *Stone Soup*. New York, NY: Aladdin Picture Books, 1997.

Buford, Bill. *Heat: An Amateur Cook's Adventures as a Kitchen Slave, Line Cook, Pasta Maker, and Apprentice to a Dante-Quoting Butcher in Tuscany*. New York, NY: Random House, 2004.

Byrn, Anne. *The Cake Mix Doctor*. New York, NY: Workman, 1999.

———. *Chocolate from the Cake Mix Doctor*. New York, NY: Workman, 2001.

———. *The Dinner Doctor*. New York, NY: Workman, 2003.

Capalbo, Carla. *The Food and Wine Lover's Companion to Tuscany*. San Francisco, CA: Chronicle Books, 2002.

Capella, Anthony. *The Food of Love*. New York, NY: Viking Books, 2004.

Carl, Joanna. *The Chocolate Frog Frame-Up*. New York, NY: Signet, 2003.

Carper, Jean. *Food: Your Miracle Medicine: How Food Can Prevent and Cure Over 100 Symptoms and Problems*. New York, NY: Harper-Torch, 1998.

Chamberlain, Samuel. *Clementine in the Kitchen*. Revised edition. New York, NY: Modern Library, 2001.

Child, Julia. *Mastering the Art of French Cooking*. Reprint edition. New York, NY: Knopf, 2001.

Clark, Robert. *The Solace of Food: A Life of James Beard*. New York, NY: Steerforth, 1998.

Colwin, Laurie. *Home Cooking: A Writer in the Kitchen*. New York, NY: Perennial, 2000.

———. *More Home Cooking: A Writer Returns to the Kitchen*. New York, NY: Perennial, 2000.

Corpening, Sara and Mary Corpening Barber. *Smoothies: 50 Recipes for High-Energy Refreshment*. San Francisco, CA: Chronicle Books, 1997.

Corriher, Shirley O. *Cookwise: The Hows and Whys of Successful Cooking*. New York, NY: Morrow Cookbooks, 1997.

Counihan, Carole, and Penny Van Esterik, eds. *Food and Culture: A Reader*. Oxford, UK: Routledge, 1997.

Coyle, Cleo. *On What Grounds,* a Coffeehouse Mystery. New York, NY: Berkley Publishing Group, 2003.

———. *Through the Grinder*. New York, NY: Prime Crime, 2004.

Crawford, Isis. *A Catered Murder*. New York, NY: Kensington Publishing, 2003.

Cunningham, Marion. *Lost Recipes: Meals to Share with Friends and Family*. New York, NY: Knopf, 2003.

Daheim, Mary. *Nutty as a Fruitcake,* a Bed and Breakfast Mystery. New York, NY: Avon, 1996.

———. *Just Desserts,* a Bed and Breakfast Mystery. Avon, 1999.

———. *Legs Benedict,* a Bed and Breakfast Mystery. Avon, 1999.

Daley, Rosie. *In the Kitchen with Rosie: Oprah's Favorite Recipes.* New York, NY: Knopf, 1994.

David, Elizabeth. *A Book of Mediterranean Food.* New York, NY: New York Review, 2002.

———. *An Omelet and a Glass of Wine.* Guilford, CT: The Lyons Press, 1997.

———. *South Wind Through the Kitchen: The Best of Elizabeth David.* New York, NY: North Point Press, 1999.

Davidson, Alan, editor. *The Wilder Shores of Gastronomy: Twenty Years of the Best Food Writing from the Journal Petits Propos Culinaires.* Berkeley, CA: Ten Speed Press, 2002.

———. *The Oxford Companion to Food.* New York, NY: Oxford University Press, 1999.

Davidson, Diane Mott. *Catering to Nobody,* a Culinary Mystery. New York, NY: Bantam, 2002.

———. *Dying for Chocolate,* a Culinary Mystery. New York, NY: Crimeline Books, 1993.

———. *Killer Pancake,* a Culinary Mystery. New York, NY: Crimeline Books, 1996.

———. *The Last Suppers,* a Culinary Mystery. New York, NY: Crimeline Books, 1995.

De Angeli, Marguerite. *Henner's Lydia.* Scotsdale, PA: Herald Press, 1998.

De Groot, Roy Andries. *Auberge of the Flowering Hearth.* New York, NY: Ecco Press, 1996.

———. *Feasts for All Seasons.* New York, NY: Random House, 2000.

———. *In Search of the Perfect Meal: A Collection of the Food Writing of Roy Andries de Groot.* New York, NY: St. Martins Press, 1986.

Duke, James. *The Green Pharmacy: The Ultimate Compendium of Natural Remedies from the World's Foremost Authority on Healing Herbs.* New York, NY: St. Martin's Paperbacks, 1998.

Edge, John, T. *Southern Belly: The Ultimate Food Lover's Guide to the South.* Athens, GA: Hill Street Press, 2002.

Editor & Publisher. *Annual Directory of Syndicated Services.* New York, NY: New York Editor & Publisher Co., annual.

Egerton, March. *Since Eve Ate Apples: Quotations on Feasting, Fasting and Food from the Beginning.* Portland, OR: Tsunami Press, 1994.

Ehlert, Lois. *Eating the Alphabet.* New York, NY: Red Wagon Books, 1996.

Ephron, Nora. *Heartburn.* New York, NY: Vintage, 1996.

Escoffier, Auguste. *The Complete Guide to the Art of Modern Cooking.* New York, NY: Wiley, 1983.

Esquivel, Laura. *Like Water for Chocolate: A Novel in Monthly Installments with Recipes, Romances and Home Remedies.* New York, NY: Anchor, 1994.

Fenster, Carol. *Wheat-Free Recipes and Menus.* New York, NY: Avery Publishing, 1997.

Field, Carol. *In Nonna's Kitchen: Recipes and Traditions from Italy's Grandmothers.* New York, NY: HarperCollins, 1997.

Fielding, Henry. *The History of Tom Jones, A Foundling.* New York, NY: Oxford University Press, 1998. Originally published in 1749.

Fisher, M. F. K. *A Considerable Town.* New York, NY: Knopf, 1978.

———. *Among Friends.* New York, NY: Knopf, 1971.

———. *The Art of Eating.* New York, NY: Vintage Books, 1976.

———. *As They Were.* New York, NY: Knopf, 1982.

———. *Consider the Oyster.* New York, NY: Duell, Sloan & Pearce, Inc. 1941.

———. *The Gastronomical Me.* New York, NY: Duell, Sloan & Pearce, Inc. 1943.

———. *How to Cook A Wolf.* New York, NY: Duell, Sloan & Pearce, Inc., 1942.

———. *The Measure of Her Powers: An M. F. K. Fisher Reader.* New York, NY: Counterpoint Press, 1999.

———. *Sister Age.* New York, NY: Alfred A. Knopf, 1983.

Fitzgerald, F. Scott. *The Great Gatsby.* New York, NY: Scribner, 1995. Originally published in 1920.

Fluke, Joanne. *Blueberry Muffin Murder:* a Hannah Swensen Mystery, New York, NY: Kensington Publishing, 2003.

———. *Chocolate Chip Cookie Murder:* a Hannah Swensen Mystery. New York, NY: Kensington Publishing, 2001.

———. *Lemon Meringue Pie Murder:* a Hannah Swensen Mystery. New York, NY: Kensington Publishing, 2004.

———. *Strawberry Shortcake Murder:* a Hannah Swensen Mystery. New York, NY: Kensington Publishing, 2002.

———. *Sugar Cookie Murder:* a Hannah Swensen Mystery. New York, NY: Kensington Publishing, 2004.

Frey, James. *How to Write a Damn Good Novel: A Step-by-Step No Nonsense Guide to Dramatic Storytelling.* New York, NY: St. Martin's Press, 1987.

Gage, Fran. *Bread and Chocolate: My Food Life In and Around San Francisco.* Seattle, WA: Sasquatch Books, 1999.

Garten, Ina. *The Barefoot Contessa Cookbook.* New York, NY: Clarkson Potter, 1999.

Geffen, Alice, and Carole Berglie. *Food Festival: The Ultimate Guidebook to America's Best Regional Food Celebrations.* Woodstock, VT: Countryman Press, 1994.

George, Elizabeth. *Write Away: One Novelist's Approach to Fiction and the Writing Life.* New York, NY: HarperCollins, 2004.

Gold, Jonathan. *Counter Intelligence: Where to Eat in the Real Los Angeles.* Los Angeles, CA: L.A. Weekly Books, 2000.

Goldberg, Natalie. *Old Friend from Far Away: How to Write a Memoir.* Louisville, CO: Sounds True, 2002.

———. *Writing Down the Bones.* Boston, MA: Shambhala, 1986.

Gordon, Nadia. *Death by the Glass: A Sunny McCoskey Napa Valley Mystery.* San Francisco, CA: Chronicle Books, 2003.

Gray, Patience. *Honey from a Weed.* Guilford, CT: The Lyons Press, 1997.

Greising, David. *I'd Like to Buy the World a Coke: The Life and Leadership of Roberto Goizueta.* New York, NY: Wiley, 1999.

Grimes, William. *Eating Your Words: 2000 Words to Tease Your Taste Buds.* New York, NY: Oxford University Press, 2004.

Grosset & Dunlap. *The Wiggles: Yummy, Yummy Fruit Salad*. Grosset & Dunlap, 2003.

Guerra, Melissa. *The Provincial Texas Kitchen Cookbook*. Linn, TX: The Provincial Texas Kitchen, Ltd. 1997.

H. W. Wilson Co. *Reader's Guide to Periodical Literature*. New York, NY: H. W. Wilson Co. annual.

Hanson, Kendall. *Writing for Trade Magazines: How to Boost Your Income by $200 to $500 Per Week. Kingston,* WA: Dixon-Price Publishing, 1999.

Harris, Joanne. *Chocolat*. New York, NY: Penguin Books, 2000.

———. *Five Quarters of the Orange*. New York, NY: Perennial, 2002.

Hemingway, Ernest. *The Garden of Eden*. New York, NY: Scribner, 1995. Originally published in 1986.

Henderson, Fergus. *The Whole Beast: Nose to Tail Eating*. New York, NY: Ecco, 2004.

Herbst, Sharon Tyler. *The New Food Lover's Companion: Comprehensive Definitions of Nearly 6,000 Food, Drink, and Culinary Terms*. Hauppauge, NY: Barron's Educational Series, 2001.

Hesser, Amanda. *Cooking for Mr. Latte: A Food Lover's Courtship, with Recipes*. New York, NY: W. W. Norton & Company, 2003.

———. *The Cook and the Gardener: A Year of Recipes and Writings from the French Countryside*. New York, NY: W. W. Norton & Company, 2000.

Hoberman, Mary Ann. *The Seven Silly Eaters*. San Diego, CA: Voyager Books, 2000.

Holman, Sheri. *The Mammoth Cheese: A Novel*. New York, NY: Atlantic Monthly Press, 2003.

Hughes, Holly, editor. The Best Food Writing Anthologies. New York, NY: Marlowe & Company, annual.

Joachim, David. *A Man, a Can, a Plan: 50 Tasty Meals You Can Nuke in No Time*. Emmaus, PA: Rodale Books, 2002.

Jones, Evan. *Epicurean Delight: The Life and Times of James Beard*. New York, NY: Knopf, 1990.

Jones, Idwal. *High Bonnet: A Novel of Epicurean Adventures*. New York, NY: Modern Library, 2001.

Kancigor, Judy Bart. *Melting Pot Memories: The Rabinowitz Family Cookbook and Nostalgic History*. Jan Bart Publications, 1999.

Kasper, Lynne Rossetto. *The Splendid Table: Recipes from Emilia-Romagna, the Heartland of Northern Italian Food*. New York, NY: Morrow Cookbooks, 1992.

Katz, Solomon H., and William Woys Weaver, eds. *Encyclopedia of Food and Culture*. New York, NY: Charles Scribner's Sons, 2002.

Kelly, Ian. *Cooking for Kings: The Life of Antonin Careme, the First Celebrity Chef*. New York, NY: Walker & Company, 2004.

Kiple, Kenneth, editor. *The Cambridge World History of Food*. New York, NY: Cambridge University Press, 2000.

Kirchner, Bharti. *Pastries: A Novel of Desserts and Discoveries*. New York, NY: St. Martin's Press, 2003.

Kurlansky, Mark. *Cod: A Biography of the Fish that Changed the World*. New York, NY: Penguin Books, 1998.

———. *Salt: A World History*. New York, NY: Penguin Books, 2003.

Lamott, Anne. *Bird by Bird: Some Instructions on Writing and Life*. New York, NY: Anchor, 1995.

Larsen, Michael. *How to Write a Book Proposal*. Cincinnati, OH: Writer's Digest Books, 2004.

———. *Literary Agents: What They Do, How They Do It, and How to Find and Work with the Right One for You*. New York, NY: Wiley, 1996.

Laudan, Rachel. *The Food of Paradise: Exploring Hawaii's Culinary Heritage*. Honolulu, HI: University of Hawaii Press, 1996.

Levin, Martin P. *Be Your Own Literary Agent: The Ultimate Insider's Guide to Getting Published*. Berkeley, CA: Ten Speed Press, 2002.

Levine, Ed. *New York Eats: The Food Shopper's Guide to the Freshest Ingredients, the Best Take Out and Baked Goods, & The Most Unusual Marketplaces in All of New York*. New York, NY: St. Martin's Griffin, 1997.

Levoy, Gregg. *This Business of Writing*. Cincinnati, OH: Writers Digest Books, 1992.

Levy, Paul. *The Penguin Book of Food and Drink*. New York, NY: Penguin USA, 1998.

Lewis, Edna. *In Pursuit of Flavor.* Charlottesville, VA: University Press of Virginia, 2000.

Lewis, Edna. *The Edna Lewis Cookbook.* New York, NY: Ecco Press, 1983.

——. *The Taste of Country Cooking.* New York, NY: Knopf, 1976.

Liebling, A. J. *Between Meals: An Appetite for Paris.* New York, NY: North Point Press, 2004.

Lin, Grace. *Dim Sum for Everyone.* New York, NY: Knopf Books for Young Readers, 2001.

Longbotham, Lori. *Luscious Lemon Desserts.* San Francisco, CA: Chronicle Books, 2001.

Lyon, Elizabeth. *Nonfiction Book Proposals Anyone Can Write: How to Get a Contract and Advance Before Writing Your Book.* New York, NY: Perigree Books, 2002.

Lyons, Nan. *Someone is Killing the Great Chefs of Europe.* New York, NY: Harcourt, 1990.

Madison, Deborah. *The Greens Cookbook: Extraordinary Vegetarian Cuisine from the Celebrated Restaurant.* New York, NY: Bantam, 1987.

——. *The Savory Way.* New York, NY: Broadway, 1998.

——. *Vegetarian Cooking for Everyone.* New York, NY: Broadway, 1997.

Malladi, Amulya. *Serving Crazy with Curry.* New York, NY: Ballantine Books, 2004.

Marken, Bill. *How to Fix (Just About) Everything: More than 550 Step-by-Step Instructions for Everything from Fixing a Faucet to Removing Mystery Stains to Curing a Hangover.* New York, NY: Free Press, 2002.

Marranca, Bonnie. *A Slice of Life: Contemporary Writers on Food.* New York, NY: Overlook Press, 2003.

Mayes, Frances. *Under the Tuscan Sun.* New York, NY: Broadway, 1997.

McCloskey, Robert. *Blueberries for Sal.* New York, NY: Puffin Books, 1976.

McGee, Harold. *On Food and Cooking: The Science and Lore of the Kitchen.* New York, NY: Scribner, 2004.

McGrath, Mike. *Kitchen Garden A to Z: Growing, Harvest, Buying, Storing.* New York, NY: Harry N. Abrams, 2004.

McNair, James. *Cold Pasta.* San Francisco, CA: Chronicle Books, 1985.

Medrich, Alice. *Bittersweet: Recipes and Tales from a Life in Chocolate.* New York, NY: Artisan, 2003.

Melville, Herman. *Moby-Dick.* New York, NY: Bantam Classics, 1981. Originally published in 1851.

Mendelson, Anne. *Stand Facing the Stove: The Story of the Women Who Gave America the Joy of Cooking.* New York, NY: Henry Holt & Company, 1996.

Mesnier, Roland. *Dessert University: More than 300 Spectacular Recipes and Essential Lessons from White House Pastry Chef Roland Mesnier.* New York, NY: Simon & Schuster, 2004.

Mettee, Stephen Blake. *The Fast Track Course on How to Write a Nonfiction Book Proposal.* New York, NY: Quill Driver Books, 2001.

Murdock, Maureen. *Unreliable Truth.* Seattle, WA: Seal Press, 2003.

Myers, Tamar. *Eat, Drink and Be Wary.* New York, NY: Signet, 1998.

———. *Parsley, Sage, Rosemary and Crime.* New York, NY: Signet, 1997.

———. *Too Many Crooks Spoil the Broth: A Pennsylvania Dutch Mystery with Recipes.* New York, NY: Signet, 1995.

Narayan, Shoba. *Monsoon Diary: A Memoir with Recipes.* New York, NY: Villard, 2003.

Nathan, Joan. *Foods of Israel Today.* New York, NY: Knopf, 2001.

Nestle, Marion. *Food Politics: How the Food Industry Influences Nutrition and Health.* Berkeley, CA: University of California Press, 2003.

Orwell, George. *Down and Out in Paris and London.* New York, NY: Harvest/HBJ, 1972.

Ostmann, Barbara Gibbs, and Jane Baker. *The Recipe Writer's Handbook.* New York, NY: Wiley, 2001.

Ozeki, Ruth L. *My Year of Meats.* New York, NY: Penguin Books, 1999.

Page, Susan. *The Shortest Distance Between You and a Published Book: 20 Steps to Success*. New York, NY: Broadway, 1997.

Parson, Russ. *How to Read a French Fry, and Other Stories of Intriguing Kitchen Science*. Boston, MA: Houghton Mifflin, 2003.

Patent, Greg. *Baking in America: Contemporary and Traditional Favorites from the Past 200 Years*. Boston, MA: Houghton Mifflin, 2002.

Pellegrini, Angelo. *The Unprejudiced Palate: Classic Thoughts on Food and the Good Life*. Guilford, CT: The Lyons Press, 1992.

Pépin, Jacques. *The Apprentice: My Life in the Kitchen*. Boston, MA: Houghton Mifflin, 2003.

Peterson, Joan, and David Peterson. *Eat Smart in Poland: How to Decipher the Menu, Know the Market Foods & Embark on a Tasting Adventure*. Madison, WI: Gingko Press, 2000.

Pomaine, Edouard de. *Cooking with Pomaine*. Washington, DC: Serif, 1993.

Pottker, Janice. *Crisis in Candyland: Melting the Chocolate Shell of the Mars Family Empire*. Palo Alto, CA: National Press Books, 1995.

Prior, Lily. *La Cucina: A Novel of Rapture*. New York, NY: Ecco, 2001.

Proust, Marcel. *Swann's Way*. New York, NY: Viking Books, 2003. Originally published in French in 1913.

Rabiner, Susan and Alfred Fortunato. *Thinking Like Your Editor - How to Write Great Serious Nonfiction and Get It Published*. New York, NY: W. W. Norton & Co., 2003.

Raichlen, Steven. *The Barbecue Bible*. New York, NY: Workman Publishing, 1998.

Rawles, Nancy. *Crawfish Dreams: A Novel*. New York, NY: Doubleday, 2003.

Rayner, Jay. *Eating Crow*. New York, NY: Simon & Schuster, 2004.

Reichl, Ruth. *Endless Feasts: Sixty Years of Writing from Gourmet*. New York, NY: Modern Library, 2002.

———. *Comfort Me with Apples: More Adventures at the Table*. New York, NY: Random House Trade Paperbacks, 2002.

———. *Tender at the Bone: Growing Up at the Table*. New York, NY: Broadway, 1999.

Riccardi, Victoria. *Untangling My Chopsticks: A Culinary Sojourn in Kyoto.* New York, NY: Broadway, 2003.

Richman, Alan. *Fork it Over: The Intrepid Adventures of a Professional Eater.* New York, NY: HarperCollins, 2004.

Richman, Phyllis. *Murder on the Gravy Train.* New York, NY: Avon, 2000.

———. *The Butter Did It: A Gastronomic Tale of Love and Murder.* New York, NY: HarperTorch, 1998.

———. *Who's Afraid of Virginia Ham?* New York, NY: Avon, 2002.

Robertson, Laurel. *Laurel's Kitchen.* Berkeley, CA: Ten Speed Press, 1993.

Roden, Claudia. *The Book of Jewish Food: An Odyssey from Samarkand to New York.* New York, NY: Knopf, 1996.

Rombauer, Irma S., and Marion Rombauer Becker. *The Joy of Cooking.* New York, NY: Scribner, 1985. Original version published in 1931.

Room, Adrian. *Dunces, Gourmands and Petticoats.* Chicago, IL: TC/Contemporary Publishing, 1998.

Roorbach, Bill. *Writing Life Stories.* Cincinnati, OH: Writer's Digest Books, 2000.

Root, Waverly, and Richard de Rochemont. *Eating in America: A History.* New York, NY: Ecco Press, 2004.

Rosenblum, Mort. *Olives: The Life and Lore of a Noble Fruit.* New York, NY: North Point Press, 1998.

Rosso, Julee, and Sheila Lukins. *The Silver Palate Cookbook.* New York, NY: Workman Publishing, 1982.

Ruhlman, Michael. *The Making of a Chef: Mastering Heat at the Culinary Institute.* New York, NY: Owl Books, 1999.

Sahni, Julie. *Classic Indian Cooking.* New York, NY: Morrow Cookbooks, 1980.

Sanger, Amy Wilson. *A Little Bit of Soul Food,* and other titles in the World Snacks series. Berkeley, CA: Tricycle Press, 2004.

Schlosser, Eric. *Fast Food Nation: The Dark Side of the All-American Meal.* New York, NY: Perennial, 2002.

Sendak, Maurice. *Chicken Soup with Rice: A Book of Months*. New York, NY: HarperTrophy, 1991.

———. *In the Night Kitchen*. New York, NY: HarperCollins, 1996.

Severson, Kim, and Cindy Burke. *The Trans Fat Solution: Cooking and Shopping to Eliminate the Deadliest Fats from Your Diet*. Berkeley, CA: Ten Speed Press, 2003.

Shapiro, Anna. *Feast of Words: For Lovers of Food and Fiction*. New York, NY: W. W. Norton & Company, 1996.

Shapiro, Laura. *Perfection Salad: Women and Cooking at the Turn of the Century*. New York, NY: Modern Library, 2001.

———. *Something from the Oven: Reinventing Dinner in 1950s America*. New York, NY: Viking Books, 2004.

Sheraton, Mimi. *Eating My Words: An Appetite for Life*. New York, NY: Morrow Cookbooks, 2004.

Silverman, Sharon Hernes. *Pennsylvania Snacks: A Guide to Food Factory Tours*. Mechanicsburg, PA: Stackpole Books, 2001.

Sinclair, Upton. *The Jungle*. New York, NY: Bantam, 1981. Originally published in 1906.

Slade, Sheryl. *A Lady at the Table: A Concise, Contemporary Guide to Table Manners*. Nashville, TN: Rutledge Hill Press, 2004.

Smalls, Alexander. *Grace the Table: Stories & Recipes From My Southern Revival*. New York, NY: Harlem Moon, 2004.

Smith, Andrew F. *Peanuts: The Illustrious History of the Goober Pea*. Champagne, IL: University of Illinois Press, 2002.

———. *Pure Ketchup: A History of America's National Condiment, with Recipes*. Washington, DC: Smithsonian Books, 2001.

———. *The Tomato in America: Early History, Culture, and Cookery*. Columbia, SC: University of South Carolina Press, 1994.

———. *The Oxford Encyclopedia of Food and Drink in America*. New York, NY: Oxford University Press, 2004.

Stein, Sol. *Stein on Writing: A Master Editor of Some of the Most Successful Writers of Our Century Shares His Craft Techniques and Strategies*. New York, NY: St. Martin's Press, 2000.

Steingarten, Jeffrey. *The Man Who Ate Everything*. New York, NY: Vintage, 1998.

Stern, Jane and Michael Stern. *Roadfood: The Coast-to-Coast Guide to 500 of the Best Barbeque Joints, Lobster Shacks, Ice Cream Parlors, Highway Diners, and Much More.* New York, NY: Broadway, 2002.

Strunk, Jr., William and E.B. White. *Elements of Style,* 4th Ed. New York, NY: Longman, 2000.

Taxel, Laura. *Cleveland Ethnic Eats 2004: The Guide to Authentic Ethnic Eats in Northeastern Ohio.* Cleveland, OH: Gray & Company Publishers, 2003.

The Asia Society. *Asia in the San Francisco Bay Area: A Cultural Travel Guide.* New York, NY: Avalon Travel Publishing, 2004.

Theophano, Janet. *Eat My Words: Reading Women's Lives through the Cookbooks They Wrote.* New York, NY: Palgrave Macmillan, 2002.

Thorne, John. *Pot on the Fire: Further Confessions of a Renegade Cook.* New York, NY: North Point Press, 2001.

Todhunter, Andrew. *A Meal Observed.* New York, NY: Knopf, 2004.

Tolstoy, Leo. *Anna Karenina.* New York, NY: Modern Library, 2000. Originally published serially from 1875–77 in Russian.

Tower, Jeremiah. *California Dish: What I Saw and Cooked at the American Culinary Revolution.* New York, NY: Free Press, 2003.

Trillin, Calvin. *American Fried.* New York, NY: Vintage, 1979.

———. *The Tummy Trilogy.* New York, NY: Farrar, Straus & Giroux, 1994.

Unterman, Patricia. *Patricia Unterman's Food Lover's Guide to San Francisco.* Berkeley, CA: Ten Speed Press, 2003.

Various. Skinny series of cookbooks. Chicago, IL: Surrey, 1990s.

Various. Williams-Sonoma series of cookbooks. New York, NY: Time-Life, 2000.

Villas, James. *Between Bites: Memoirs of a Hungry Hedonist.* New York, NY: Wiley, 2002.

———. *Stalking the Green Fairy: And Other Fantastic Adventures in Food and Drink.* New York, NY: Wiley, 2004.

Visser, Margaret. *Much Depends on Dinner: The Extraordinary History and Mythology, Allure and Obsessions, Perils and Taboo, of an Ordinary Meal.* New York, NY: Grove Press, 1999.

Volland, Susan. *Love and Meatballs.* New York, NY: New American Library, 2004.

Walsh, Robb. *Are You Really Going to Eat That?* New York, NY: Counterpoint Press, 2003.

Wells, Patricia. *A Food Lover's Guide to Paris.* New York, NY: Workman Publishing, 1999.

Werlin, Laura. *New American Cheese.* New York, NY: Stewart, Tabori & Chang, 2000.

———. *The All American Cheese and Wine Book.* New York, NY: Stewart, Tabori & Chang, 2003.

Wexberg, Joseph. *Blue Trout and Black Truffles: The Peregrinations of an Epicure.* Chicago, IL: Academy Chicago Publishers, 1985.

Wharton, Edith. *The Age of Innocence,* New York, NY: Modern Library, 1999. Originally published in 1920.

Whitman, Joan and Dolores Simon. *Recipes Into Type: A Handbook for Cookbook Writers and Editors.* Newton, MA: Biscuit Books, Inc., 1993.

Winston, Lolly. *Good Grief.* New York, NY: Warner Books, 2004.

Wolke, Robert. *What Einstein Told His Cook.* New York, NY: W.W. Norton & Company, 2002.

Wood, Monica. *Description* (the Elements of Fiction Writing series). Cincinnati, OH: Writer's Digest Books, 1999.

Wyler, Susan. *Great Books for Cooks.* New York, NY: Ballantine Books, 1999.

Young, Grace. *Wisdom of the Chinese Kitchen.* New York, NY: Simon & Schuster, 1999.

Zinsser, William. *Writing About Your Life: A Journey Into the Past.* New York, NY: Marlowe & Company, 2004.

———. *Inventing the Truth: The Art and Craft of Memoir.* Boston, MA: Mariner Books, 1998.

———. *On Writing Well: The Classic Guide to Writing Nonfiction.* New York, NY: HarperResource, 2001.

Selected Web Sites

Magazines

- *AAA Traveler*—http://www.ouraaa.com/traveler/
- *AARP* magazine—http://www.aarpmagazine.org
- *Bon Appétit (Epicurious)*—http://www.epicurious.com
- *Cleveland Magazine.Com*—http://www.clevelandmagazine.com
- *Conde Nast Traveler*—http://www.cntraveler.com
- *Cook's Illustrated.Com*—http://www.cooksillustrated.com
- *Cooking Light*—http://www.cookinglight.com
- *Eating Well: The Magazine of Food and Health*—
  http://www.eatingwell.com
- *Esquire*—http://www.esquire.com
- *Family Circle*—http://www.familycircle.com
- *Fine Cooking*—http://www.taunton.com/finecooking
- *Food & Wine*—http://www.foodandwine.com
- *Food History News*—http://www.foodhistorynews.com
- *Gastronomica: The Journal of Food and Culture*—
  http://www.gastronomica.org.
- *Gourmet*—http://www.epicurious.com
- *GQ*—http://us.gq.com
- *Health*—http://www.health.com/health
- *House and Garden*—http://www.houseandgarden.com

➡ *Islands: The Leading Guide to Island Travel*—http://www.islands.com

➡ *Life* magazine—http://www.life.com

➡ *Martha Stewart Living*—http://www.marthastewart.com

➡ *National Geographic Traveler*—
http://www.nationalgeographic.com/traveler

➡ *Natural Foods Merchandiser*—http://www.naturalfoodsmerchandiser.com

➡ *New York Metro.Com*—http://www.newyorkmetro.com

➡ *Newsweek*—http://www.newsweek.com

➡ *Northern Ohio Live*- http://www.northernohiolive.com

➡ *Oprah*—http://www.oprah.com

➡ *Pig International.Com*—http://www.wattnet.com/pigi/home.cfm

➡ *Real Simple* magazine—http://www.realsimple.com

➡ *Restaurants and Institutions*—http://www.rimag.com

➡ *Safeway Select*—http://www.Safeway.com/Safeway_Select.asp

➡ *Sante* magazine—http://www.sante-mag.com (in French)

➡ *Saveur*—http://www.saveur.com

➡ *Seafood Business*—http:// www.seafoodbusiness.com

➡ *Simple Cooking*—http://www.outlawcook.com

➡ *Slow Food*—http://www.slowfood.com

➡ *Southern Living*—http://www.southernliving.com

➡ *Sunset: Life in the West*—http://www.sunset.com

➡ *Taste of Home*—http://www.tasteofhome.com

➡ *Texas Monthly*—http://www.texasmonthly.com

➡ *The New Yorker*—http://www.newyorker.com

➡ *Time Out*—http://www.timeout.com

➡ *Travel & Leisure*—http://www.travelandleisure.com

➡ *Vogue*—http://www.style.com/vogue

➡ *Where*—http://www.wheremagazine.com

➡ *Woman's Day*—http://www.womansday.com

➡ *Yoga Journal*—http://www.yogajournal.com

Newspaper Food Sections

•❖ Gourmet Spot—http://www.gourmetspot.com/newspapers.htm

Web Sites

•❖ Chowhound.Com—http://www.chowhound.com (non-commercial information on great eating around the world)

•❖ Chef Talk Cooking Forums—http://www.cheftalkcafe.com/forums/

•❖ City Search—http://www.citysearch.com (online city guides with restaurant reviews)

•❖ Bruce Cole, Sauté Wednesday—http://www.sautewednesday.com/

•❖ Tyler Cowen's Ethnic Dining Guide—http://www.gmu.edu/jbc/Tyler/ethnic.html

•❖ Egullet Culinary Institute (eGullet)—http://www.egullet.com (bulletin board and discussion groups for cooking, restaurant reviews, and travel; cooking classes in the Egullet Culinary Institute forums)

•❖ Food Newsgroups—http://www.foodweb.com/w.w.bites/foodnewsgroups.html

•❖ Forbes.Com—http://www.forbes.com (business and finance magazine, runs some food writing)

•❖ Hungry Monster—http://www.hungrymonster.com (more than 400,000 restaurant listings; reviews, menus, food glossary, prices, maps, and recipes)

•❖ Leite's Culinaria—http://www.leitesculinaria.com/index.html (David Leite)

•❖ Literary Marketplace—http://www.literarymarketplace.com (lists literary agents alphabetically by name)

•❖ Msn.com—http://www.msn.com (online news magazine, occasionally runs food writing)

•❖ Phantom Gourmet—http://www.phantomgourmet.com (site of New England–based restaurant critic)

•❖ Publishers Marketplace—http://www.publishersmarketplace.com (Web pages for writers and agents to promote themselves)

- Sally's Place—http://www.sallys-place.com (online food and drink news, reviews, recipes, restaurants, and travel)
- Slate magazine—http://www.slate.com (online news magazine, runs food writing)
- John Thorne Simple Cooking—http://www.theoutlawcook.com

Food Writing and Writing Classes

- Book Passage—http://www.bookpassage.com (lists conferences on writing, sometimes food writing)
- Gotham Writers' Workshop and Writing Classes.Com— http://www.writingclasses.com (online classes in nonfiction writing)
- Media Bistro.Com—http://www.mediabistro.com/courses/cache/ menu_1.asp
- Shaw Guides—http://www.shawguides.com (writing classes around the country)
- Symposium for Professional Food Writers at the Greenbrier— http://www.greenbrier.com/foodwriters/
- Virtual University—http://www.vu.org/ (online English classes)
- Virtual Student—http://www.virtualstudent.com/ (online English classes)
- Writer's College—http://writerscollege.com
- Writing Salon, San Francisco—http://www.writingsalons.com
- Writer's Digest—http://www.writersdigest.com

Associations and Non-Profits

- The American Culinary Federation, Inc.—http://www.acfchefs.org (promotes the culinary profession)
- American Institute of Wine & Food—http://www.aiwf.org (a non-profit devoted to improving appreciation, understanding, and accessibility of food and drink)
- Association for the Study of Food and Society—

http://www.food-culture.org (international organization dedicated to academic study of food, culture, and society)

●◆ Association of Food Journalists—http://www.afjonline.com

●◆ Les Dames d'Escoffier—http://www.ldei.org/homeFrameset.asp (women's organization for food industry professionals, food writers and researchers)

●◆ COPIA, The American Center for Wine, Food & the Arts— http://www.copia.org (cultural museum and education center dedicated to understanding wine, food and the arts in American culture)

●◆ International Association of Culinary Professionals— http://www.iacp.com

●◆ The Research Chefs Association—http://www.researchchef.org (professional group for food research)

●◆ Slow Food—http://www.slowfood.com (studies effects of fast food on society and life)

●◆ Women Chefs and Restaurateurs—http://www.womenchefs.org (promotes the education and advancement of women in the restaurant industry)

Cooking Schools and Classes

●◆ L'Academie de Cuisine, Gaithersburg, MD.— http://www.lacademie.com

●◆ California Culinary Academy—http://www.baychef.com

●◆ Cooking Schools.com—http://www.cookingschools.com/search-saver/

●◆ The Culinary Institute of America, St. Helena, Calif., and Hyde Park, N.Y.—http://www.ciachef.edu

●◆ Star Chefs' Culinary School Finder—http://www.starchefs.com/ cooking_school_finder.html

●◆ The French Culinary Institute— http://frenchculinary.com/subpages/amateur/foodwriting.html

●◆ The New School of Cooking Los Angeles— http://newschoolofcooking.com/

●◆ La Varenne École de Cuisine, France—http://www.lavarenne.com

- ➻ Shaw Guides—http://www.shawguides.com (contains listings of cooking schools)
- ➻ Sur La Table cooking school—http://www.surlatable.com/cooking/index.cfm

Food Studies

- ➻ New York University Graduate program in food studies and food management—http://education.nyu.edu/nutrition/

Online Cookbook Stores

- ➻ Jessica's Biscuit Ecookbooks.com—http://www.ecookbooks.com/index.html
- ➻ Foodbooks.com—http://www.foodbooks.com/
- ➻ Cookbooks We Love—http://www.cookbookswelove.com/

Government Sources

- ➻ U.S. Copyright Office at the Library of Congress, (202) 707-9100—http://www.copyright.gov
- ➻ The Food and Nutrition Information Center of the U.S. Department of Agriculture, (301) 504-6409—http://usda.gov

Index

Note: **Bold** page numbers indicate a lengthy discussion of that topic.

writing skills. *See also* education
books about, 96
developing stories, 91–96
importance of, 3–4, 49
memoirs and, 193–95
query letters and, 85–86

Yan, Martin, 145

Zoloth, Joan, 139